The Uses
of Grammar

The Uses
of Grammar

Judith Rodby
California State University, Chico

W. Ross Winterowd
Emeritus, University of Southern California

Oxford   New York
OXFORD UNIVERSITY PRESS
2005

Oxford University Press

Oxford   New York
Auckland   Bangkok   Buenos Aires   Cape Town   Chennai
Dar es Salaam   Delhi   Hong Kong   Istanbul   Karachi   Kolkata
Kuala Lumpur   Madrid   Melbourne   Mexico City   Mumbai   Nairobi
São Paulo   Shanghai   Taipei   Tokyo   Toronto

Published by Oxford University Press, Inc.
198 Madison Avenue, New York, New York 10016
www.oup.com

Library of Congress Cataloging-in-Publication Data

Rodby, Judith.
    The uses of grammar / Judith Rodby, W. Ross Winterowd.
        p. cm.
    Includes index.
    ISBN-13: 978-0-19-517508-0
    ISBN 0-19-517508-5
        1. Grammar, Comparative and general. 2. Linguistic analysis (Linguistics) I.
    Winterowd, W. Ross. II. Title.

P151.R69 2004
415—dc22   2004053166

Printing number: 9 8 7 6 5 4 3 2 1

Printed in the United States of America
on acid-free paper

Contents

11 Adjectivals: Adjectives, Nouns, Prepositional Phrases   155

12 Adjectivals: Clauses   170

17 Using Grammar   250

Preface

The Uses of Grammar is the result of a painstaking process of field-testing in the class-room, refinement on the basis of student feedback, further testing, and further refine-ment. The authors' goal was to create the ultimately teachable textbook—without sacrificing intellectual and scholarly integrity.

FORMS, FUNCTIONS, USES

Three questions constitute the superstructure of this book. What are the *forms* in the grammar of American English? How do those forms *function* in that grammar? And how are those forms *used* in speaking and writing—for various audiences in diverse situations to achieve the desired purposes?

FEATURES

We believe that these features will make *The Uses of Grammar* effective and interesting:

- Boxed materials, including "Challenger" and "For Discussion" items, will stretch the students' understanding of the principles presented in the text and encourage classroom discussion of concepts.

- The examples illustrating principles and the items in the exercises throughout the text reflect real-life language use: quotations from celebrities, periodicals, literature, and a wide array of "everyday" language users.

- The end-of-chapter "Passages for Analysis" sections allow students to think about and analyze the uses of forms and functions in contexts that are more extensive than the snippets given in the exercises.

- The Instructor's Manual accompanying *The Uses of Grammar* contains (1) an alternate table of contents, enabling instructors to base their courses on the traditional structure, moving from parts of speech to phrases, clauses, and sentences; (2) answer keys to all of the exercises in the book; and (3) some of the authors' ideas about teaching grammar.

- A companion website is available online (www.oup.com/us/usesofgrammar). Its base consists of (1) additional exercises keyed to the sections of chapters in the book; (2) answer keys to these exercises; (3) a "chapter" on the system of punctuation; and (4) an extended discussion of English as a second language. The website will grow in response to adopters' feedback and the need to address issues regarding language and teaching that arise on occasion (e.g., issues about public figures' use of language).

LANGUAGE LEARNING AND ENGLISH AS A SECOND LANGUAGE

One of the most important uses of grammar is understanding the processes whereby people learn languages. English as a second language (ESL) is an educational, social, and political problem. What are the most effective ways of teaching speakers of other languages to be fluent in English? What are the social consequences, particularly in the United States but also worldwide, of the inability to speak English? Should English be the official language of the United States?

The problems of ESL are implicit subjects throughout the chapters of this book, and Chapter 17 directly addresses ESL, as do materials at the companion website.

THE FLEXIBILITY OF THIS BOOK

The structure of *The Uses of Grammar* results from our many years of teaching undergraduate grammar courses, Judith Rodby at California State University–Chico and Ross Winterowd at University of Southern California. The traditional structure of grammar textbooks moves from the smallest unit to the largest: parts of speech (nouns, verbs, adjectives, adverbs, etc.) through phrases and clauses to sentences. There are, of course, good reasons for preferring this structure—not the least of which is what we call "the grammarian's dilemma" or "the grammatical circle": you can't understand the whole without understanding the parts, and you can't understand the parts without understanding the whole. Our way out of this dilemma is the structure we have chosen for this book. But there is no reason in principle why students and teachers should not begin with an understanding of parts of speech and work upward, toward the structure (the syntax) of sentences. For this reason, we have provided an alternate table of contents in the Instructor's Manual.

AN ATTITUDE TOWARD GRAMMAR

When mathematicians speak of the *elegance* of their subject, they are thinking about the underlying consistency and neatness and about the fundamental simplicity of the field: from a handful of basic principles, mathematicians develop theories and equations that attempt to explain the nature of the universe.

Consider the elegance of grammar. The articles that you read in the newspaper this morning, the novel by Dickens that you enjoyed last week, the speech delivered by your senator on the Fourth of July, the instructions for operating your new computer— underlying these and all other uses of the English language are just eight basic patterns that make up sentences and the structures derived from sentences. One of our main goals in this book is to change attitudes toward grammar. It is not a dull, nit-picking subject; it is as elegant as mathematics or music.

THE ONGOING PROCESS

Some wise person said, "No piece of writing is ever finished. It's just abandoned." Or, to state the idea as a cliché, there's always room for improvement. We urge users of this book to contact us through the companion website with suggestions for revision. What should we delete? What should we add? What should we change to make explanations clearer? What should we rearrange?

ACKNOWLEDGMENTS

The suggestions of reviewers were a significant factor in our revisions and refinements of this book, and we express our sincere appreciation to Douglas Biber, Northern Arizona University; Daniel R. Davis, University of Michigan–Dearborn; William Gustafson, Southern Connecticut State University; Charles Hill, University of Wisconsin–Oshkosh; Paul Justice, San Diego State University; William Provost, University of Georgia; William Roberts, University of Massachusetts–Lowell; Lois Spitzer, University of Nebraska; and Beth Rapp Young, University of Central Florida.

We have been particularly fortunate in working with our editor, Janet M. Beatty, whose commitment to the project and guidance in bringing the manuscript to its completed state were invaluable. Jan is a member of a professional group that is growing appreciably smaller: editors who are book people, committed to the art, ethics, and responsibilities of publishing.

We are indebted to Brian Kinsey, who patiently and efficiently guided us in preparing the manuscript for publication. Brenda Griffing, who edited our manuscript, meticulously eliminated inconsistencies, revised murky prose, and made us aware of omissions here and there.

Finally, we are delighted to have our book appear under the Oxford University Press colophon.

Judith Rodby
W. Ross Winterowd

1

The Uses of Grammar

CHAPTER PREVIEW

- Grammar describes a language in use. Grammars are made of rules that constitute the language (constitutive rules) and rules that attempt to regulate the language (prescriptive rules).

- The history of English grammar shows us how grammars have developed and how they have been used. In the eighteenth century, for example, grammars were used to try to purify and preserve English.

- Knowing grammar may help you to use English effectively. Grammar helps you to understand how language forms are used and why people think some language forms are right and others wrong.

WHAT IS GRAMMAR?

For the moment, we ask that you set aside all of your previous conceptions about grammar and follow our explanation of what "grammar" means in terms of this book. A grammar of a language (in this case, English) is a description of that language. This description does not make value judgments. For instance, grammar as a description of English would not state that the word "gentleman" is better or more elegant or more polite than the word "geezer." Both "gentleman" and "geezer" are part of the grammar of English. The description would include both *Me and him ain't going to the game* and *He and I are not going to the game,* because both these sentences are part of the English language. In other words, grammar describes the *forms* of a language that are actually used by native speakers.

Grammar also explains how the forms of language function in units we call sentences. For example, in the sentence *The teacher was unhappy about the test,* the words *the* and *teacher* form a noun phrase that functions as a subject in the sentence.

Grammar (as usage) is to language as sociology is to any society it studies. Through sociology you learn the norms and customs of a given society and what is acceptable and unacceptable in behavior. Through grammar as usage, you learn what language is appropriate in given situations and what is inappropriate (or even taboo). Grammar as usage helps explain why sometimes the word *gentleman* is preferable to the word *guy,* why sometimes the sentence *I must leave immediately* is preferable to the sentence *I've got to go right now,* and why sometimes the reverse is the case.

WHY STUDY GRAMMAR?

There is at least one good reason for studying grammar. Knowledge of grammar can help one use language effectively. Grammar helps one to think about how language structures are used to get meaning across (and use of language is a major factor in an individual's success or failure in a career and in society).

For DISCUSSION

As you work through this book, take time periodically to respond to this question: Are you aware of using grammar as you write? If so, what do you use, and when in your writing process do you apply any such tool? Does grammar help or hinder you? Does it get in the way because you are anxious about correctness or structure? As you write in a variety of contexts, take notes on what you actually do with and without grammar knowledge. Pay very close attention and note the specifics. You may be surprised by what you find.

HISTORY OF THE USES OF GRAMMAR

Before we get into the detailed study of the grammar of English, it will be useful to provide some historical context, and so we ask why various grammars have been written and how they have been used.

The Greeks and the Romans

Our story begins with the Greeks in the first century BCE, when the first grammars (i.e., grammar books) were written. The most famous of the Greek grammarians was Dionysius Thrax, who, using the works of Homer (*Iliad* and *Odyssey*) as his standards, wrote *The Art of Grammar* to aid in the study of literature and to preserve the purity of the language. A momentous fact of history, the importance of which will become apparent, is that the Romans adopted and adapted the Greek grammar to their own language, Latin. And we should note that Dionysius wanted to *preserve* the Greek language, to keep it from change. We will see that this motive—preserving language—is an idea that occurs throughout history.

In their structure, Greek and Latin differed. For example, Greek had three ways to express number: singular (only one item), dual (two items), plural (more than two items). If this were the case in English, we would talk about *one dog* and *several dogs,* but we would need a different form for talking about two of them (*two doga?*). Like English, Latin had only singular and plural—and this is but one instance of the differences in the two languages. Clearly, then, using Greek grammar as the basis for Latin grammatical analysis involved a good deal of adjustment—even wrenching.

For DISCUSSION

Do you think language is decaying? What is your evidence, pro or con? At one time *disinterested* and *uninterested* conveyed different meanings. *Disinterested* meant "unbiased, without prejudice or prejudgment"; thus one would want a *disinterested* judge, but not an *uninterested* judge. Now many people use *disinterested* as a synonym for *uninterested*. Does this usage represent language decay. Why or why not?

Throughout the Middle Ages the works of Latin grammarians, based on the Greek analyses of language, were used to teach Latin in the schools. During the Middle Ages and into the Renaissance, education to a great extent meant learning Latin and Latin grammar.

The Latin Influence on English Grammar

Now, in this brief history, we arrive at a watershed moment—the use of Latin grammar (which was based on Greek) to create grammars of English. In the eleventh century, Aelfric, abbot of Eynsham Monastery, wrote a Latin grammar and proposed that this work serve as the basis for a grammar of English. (Aelfric's English was, of course, Anglo-Saxon, which to us sounds like an utterly foreign language.) With Aelfric, the long tradition of basing English grammar on that of Latin began. Here is just one example.

In Latin, the form of the noun changes with the different functions in sentences, and this change in word forms according to function allows Latin to be more flexible in its syntax (sentence structure) than English. For example, both *canis hominem mordet* and *hominem canis mordet* mean *dog bites man* because *canis* is the subject form of the noun, and *hominem* is the object form of *homo*. But in English, *dog bites man* and *man bites dog* are exact opposites. (To express *man bites dog* in Latin, one would say *canem mordet homo* or *homo mordet canem.*)

In Latin, nouns have as many as six forms, depending on their use as subjects, objects, and so on. In short, Latin showed the function of nouns by changing their forms; English shows the function of nouns by their positions in the sentence.

Although there are many other examples of Latin influence on English grammar, perhaps the most important is the choice of the language use on which to base the grammar. Dionysius Thrax and other Greeks used the works of Homer as their basis; Roman grammarians used the works of Cicero and Virgil, who wrote in Latin. English grammars followed this tradition, basing their analyses and commentaries on the writings of established authors and the speech of educated classes.

The problem, of course, is that a grammar should analyze and describe all levels of usage. Here is an analogy. If a sociological study of the American people were based only on college graduates, we would have a false idea of the values and living conditions of the population. A grammatical study based only on literature and the usage of educated people gives a false picture of the English language.

In the eighteenth century, Robert Lowth and other grammarians who thought that Latin was superior to English put much of their energy into what they believed was purifying and preserving the language, condemning usages like *It's me* and *Who is this for?* These usages, which the grammarians considered vulgar, are perfectly normal English, but they might not be appropriate in all situations.

The English literati had aspirations of standardizing and refining English. They also wanted to stop the language from changing. The essayist Jonathan Swift, for example, wrote that "it is better that a Language should not be wholly perfect than that it should be perpetually changing." One method of standardizing English was to try to make it systematic and to borrow the rules for the system from Latin.

Noah Webster: Grammar as a Description of Language

And now an American hero enters the scene: Noah Webster (1758–1843).

While he was teaching school in Goshen, New York, Webster became dissatisfied with available textbooks on language; he wanted instruction to reflect both the American version of English and American values. Thus, he set out to write *A Grammatical Institute of the English Language,* the three parts of which were a spelling book, a grammar book, and a collection of readings. (One indication of Webster's influence is the estimate that one hundred million copies of his spelling book were sold!)

Webster is most famous for his dictionary (indeed, "Webster" and "dictionary" are almost synonymous), in which he enunciated the then revolutionary principle that "grammar is formed on language, and not language on grammar." In other words, Webster was saying that a grammar should describe the language used, not dictate what should be used.

FOR DISCUSSION: POLITICAL CORRECTNESS AND LANGUAGE CHANGE

You know that some words and phrases are taboo. For example, in my vocabulary are words that I could not include in this discussion, for if I listed them, they would offend many readers and would adversely affect the sales of the book. Usually such taboo words have to do with sex or excretory functions, or they are blasphemous (showing lack of respect for God or other holies). But there are other words that out of context seem perfectly acceptable—for instance, *fairy*. Editors of such publications as newspapers, magazines, and textbooks ban the use of this term because it connotes homosexuality in a derogatory way and thus might offend a group of readers. Editors suggest "elf" as a synonym. Hence, "the tooth fairy," so common among children of an earlier generation, must become "the tooth elf," and "fairy tale" would, presumably, be replaced by "elf tale."

Scholar Diane Ravitch has compiled a list of terms that some people think are potentially offensive to groups of readers. Among these are

- *Adam and Eve,* to be replaced by "Eve and Adam," to demonstrate that males do not have precedence.
- *Chief Sitting Bull,* a relic of domination of Native Americans should be replaced by the chief's actual name, Tatanka Iyotake.
- *Egghead,* to be replaced by "intellectual."
- *Insane,* to be replaced with "a person who has an emotional disorder or psychiatric illness."
- *Snowman* is sexist and should be replaced with "snowperson."

What do you think of about this policing of language? Is it justified, or is it silly? Explain your attitude. Can you think of other words and phrases that have become politically incorrect?

During the nineteenth century and well into the twentieth, a strange situation prevailed. While scholars were studying the evolution and actual use of languages, students in classrooms throughout America were being given a simplified version of grammar that evolved from the attitudes of the Latin grammarians.

Now in this brief history, we move forward from the nineteenth century to the twentieth and the coming of modern language studies.

Structuralism

Of great importance in the history of grammar was the coming of structuralism, starting with the publication in 1916 of *Course in General Linguistics,* by the Swiss scholar Ferdinand de Saussure, who made the important distinction between the language itself (*langue*) as a system and the individual use of that system (*parole*). (You and your friends speak *la langue;* but each of you has his or her own version, that is, *parole.*) Analogically, Beethoven's Ninth Symphony is a complete "system" with its own unvarying structure. Performances of the symphony differ, however, according to the interpretations of various conductors—but they are, nonetheless, still "Beethoven's Ninth." You and I speak the same language (*langue*), English, but your individual use of that language (*parole*) is different from mine. The task of the structural linguist was to describe *la langue.* Here is the important point: native-born Americans speak the language (*la langue*), but each person has his or her own version of it (*parole*).

Compare *la langue* to the range and variety of foods available in a supermarket—everything from asparagus to zucchini. You and I shop in this supermarket, but each of us brings a personal assortment to the checkstand. Your basket contains tofu, but mine doesn't; mine contains a can of mackerel, but yours doesn't. We can compare *parole* to the array of items that each of us has chosen from the large selection in the supermarket.

The next momentous development was the adaptation of the theories of behavioral psychology for the study of grammar.

Behaviorism

Leonard Bloomfield (1887–1949) incorporated behavioral (stimulus-response) psychology into his theory of language. Trying for empirical rigor, he excluded mental and conceptual categories from his work, considering only language phenomena that could be observed, thus eliminating from grammar the science of meaning, or semantics.

Behavioral psychology, now abandoned, had severe limitations as an explanation for human motives and actions, and the same limitations made the behavioral study of language less than satisfactory. For example, according to the behavioral model, children learn language through imitation. Little Jane hears Mama say, "Eat your spinach," and Jane tries to imitate that sentence. However, studies of language development clearly demonstrate that Jane is not merely imitating; she is developing a "grammar" in her brain and is using it to make sense of language and to begin to work with it. Mama says, "Eat your spinach," and Jane responds, "I *eated* my spinach." Jane has never heard Mama or anyone else use *eated* as the past form of *eat,* so something other than imitation is clearly going on in Jane's development of language. As we will several times point out in this book, it is obvious that humans have a genetically endowed "grammar" in their brains, just as they have a genetically endowed sense of sight.

In spite of the limitations of the theoretical framework he applied to language, Bloomfield did further the rigorous study of the structure of language.

The next development in our history has been the attempt to account for the "grammar in the brain," of which we just spoke. Thus, in the next section of this chapter, we turn to universal grammar.

FOR DISCUSSION: LANGUAGE AS STIMULUS-RESPONSE

Pause for just a moment to consider what it means to view language as mere stimulus-response. I utter the stimulus "Stop!" and you respond by stopping. So far, so good. But then I point to a building on the corner and say "apartment house." You observe the building; you see people coming and going; you conclude that several families must live in this building and that, hence, a multifamily dwelling is an apartment house. However, overnight a transformation takes place. All of the residents of the building sign a document and pay money, and now the building is no longer an apartment house; it is a condominium. In other words, language has changed the nature of the building. How can one explain this change except through meanings? The building is constructed not only of steel and bricks, but also of words.

Can you think of other examples of ways in which language is far more than a matter of stimulus and response?

Transformational or Universal Grammar

A momentous revolution in the study of grammar came in 1957, when Noam Chomsky published *Syntactic Structures*—the beginning of transformational grammar,[1] which was a reaction against the structuralism represented by Bloomfield. Chomsky's goal was to study linguistic competence, not individual performance. What is meant by "competence"? In transformational grammar, competence is really the grammar that you and I have in our heads. We are able to produce and understand language; therefore, we must have some kind of mental system for that language ability. A useful analogy (if not pushed too far) is the computer. To develop a computer that uses language as do humans, scientists must devise a set of rules (a program) that will allow the computer to do what HAL did in *2001: A Space Odyssey,* using language in the same way a human would. Anyone who has used a telephone knows that computers now can give canned, standard responses but cannot carry on conversations about the weather or the World Series. It must be the case that we humans have a built-in and inborn set of "rules" that allow us to use language. Discovering these rules is the ultimate goal of transformational grammar. Chomsky and his followers are attempting to explain and describe human language ability.

Currently, linguists are working on "universal grammar," writing rules that represent language "principles" that seem to be innate and universal. For example, it would seem to be a principle that all languages have verbs. Linguists are also working on writing grammar rules that describe the "parameters" or particular rules for specific human languages such as English. Word order in sentences is an example of a parameter because word order differs from one language to another.

Three Views of Grammar

From this brief excursion, three views of grammar and its uses will become obvious:

1. Until about the mid-nineteenth century, the main concern of most grammarians was preserving and purifying the language. (The residue of this movement, still evident in some textbooks, was what might be called "traditional grammar.")

2. During the nineteenth century and the first half of the twentieth century, linguists (actually, a fancy term for scholars of grammar and other aspects of language) began to provide descriptions of languages as people used them. (The result was descriptive grammar or, to use the jargon of the trade, "structural linguistics.")

3. By the mid-twentieth century, linguists had begun to focus on the mind's ability to produce language. (The result was the set of terms listed in footnote 1. All of these terms refer to an evolving body of theory.)

---

[1] Several terms denote the grammatical revolution begun by Chomsky (transformational grammar, generative grammar, transformational-generative grammar, and universal grammar). We will use the term *universal grammar,* without attempting to sort out the distinctions implied by all four terms.

As you go through the chapters of *The Uses of Grammar,* you will find that they incorporate the insights gained from traditional grammar, from structural linguistics, and from transformational grammar. We think that you will make significant gains in both your understanding of the English language and your ability to use it effectively.

USING GRAMMAR: USAGE

Knowing grammar can help you use language more effectively: you will have words and terms, a metalanguage, that will help you talk about and analyze your own grammar use; you will have knowledge that will help you make choices about your use of language.

Grammar books (such as this one) usually contain two types of statements about the language. One type sets forth or describes what is—for example:

1. A sentence consists of a subject and a predicate.

Subject	Predicate
Dogs	bark.
The cats in the yard	yowled all night.

The other type explains what should be—for example:

2. In formal academic writing (e.g., doctoral dissertations), contractions (*isn't* for *is not, can't* for *cannot*) are usually unacceptable, but they may be preferred in informal writing such as letters to friends.

The first type of grammatical statement (describing what *is*) we call a constitutive rule. The other type of rule (stating what *should be* in language use) we call a regulative rule.

Constitutive Rules

Constitutive rules, those that describe what is, are exemplified by the game of chess, which is nothing but the constitutive rules that regulate what players can and cannot do with each piece. Thus, one chess rule says that bishops can move any number of spaces diagonally. If someone moves a bishop horizontally or vertically, he or she is simply not playing chess. Suppose one of the bishop pieces from a set is lost. The players can agree that a paperclip or a thimble can replace the missing bishop; the shape and size of the piece is irrelevant; the constitutive rule whereby the piece functions is essential.

Regulative Rules

A rule such as "Contractions are unacceptable in formal academic writing" tells language users what is considered to be "proper" English (by the writer of the rule, that is). Thus it is not constitutive, but regulative.

Rules

- Constitutive rules make up grammar. Grammar is a body of rules, just as chess is. To the question "What is grammar?" we could answer, "A system made up of constitutive rules."
- Regulative rules state what language structures should be used. The following sentences are all English:

  You are not a certified teacher.

  You aren't a certified teacher.

  You ain't a certified teacher.

  The first is appropriate in, for instance, an official statement about certification; the second might be used in a conversation; the third is an example of a dialect that would probably be judged inappropriate in most formal situations.

Regulative Rules and Prescriptive Grammar

One famous regulative rule (often referred to as a prescriptive rule) is this: Do not end a sentence with a preposition (e.g., *of, with*). The following sentences violate that rule:

Fudge is the candy I was thinking *of.*

Marge is the person I'm going *with.*

However, we know that both sentences are perfectly normal English.

Another regulative rule states that *shall* is to be used to express the future with first person pronouns (e.g., *I, we*) and that *will* should be used with second and third persons (*you, they*). The following perfectly normal English sentences violate that rule:

I *will* cook the hamburgers.

They *shall* shuck the corn.

The problem with regulative or prescriptive rules is just this: they do not take the speaker's purpose or situation into account. For example, when I am at home, chatting with my family, I would be quite likely to say something like *I know who you're talking about.* A prescriptive grammarian would say that the *who* in the sentence should be *whom* and that the sentence should not end with a preposition (*about*). Thus, the "correct" form of the sentence would be *I know about whom you are talking.* But in conversation with friends and family the "correct" form sounds too stuffy; I would be much more comfortable with the "incorrect" form. On the other hand, if I were addressing the students in one of my classes, I would say, *I know whom you are talking about,* changing the form *who* to *whom,* but still ending the sentence with a preposition. Even in a formal situation, the "correct" sentence *I know about whom you are talking* seems stilted, stuffy, phony.

FOR DISCUSSION

My grandson, Christopher Winterowd, characteristically says "Him and me" did this or that. Once when I corrected him, he responded, "Oh, Grandpa, I know that. When I'm in school I would say 'he and I,' but me and my buddies don't talk grammar all the time."

In what ways does Chris's statement show a sophisticated understanding of language? Was I right in correcting him? Explain.

It is useful to understand the development of the regulative rules, making up prescriptive grammar, which sets forth hard and fast rules about what is right and what it wrong, usually ignoring context or the purpose of the speaker or writer.

When people say to us, "Oh, you teach English; I had better watch my grammar," what they mean is that they feel the need to be vigilant about regulative rules (because they assume that we listen for error and have some kind of regulative role to play). While native speakers of a language are generally not conscious of constitutive rules, they may be very aware of prescriptive or regulative rules.

FOR DISCUSSION

The following ideas about grammar have prevailed from the Latin grammarians through the ages; there are vestiges even today in some textbooks.

- That there is an absolute right and wrong in language use regardless of purpose and situation. (The subjective complement is *always* in the subjective case. Therefore, *It is I* is correct, and *It is me* is incorrect.) In other words, grammar regulates language.

- That grammar and logic coincide (Since two negatives make a positive, *I don't have no money* must mean *I have some money*.) In other words, grammar follows the rules of logic. If someone told you "I don't have no money," would you assume that the person is announcing the possession of at least some money?

- That literature, not common usage of the language, sets the standards for grammar. This doctrine removes grammar from the realm of public discourse and places it in a rarefied realm all its own.

> • That definitions ("A noun is the name of a person, place, or thing") and drills (such as filling in the blanks) are necessary for improving one's use of language.
>
> Which of these beliefs about the uses of grammar have you been taught or exposed to? We would argue that even though knowing *about* language is useful, the best way to become a better communicator is to use language. Grammar can help speakers and writers fine-tune their language for use in various situations. What do you think?

Prescriptive rules may also serve to preserve or even to define social class boundaries. For example, adherence to rules about when to use *he* and *him* or *I* and *me* (in other words, rules about the forms of pronouns) identifies a speaker as a member of the educated middle-class in many areas of the United States. Many middle-class urban adults would neither say nor find acceptable the phrase "Me and him are going to dinner." (It is unlikely, however, that they would say this phrase was NOT English. The rule violated is not a constitutive one for most of us.) Interestingly, and not surprisingly, these rules for pronoun usage are derived from Latin.

Many of our attitudes about good and bad grammar and language come from rules developed 50, 100, or 150 years ago. Indeed, regulative rules are still used to slow down changes in a language.

USING GRAMMAR: LANGUAGE LEARNING

If you plan to be a teacher, knowing the grammar of English will be invaluable, for you will almost certainly have students who are learning English as a second language. (For example, in one high school district in Southern California, the native languages of the students include English, Spanish, Vietnamese, Chinese, Cambodian, and Thai.) Your knowledge of grammar will help you to understand the "errors" that these students make when they speak or write English and will give you the knowledge to help them advance in their mastery of the language.

If you do not plan to be a teacher, you nonetheless live in a multicultural society, and you are surrounded by people whose first language is not English. In a metropolitan area such as Chicago or Los Angeles, many recent immigrants do not speak English at all. Understanding grammar will give you insight into the struggles of new arrivals to become fluent in English. If more people understood the workings of language and language learning, much of the resentment toward "foreigners" would disappear. Grammar can be an instrument for expanding tolerance.

As we all know, English as a second language (ESL) is a politically hot topic, debated by politicians and making a plank in the platforms of candidates. Unfortunately, most politicians and their constituents have no knowledge of the problems and processes of language learning, with the result that language learners are shuffled about from program to program as politicians mandate educational changes based on fears and myths. Knowledge of how people learn languages is thus an important aspect of what used to be called "civics," the social science that deals with the rights and duties of citizens.

Finally, a brief survey of language learning is a good introduction to the workings of grammar.

Native speakers of English (or any other language) generally are not conscious of using the grammatical rules of their language; but second-language learners, especially adults, may focus on their knowledge of language rules as they attempt to speak or write. Furthermore, people learning a language often inadvertently formulate a rule incorrectly. For example, a learner might say, "He was sing a song." In the absence of context, it is impossible to tell whether the person meant "He was singing a song" or "He sang a song."

Fortunately, learners aren't stuck with incomplete or incorrect rules; learners' rules are highly malleable. As language learners acquire more information about the language, they can and do formulate new rules and change old ones. For example, a learner may have formulated the following rule: "When you want to make a sentence negative, insert *not*." This rule would produce a variety of sentences, some of them, from the viewpoint of a typical native speaker of English, correct and some incorrect:

> I am not hungry. [a perfectly normal English sentence]
>
> I not eat pork. [a sentence typical of someone not fluent in English, that is, a language learner]

For second-language learners (especially adults), acquiring and using grammatical knowledge about a language can be a more or less conscious process. In language classes, learners might be taught explicitly about when to use *do* in forming negatives

LANGUAGE LEARNING

- Knowing grammar helps teachers assist students learn English, gives one an understanding of nonnative speakers in this multicultural society, and helps one understand how language use can become a public issue, the cause of political debate.

- Native speakers of English are usually not conscious of the rules of grammar. When they speak or write, they "do what comes naturally," without pondering how, for instance, to form negative sentences.

- Learners can use rules to help them master a second language. The more thoroughly they master the second language, the less they rely on or think about the rules.

For DISCUSSION

It may surprise you to know that *glamour* and *grammar* are closely related, and that *glamour* was once associated with magic. In the early eighteenth century, Scottish speakers of English altered *grammar* to create *glamour*, which meant enchantment or spell. The word "spell" itself relates both to correctness in language and to the magic of language. In one sense "spell" has to do with the forms of words: the longest river in the United States is *spelled* M-I-S-S-I-S-S-I-P-P-I. But "spell" also describes words used to invoke magical powers. What attitudes do people you know have about grammar and its power? Do they think grammatical knowledge is important—do they attribute much power to knowing grammar rules?

(I *do* not eat pork); they might have a native-speaking friend who corrects statements like "I not eat pork." In addition, they may live in an English-speaking environment where they hear *do* and *did* used repeatedly. All of these sources are valuable to the newcomers' learning; and as they reformulate their rules, they use these rules to produce sentences. Undoubtedly as learners become increasingly adept in English, they also become less conscious of applying grammar rules when they speak.

Second-language learning is such an important topic that we end this book with a chapter on that subject.

In this book, we recognize that language and grammar are always associated with power. The ability to speak and write in accepted ways is often a requisite for entry into a career and acceptance by social groups. Grammar is not a magical elixir for the problems of communicating, but it is, as you will see, an important tool, useful for understanding language and its use.

CHAPTER REVIEW

Summarize what the chapter says about these key concepts:

- Traditional grammar
- Descriptive grammar
- Universal grammar
- Constitutive rules
- Prescriptive rules
- Regulative rules
- Second-language learning and the development of rules

C H A P T E R

Getting Started:
Some Important Concepts

CHAPTER PREVIEW

- Grammaticality is one of the most important concepts in this book. A grammatical sentence is one that would be spoken or written by a native speaker of English and would be judged grammatical. Native speakers know what is grammatical and what is not; they do not need to know grammar terms to analyze a sentence and determine that it is or is not grammatical. An ungrammatical sentence is one that a native speaker would not generate.

- Descriptive grammar considers all of the sentences in a language, not just those that purists consider correct.

- A grammatical sentence can be either appropriate or inappropriate. Appropriateness often depends on the level of formality of the sentence. *Let's grab some chow* is informal; *We shall dine at seven* is extremely formal. Both sentences are grammatical, but they would not be appropriate in the same situations.

- Grammatical judgments are seldom cut and dried; they are usually not questions of absolute right or absolute wrong. For example, the sentence *Timothy is in hospital* would seem perfectly grammatical to a British speaker of English, but might well seem ungrammatical to a speaker of American English, who would prefer *Timothy is in the hospital.*

- The parts of sentences can be talked about as forms or as functions. Forms are word classes or parts of speech such as noun, verb, and adjective. Functions are the work a structure does in a sentence: subject, object, and complement, for example, are terms for functions in a sentence. In *Dogs chase cats,* the word *dogs* is a noun functioning as subject of the sentence.

- Sentences can be divided into subjects and predicates.

SUBJECT	PREDICATE
My cat	likes tuna fish.

- They can also be broken into phrases.

SUBJECT

PREPOSITIONAL PHRASE   PREDICATE

For her dinner, my cat   likes tuna fish.

- The eight classes of words in a language fall into two categories:

   a. Form-class words

      Nouns: e.g., man, Alvin, love

      Verbs: e.g., sing, see, become

      Adjectives: e.g., pretty, horrible, intelligent

      Adverbs: e.g., quickly, reluctantly

   b. Function (structure) words

      Pronouns: e.g., I, you, he, she, it, we, they

      Prepositions: e.g., in, of, above, under

      Conjunctions: e.g., and, but, because, if

      Interjections: e.g., darn! golly! rats!

      Determiners: e.g., the, a, these, those, his, hers

      Modal auxiliaries: e.g., will, should, could

- By addition, deletion, movement, and substitution, sentences can be changed. To *Monkeys eat bananas,* I can add a word, *Do monkeys eat bananas?,* creating a question. Deleting a word creates a command or imperative sentence: *Eat bananas!* Through addition and movement, I can create another type of sentence, a passive: *Bananas are eaten by monkeys.* And, of course, I can make substitutions: *Monkeys eat them.*

SYMBOLS USED IN THIS BOOK

The symbols that we use throughout this book will save verbiage.

    An asterisk (*) before a language structure means that, *in our opinion,* the structure in question is ungrammatical (i.e., is not English). (For a definition of *grammaticality,* see below.)

    *Rudolf not going this day. [Rudolf isn't going today.]

    A question mark (?) before a language structure means that we are undecided about its grammaticality or its appropriateness.

    ?To who did Marvin give the book? [In formal usage, the sentence would read differently. Here: *To whom did Marvin give the book?*]

> When we want to indicate that we are approximating spoken language, we use slash marks.
>
> > Gustav, a German who was just learning English, said /Vell, I vahnt to read zee book/ (Well, I want to read the book).
>
> An arrow (→) means "consists of" or "is made up of." Thus, *Sentence* → *Subject + Predicate* means "A sentence is made up of (or consists of) a subject and predicate."

GRAMMATICALITY: WHY IS THIS A VERY IMPORTANT CONCEPT?

In the heading for this section, we use the intensifier *very* to stress the importance of the concept that we are about explain. To follow much of what we will be saying throughout this book, readers must understand what we mean by the terms *grammatical, ungrammatical,* and *grammaticality.*

A good descriptive grammar sets forth the features of a language. Insofar as it is accurate and complete, it is valid and useful. Thus, a descriptive grammar would contain analyses of such common American English sentences as these, all of which violate "rules" of prescriptive grammar:

1. Me and him played chess until midnight. [Formal English: He and I played chess until midnight.]

2. My father be home at five every day. [Formal English: My father is home at five every day.]

3. Me, I'd just as soon not go to the game tonight. [Formal English: I'd prefer not to go to the game tonight.]

4. Wanting to make sure we had enough money, the bank was our first stop. [Formal English: Wanting to make sure we had enough money, we stopped first at the bank.]

5. Airlines like customers who they sell first-class tickets to. [Formal English: Airlines like customers to whom they sell first-class tickets.]

6. Neither of us are willing to stop. [Formal English: Neither of us is willing to stop.]

7. Everyone has their own opinion about the candidate. [Formal English: Everyone has his or her own opinion about the candidate.]

8. The child not only wants a new bicycle, but also a TV. [Formal English: The child wants not only a new bicycle, but also a TV.]

The point is this: hearing or reading any of these sentences, we would conclude that the speakers or writers were fluent in English. In other words, all of the sentences are perfectly normal English. (Some people might prefer the formal versions, but that has nothing to do with whether the sentences are English or non-English.)

Since a grammar of English is a description of the language, any sentence that we assume has been spoken or written by a person fluent in English is, in our terms, *grammatical*. Grammaticality has nothing to do with politeness or appropriateness in language; the term simply means that a sentence (or passage) is English. The following are not English, and therefore are ungrammatical:

1. *Moby Dick* is very great book. [Native speakers of many languages other than English often omit the indefinite article (*a*).]

2. *In the fourteenth century, one half of the population of Europe starved from bubonic plague. [The German, verb for *to die* is *sterben*. A German writer guessed (wrongly) that the English *starved* was close enough.]

3. *The pasta no ready yet.

4. *Several from the books were best sellers in France. [The English idiom is *several of*, not *several from*.]

Because we assume that a native speaker would not say or write these four sentences, we judge them as ungrammatical. We should not confuse grammaticality with appropriateness. Perfectly grammatical English sentences can be either appropriate or inappropriate, depending on circumstances. For example, "It is my express desire that you complete your homework before you retire for the night" is perfectly grammatical, but do you think it would be appropriate for a father to say this to his nine-year-old daughter?

Exercise 2.1

In your own words, explain *grammaticality*.

Grammaticality, Appropriateness, and Formality

In addition to grammaticality, appropriateness and levels of formality are very important to what we will be saying throughout this book.

The following sentences are perfectly grammatical; that is, we would take them to be produced by a native speaker of English, not by a person who just learning the language.

1. Me and him went to the store.

2. Airlines like customers who they sell first class tickets to.

3. The child not only wants a new bicycle, but also a TV.

Me and him went to the store may be appropriate in some dialects of English. (See pages 8–11 in Chapter 1.) In some geographical areas or in some groups, the rule for pronouns in subject position may either allow for or require *me and him* (rather than *he and I*). We could say that the prestige dialect, Standard American English (SAE), requires *he and I* in subject positions, but other dialects have different rules for pronouns. No one would say that *Me and him went to the store* is not an English sentence.

The second and third sentences bring up not only issues of prescriptive grammar, but also problems of formality and context of use. Prescriptivists would be unlikely to accept the sentence *Airlines like customers who they sell first-class tickets to;* they would want the sentence to read *Airlines like customers to whom they sell first-class tickets.* Prescriptivists would consider the sentence ending in *to* as an English sentence; they would just think it was a bad English or an inappropriate English sentence for a formal written context.

The issue of appropriateness is also tricky. Very formal language may be inappropriate in informal situations. Perfectly grammatical English sentences can be either appropriate or inappropriate, depending on the circumstances. For example, as we have already seen, *It is my express desire that you complete your homework before you retire for the night* is perfectly grammatical but in most families it would be an inappropriate way for a father to speak to a child in elementary school. The child would think that the father was angry or making fun of him or her. If we heard or read the sentence *A child not only wants a new bicycle, but also a TV,* we would conclude the speaker or writer was fluent in English. The sentence is a perfectly normal English sentence. Some people might prefer the more carefully composed and edited version *A child wants not only a new bicycle but also a new TV* in a formal letter or document.

Our point is this: before we make judgments about language, it is important to think about the situations—who is speaking or writing, to whom, and for what purpose? Language is not simply grammatical or ungrammatical—it is also formal and informal, conventional and unconventional, standard or nonstandard, and appropriate or inappropriate. Grammar rules and theory help us to talk and think about these very important distinctions.

G RAMMATICALITY, APPROPRIATENESS, AND FORMALITY

- If, in your opinion, a sentence would be uttered by a native speaker, you then will conclude that the sentence is grammatical. *I ain't got time for them jobs* is, in our opinion, a grammatical sentence. **I no have no time for that jobs* is not a grammatical sentence, since we don't think it would be uttered by a native speaker.

- Both of the following sentences are grammatical: (1) *The professor is nuttier than a fruitcake.* (2) *The professor is extremely eccentric.* The informal first sentence would be appropriate in a conversation among college classmates. The formal second sentence might be appropriate in a discussion with a dean or department chair.

FOR DISCUSSION: MALAPROPISMS

A malapropism is the misuse of a word or phrase, often resulting in humor. The term is derived from the name of Mrs. Malaprop, a character in Richard Brinsley Sheridan's play *The Rivals* (1775). Speaking of countries that shared a border, she talked of the *geometry* of *contagious* countries, where a better informed person would have said *geography* and *contiguous*. She wanted her daughter to *reprehend* her meaning rather than *apprehend* it. (*Reprehend*, of course, means "to voice disapproval or criticize.")

Shakespeare often used malapropisms to create humor in his plays. The character Elbow in *Measure for Measure* is a regular user of malapropisms. For example, he uses *benefactors* when he means *malefactors*. In *Much Ado About Nothing*, the foolish constable, Dogberry, responds in this way when he is called an ass: "Dost thou not suspect my place. Dost thou not suspect my years?" Of course, Dogberry means *respect*, not *suspect*.

As Louis B. Mayer (of Metro Goldwyn Mayer fame) departed for a voyage to Europe, he called from the deck of the ship, "Bon Voyage." Why is that a malapropism?

Why is the sentence (attributed to Yogi Berra) "It's déjà vu all over again" a malapropism?

Grammatical Judgments

Throughout this book, we will make judgments about grammaticality and usage, just as you will during the time you study grammar and as you unconsciously have done from the time you began to use language. It is important to understand that many of the judgments you make and those we make are not absolutes and are open to questioning. For example, if you are unfamiliar with the British use of English, you might judge the following sentence as ungrammatical: *Louella is on holiday.* The American equivalent would be *Louella is on vacation.* If you were familiar with both British and American English, you would judge both sentences as grammatical. In central Utah, the sentence *Yesterday we visited Greg and them* (meaning "Greg and the rest of his family") would be perfectly normal and hence grammatical, but someone unfamiliar with the dialect spoken in this region of Utah might well judge the sentence ungrammatical.

The way to avoid fruitless squabbles about right and wrong and grammatically or ungrammaticality is to realize that often in the study of language, we deal with probabilities and uncertainties.

FORM AND FUNCTION

You may be familiar with a set of terms for parts of speech or language forms: verb, noun, adjective, adverb, conjunction, preposition. Many grammars of English are organized on the basis of these language forms. This grammar is largely organized around the functions of these forms in the sentence. Let's look at some illustrations of the form and function distinctions:

For example, the word *grammar* (form = noun) can function in many different ways:

Grammar is fun. [subject]

Students enjoy grammar. [object of the verb]

Students have fun with grammar. [object of preposition]

Conversely, often functions can be fulfilled by a variety of language forms. Let's look at a variety of forms or structures that can function as a subject:

Grammar is fun. [one-word noun phrase]

The last grammar exercise is fun. [several-word noun phrase]

Learning grammar is fun. [nonfinite verb phrase]

What I do with grammar is fun. [noun clause]

SENTENCES: SUBJECT AND PREDICATE

In this grammar we will be analyzing sentences and their constituents. As a basis for understanding sentences, you must first know about the two main sentence parts, subject and predicate. First, we will work inductively and see what you know already know about sentences and their parts. Each of the following sentences is divided into two parts. Some of these divisions should strike you as odd or unjustified, and some should seem natural and justified. Which of the divisions seem justified?

1. Dick   and Jane played checkers.
2. Mother and Father   painted the kitchen.
3. Spot gnawed on   a bone.
4. The boy who saw Dick cheat on the exam   told the teacher.
5. The test   that Dick took was very difficult.
6. The children have   been wailing.

If you are a native speaker of English, your intuitive knowledge of the English language probably gave you ideas about what goes with what in the sentences. Intuitive knowledge helped you find the subject and predicate "units" that make up sentences. (In case you want to verify your intuition, you can find the correct divisions on page 28.)

As we have just seen, the two main structures in a sentence are subject and predicate. The subject of a sentence is either one word or a word group, and the predicate, likewise, is either one word or a group of words. The subject states the topic of the sentence, and the predicate gives information about what the subject does or brings about or what changes it undergoes or what happens to it.

Subject	Predicate
Fish	swim.
Humans	talk.
Most politicians	accept contributions.
"The university	charges too much for parking." (Student)
"Adults	find pleasure in deceiving a child." (Elias Canetti)
"Good fortune	has always trailed Michael Jordan." (John Gregory Dunne, *The New York Review of Books*, July 15, 1999)
"Gene Hackman's character	remarks that watching an Eric Rohmer [film] is like watching paint dry." (*Los Angeles Magazine*, August 1999)

To graphically represent the relationships of units within the sentence we can use the diagram system developed by Alonzo Reed and Brainerd Kellogg, *Higher Lessons in English*, published in 1909. Reed-Kellogg diagrams are still widely used. Diagrammatically, we can represent subject and predicate as in Figure 2.1.

Figure 2.1   Reed-Kellogg diagram of *Most politicians accept contributions*. The vertical line cutting through the horizontal line separates the subject from the predicate; the vertical line between *accept* and *politicians* separates the direct object from the verb *accept*. *Most*, on the slant line, modifies *politicians*.

Exercise 2.2

Draw a line between the subjects and the predicates of the following sentences.

> **Examples**
> 1. Bored people | watch TV.
> 2. "No song or poem | will bear my mother's name." (Alice Walker)
> 3. "Medication without explanation | is obscene." (Toni Cade Bambara)

1. Dick sneezes.
2. Jane hates liver.
3. The whole family thinks that cats are cute.

4. "I claim the right to contradict myself." (Federico Fellini)

5. "The accomplice to the crime of corruption is frequently our own indifference." (Bess Myerson)

6. "The ideology of capitalism makes us all into connoisseurs of liberty—of the indefinite expansion of possibility." (Susan Sontag)

7. "The catholicity of Christianity integrates the small and touching household gods into the worship of saints, and local cults." (Emmanuel Levinas)

8. "Large department stores, with their luxuriant abundance of canned goods, foods, and clothing, are like the primary landscape and the geometrical focus of affluence." (Jean Baudrillard)

CHALLENGER[1]

Find the subject and predicate division in the following sentence: "One chill May day in Newfoundland I met Birgitta Wallace, a Swedish archaeologist for Parks Canada." (Prijt Vesilind, *National Geographic*, May 2000)

PHRASES

Sentences can also be divided into units called phrases. A phrase consists of one word or more than one word. When a phrase consists of more than one word, the group of words acts together as a part of the sentence. For example, in the sentence *Most boys in Utah like rutabagas,* the words *Most boys in Utah* form a noun phrase. A noun phrase functions just like a single noun; in the sentence above, it is the subject of the sentence.

One way to see if a unit is a noun phrase is to substitute a single word for the phrase:

Most boys in Utah like rutabagas.

They like rutabagas.

The following ungrammatical sentences show us that the words *Most* and *in Utah* are part of the noun phrase:

*They in Utah like rutabagas.

*Most they in Utah like rutabagas.

In the sentence *The ducks quack loudly in City Park,* the group of words *in City Park* is a prepositional phrase. The word *in* is a preposition and the head of the phrase. We

---

[1] Challengers are intended to extend your understanding beyond the sentences you have already practiced.

know that *in* is the head word of the phrase *in City Park* because if we delete this preposition, the whole sentence will be ungrammatical: **The ducks quack loudly City Park.* In the sentences above, the predicate is also a verb phrase and the subject is a noun phrase.

Phrases and phrase structures are associated with another method of diagramming: branching trees, as in Figure 2.2.

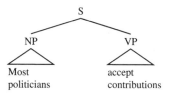

Figure 2.2 Branching tree diagram of *Most politicians accept contributions.* In this diagram, S = sentence. NP is, of course, noun phrase, and VP is verb phrase. Be aware that this terminology creates a small problem. In relation to branching tree diagrams, VP (verb phrase) is the equivalent of predicate. This is the case only with branching tree diagrams.

For displaying some principles of grammar (e.g., hierarchies of grammatical relationships and structures that are embedded inside other structures), branching tree diagrams are better than Reed-Kellogg diagrams. As we progress though this grammar section of the book, the reasons for using Reed-Kellogg or branching tree or both will become obvious.

We will use diagrams throughout this book, simply to give a visual representation of the principles that we will be discussing. If the diagrams help you understand grammar, they have served their purpose; don't get bogged down in the details.

THE PARTS OF SPEECH

It is conventional and convenient to classify the words in the language according to what has been called "the parts of speech."

One interesting fact about the parts of speech is that some categories can gain new members, but others are finite lists to which no new members are added. We can invent new nouns, such as "glebbiness": *The glebbiness of the room was disgusting.* You might protest that you don't know the meaning of "glebbiness," but you don't know the meanings of all nouns found in dictionaries. (Can you define, for example, *epigone, philogyny, ailurophobe?*) New nouns constantly enter the language. *Ecoterrorism* is now part of the language, but this noun is so recent that it is not listed in the Britannica version of the Merriam Webster dictionary. And what about *cookie,* not something you eat, but a mini-program planted in your computer to enable advertisers to send you spam, that is, junk e-mail? Notice that *spam* has a verb equivalent: *Someone spammed me* (i.e., sent unwanted messages).

We can invent new verbs (We *friddled* the old rug), and new verbs constantly enter the language. For example *nuke,* which first appeared in 1967 (I *nuked* the potato in the microwave), and *zap,* which entered the language in 1942 (USC *zapped* UCLA in the game yesterday). Such is also the case with adjectives and adverbs.

However, pronouns (*I, you,* etc.), prepositions (*on, above, into,* etc.), conjunctions (*but, because, so,* etc.), determiners (*the, these, his, her*), and modal auxiliaries (*would, could, should, will*) are closed lists; no new members are added or can be added. Frequently nouns, verbs, adjectives, and adverbs are called *form words,* and pronouns, prepositions, and conjunctions are called *function words.*

Interjections, words that express emotion or feelings, are in a class by themselves. Some words used as interjections also belong to the form-word categories:

> *Goodness,* I wish I had a million dollars.

> *Man,* that was a close call.

Other words are used only as interjections:

> *Gosh,* I'm tired.

> *Whoopee,* I won the lottery!

> *Golly,* I wish you'd be more careful!

Form-Class Words

Nouns

Nouns are words that can fill the vacant slot in the following sentence: (*The*) _____ *can endure.* Thus, *love, state, freshness, apple,* and countless other words will fit into the slot without creating nonsense. Even if we insert, for instance, the word *steak,* the sentence may seem a bit odd, and we might ask the person who spoke it to explain what he meant, but we would know that the sentence is perfectly acceptable English.

Also, as you know, the articles—*a, an,* and *the*—often precede nouns and are a tipoff to the members of the noun class: *the* love, *a* state, *an* apple.

In Chapter 8, you will find a complete discussion of the noun category.

Verbs

Verbs convey actions—*to run, to think*—and what has traditionally been called "states of being." These definitions are problematic, but they will suffice until we arrive at the detailed treatment of verbs in Chapter 5.

One characteristic of verbs is that they change tense: *run/ran, think/thought, walk/walked.*

Adjectives

For the moment, the following definition will be enough: "An adjective is a word that modifies a noun":

> *bad* vibes

> *good* luck

> *filthy* rich

> *noxious* fumes

In Chapter 11, you will find a complete discussion of adjectives, but the incomplete definition above will get us started.

Adverbs

A useful, though incomplete, definition is that adverbs are words used to modify verbs:

run *quickly*

sob *bitterly*

run *fast*

dine *often*

In Chapter 13, you will find a complete discussion of adverbs.

Function Words (Structure-Class Words)

Pronouns

Pronouns are words that can replace nouns in sentences:

Walter croons the blues. *He* croons the blues.

He sees *Henrietta*. He sees *her.*

The *women* protested. *They* protested.

Fraud is a problem. *That* is a problem.

The category "pronouns" breaks down into several subcategories. For example, pronouns are used to ask questions: <u>*What* are you doing?</u> Chapter 9 deals with the whole class in depth.

Prepositions

Prepositions are words that join one word or phrase to another:

the United States *of* America

the rain *in* Spain

the dog lying *on* the carpet

the canopy *over* the altar

In Chapter 15 you will find a complete discussion of prepositions.

Conjunctions

One type of conjunction joins sentence elements or sentences. The coordinating conjunctions, *and, but, for, nor, or, so,* and *yet,* are used as follows.

Jack *and* Jill [joining two nouns]

Jack fell down *and* broke his crown. [joining two phrases]

Jack fell down and broke his crown, *and* Jill came tumbling after. [joining two sentences]

Jack liked water, *but* Jill preferred milk. [joining two sentences]

Jack spilled the water, *so* Jill had to refill the bucket. [joining two sentences]

Do you prefer the chocolate *or* the vanilla? [joining words within a sentence]

(Regarding coordinating conjunctions, see pages 237–240.)

Subordinating conjunctions (e.g., *because, if, although*) join sentences in a particular way. For example, here are two sentences: *Jack fell down. He stubbed his toe.* With a subordinating conjunction we can join these sentences to show cause: *Jack fell down because he stubbed his toe.* For another example of such sentence joining with a subordinating conjunction, we start with two sentences: *Jack was cheerful. He had fallen down.* Joined with a subordinating conjunction, these sentences show a complete meaning: *Jack was cheerful although he had fallen down.*

For more on subordinating conjunctions, see pages 202–205.

Correlative conjunctions are the sets *both . . . and, either . . . or,* and *neither . . . nor.* You will see them in sentences such as this one: *You must choose either the black one or the white one.* (See pages 240–241.)

Determiners

Determiners are elements of a noun phrase. That is, they come before a noun and modify or determine that noun.

The large turtle is sitting on *that* pile of rocks with *his* nose in *the* freezing water.

Modal Auxiliaries

Modals are a category of auxiliary verb that reflects the speaker or writer's attitude toward the verb.

Sonya *will* climb the mountain. She *could* go to ocean this summer as well, but she knows she *should* travel to see her brother.

SUBSTITUTION, ADDITION, DELETION, MOVEMENT

The verb is the pivot around which other elements in the sentence move. By substituting, adding, deleting, and moving sentence parts, we can revise our sentences and change their meaning. Take the statement *Kids eat spinach.* By adding the word *do,* we can make this statement into a question: *Do kids eat spinach?*

The relationships among the following sentences are apparent. All relate *kids* to *eating* and to *spinach.* Note the changes from the basic sentence pattern.

Kids eat spinach.

Kids don't eat spinach. [addition]

Do kids eat spinach? [addition]

Spinach is eaten by kids. [addition, movement]

Eat spinach! [deletion]

The changes also allow the speaker to alter the emphasis placed on various elements in the sentence. We do not mean to suggest that speakers or writers first generate basic sentences and then change them. Common sense and our experience with language tells us that they do not. The point is that underlying a transformed sentence and the corresponding basic sentence are the same relationships.

For example, in both *Dogs chase cats* and *Cats are chased by dogs,* the dogs are doing the chasing and the cats are being chased. The same basic relationships underlie *Gertrude seems morose, Gertrude doesn't seem morose,* and *Does Gertrude seem morose?* Each sentence relates *Gertrude* to the quality of *moroseness.*

As you will see, in some sentences and phrases, conjunction brings about deletions and substitutions.

Exercise 2.3

The sentences below have been produced by adding two basic sentences together. Make appropriate deletions and substitutions. Discuss the possibilities in class. How do the changes affect the meaning (emphasis, tone, connotation, etc.)?

Examples
a. Albert has pneumonia, and Albert is in the hospital.

Albert has pneumonia and is in the hospital. [deletion]

b. Cary studies hard, but Cary also likes sports.

Cary studies hard, but she also likes sports. [substitution]

1. The lodge members observed a minute of silence, and then the lodge members began the meeting.

2. Senior citizens often attend concerts, and senior citizens always enjoy the music.

3. The poems in the anthology were written in the twentieth century, and the poems in the anthology are incomprehensible.

4. The chapter devoted to Franz Kafka is interesting because in his fiction Franz Kafka used Freudian concepts.

5. Dorothy Kirsten was the perfect Isolde because Dorothy Kirsten was thoroughly Teutonic.

PASSAGES FOR ANALYSIS

Find the subject and predicate divisions in the sentences in the following passages.

1. "It was always very cold on that lake-shore [of Lake Tahoe] in the night, but we had plenty of blankets and were warm enough. We never moved a muscle all night, but waked at early dawn in the original positions, thoroughly refreshed, free from soreness, and brim full of friskiness. There is no end of wholesome medicine in such an experience. That morning we could have whipped ten such people as we were the day before—sick ones at any rate. But the world is slow, and people will go to 'water cures' and 'movement cures' and to foreign lands for health. Three months of camp life on Lake Tahoe would restore an Egyptian mummy to his pristine vigor, and give him an appetite like an alligator. I do not mean the oldest and driest mummies, of course, but the fresher ones." (Mark Twain, *Roughing It,* 1871)

2. "Every promise of the soul has innumerable fulfillments; each of its joys ripens into a new want. Nature, uncontainable, flowing, forelooking, in the first sentiment of kindness anticipates already a benevolence which shall lose all particular regards in its general light. The introduction to this felicity is in a private and tender relation of one to one, which is the enchantment of human life; which, like a certain divine rage and enthusiasm, seizes a man at one period and works a revolution in his mind and body; unites him to his race, pledges him to domestic and civic relations, carries him with new sympathy into nature, enhances the power of the senses, opens the imagination, adds to his character heroic and sacred attributes, establishes marriage and gives permanence to human society." (Ralph Waldo Emerson, "Love")

SUBJECT AND PREDICATE ANSWER KEY (for page 20)

Subject (Noun Phrase)	Predicate (Verb Phrase)
Dick and Jane	played checkers.
Mother and Father	painted the kitchen.
Spot	gnawed on a bone.
The boy who saw Dick cheat on the exam	told the teacher.
The test that Dick took	was very difficult.
The children	have been wailing.

CHAPTER REVIEW

In your own words, explain the following concepts that this chapter developed:

- An asterisk before a word, phrase, or sentence
- A question mark before a word, phrase, or sentence

- A word, phrase, or sentence that is placed between slant marks, such as /duh boid flew away/
- Grammaticality
- Descriptive grammar
- Appropriateness and formality
- The distinction between form and function
- Subject and predicate
- Phrases
- Substitution, addition, deletion, movement
- Sentence diagrams
- Function words and form class words
- Parts of speech

C H A P T E R 3

The Forms of Words: Morphology

CHAPTER PREVIEW

- Words in the English language come from a variety of sources. For instance, English borrows words from other languages (e.g., *rodeo* from Spanish) and forms new words (1) by combining two or more words (*gaslight* from *gas + light*); (2) by using the first letters of phrases to form acronyms (*laser* from *l*ight *a*mplification by *s*timulated *e*mission of *r*adiation); (3) by blending parts of two or more words to form a new word (*smog* from *sm*oke + f*og*); (4) by using abbreviations as words (*Gen., Lt., Prof.*); (5) by removing a part of one word to create another word, a process known as *back-formation* (*burgle* from *burglar*).

- Morphemes are parts of words that change meanings, make one part of speech into another, and show such grammatical functions as tense and plurality. For example, the morpheme *un-* makes a positive into a negative (happy, *un*happy), the morpheme *-ful* changes a noun into an adjective (beauty, beauti*ful*), and the morpheme *-s* makes a singular into a plural (dollar, dollar*s*).

- Some morphemes are free and can be used as words or as parts of words: My love is *like* a red red rose/My love is rose*like*. Morphemes at the beginnings of words are called prefixes: *dis*honor, *in*human. Morphemes at the ends of words are suffixes: typ*ed*, reliabil*ity*.

- Derivational morphemes change the part of speech category to which words belong. For example, the suffix *-ly* often changes adjectives into adverbs: quick action, quick*ly* acting.

- Inflectional morphemes indicate such grammatical functions as tense and agreement. The suffix *-ed* changes present tense *work* into past tense *worked*. The suffix *-s* shows that in the following sentence the verb *work* agrees with its subject: *Herbert works.*

THE LEXICON

Lexicon means (1) "dictionary," (2) the words of a language, and (3) the words in a person's vocabulary. The English lexicon consists of some 450,000 words, of which the average high school graduate knows about 60,000; no one has mastered the complete English lexicon.

You can do some quick research. Flip your desk dictionary open to any page, and count the number of words on that page that are not part of *your* lexicon. I have just flipped my desk dictionary open to page 377. Here are some of the words on that page that are not part of my lexicon: endospore, endosteum, endrin, energrid, enfilade, enfleurage. Of the sixty-five words defined on that page, only thirty-five are part of my lexicon, and of the thirty-five, many are words of which I know the meaning, but which I would never use in my own speech or writing (e.g., *enfetter*, meaning to bind in chains, as to enfetter a criminal).

SOURCES OF WORDS IN THE ENGLISH LEXICON

Where do those 450,000 words that make up the English lexicon come from? If you'll think about it, you probably already know the answer to that question, but let's take a look at just a few of the languages from which English has derived its vocabulary.

Old English (Anglo-Saxon)

Many of our words trace their lineage back to the great-great-grandparents of Modern English: Old English (or Anglo-Saxon).

> *child* from *cild* [pronounced roughly /chilled/]
>
> *dream* from *dream* [pronounced /dray ahm/]
>
> *egg* from *aeg* [pronounced /egg/]
>
> *free* from *freo* [pronounced /fray oh/]
>
> *good* from *god* [pronounced /goad/]

Languages Other than English

- African languages: apartheid (Afrikaans), banana (Woloff), gumbo (Kongo), okra (Ibo)
- French: beauty, chauffeur, domain, ecstasy, fort, garage, honor, lake, mutton, pork, restaurant
- German: berg (mountain), blitzkrieg, Donner (thunder) and Blitzen (lightning), flak (an acronym from *f*lugzeug*a*bwehr*k*anone, antiaircraft gun), Führer, sauerkraut, wiener
- Hawaiian: aloha, lanai, lei, wahine
- Japanese: futon, hara-kiri, kamikaze, kimono, sushi, tatami, tsunami

- Native American: papoose (Narraganset), pemmican (Cree), powwow (Narraganset or Massachuset), tepee (Dakota), tomahawk (Virginia Algonquian)
- Spanish: bracero, chili, hacienda, lariat, ranch, rodeo, serape, siesta, tamale

And, of course, this is only a small sampling of the words that English has borrowed from virtually the whole spectrum of world languages.

Exercise 3.1

Find a word currently in use in English that comes from each of the following languages: Hindu, Hebrew, Italian, Korean, Tagalog.

Compounds

Another source of words in the lexicon is compounding: joining two or more words to make a new word. The classic example of a compound in English is *bookkeeper:* book + keeper. There are countless others: grape + fruit, rein + deer, gold + fish, bath + robe, bath + room, break + through, cup + cake. Some compounds are written with hyphens: commander-in-chief, mother-in-law, happy-go-lucky.

Acronyms

Acronyms are formed by using the first letters of phrases. Very much in the public's awareness right now is the acronym AIDS (Acquired Immunodeficiency Syndrome). An acronym coined in the 1960s is LEM (lunar excursion module). Other common acronyms are UNESCO (United Nations Educational, Scientific, and Cultural Organization), ASCII (American Standard Code for Information Interchange), RAM (random access memory), and NASA (National Aeronautics and Space Administration). Many acronyms are not pronounced as single words, but each letter is pronounced. Thus, UCLA is not /ukluh/, but U-C-L-A, and USC is not /usk/, but U-S-C. One acronym that has become the name of a restaurant chain is TGIF.

Exercise 3.2

Find five acronyms (other than those already listed in this chapter) that are currently used in American English.

Blends

Blends are words that result from fusing parts of other words. One famous blend comes from *Alice in Wonderland: chortle,* resulting from *ch*uckle + sn*ort*. The blend most in use right now is *smog,* from *sm*oke + f*og*. Others are *motel* (*mo*tor + ho*tel*), *infomercial* (*info*rmation + com*mercial*), *cranapple* (*cran*berry + *apple*), and *pluot* (*plu*m + apric*ot*).

Abbreviations

Some abbreviations replace the full word forms, particularly in titles. For example, *Mrs.* is an abbreviation for *mistress,* and using the full form would seem strange, *Mistress* Smith rather than *Mrs.* Smith. In addressing a letter to a physician, one would use the abbreviation *Dr.,* not the full word *doctor.* Other common abbreviations are *M.A.* for master of arts, *Ph.D.* for *philosophiae doctor* or doctor of philosophy (not, as some students claim, "Piled Higher and Deeper").

Back-Formations

Back-forming results from removing part of a word to create a new word. For example, *alp,* meaning "mountain," is a back-formation from *Alps,* the European mountain system, and *swindle* is a back-formation from *swindler,* a word derived from the German *Schwindler,* meaning "giddy person."

MORPHEMES

Morphemes are parts of words that change meanings, make one part of speech into another, and show such grammatical functions as tense and plurality. For example,

- The morpheme *un-* changes a positive into a negative: easy/*un*easy
- The morpheme *-ish* changes nouns into adjectives: a boy/a boy*ish* grin
- The morpheme *-ed* changes a present tense verb into past tense: walk/walk*ed*
- The morpheme *-s* changes a singular noun into a plural: one dollar/ten dollar*s*

A word, of course, can contain more than one morpheme: *un*glamour*ous*, *be*numb*ed*.

Bound and Free Morphemes

Some morphemes are bound; that is, they cannot occur alone, but only as parts of words. Both *un-* and *-ish* are bound morphemes. Free morphemes are actually words. *Man* is a word-morpheme: The *man* ate caviar. But it can also occur as a morpheme in words: *man*hood, *man*power, and *man*hole.

Prefixes and Suffixes

As you have already seen, some morphemes occur at the beginnings of words: *un*happy, *pre*view, *dis*tasteful. These are prefixes. Morphemes that occur at the ends of words are suffixes: ail*ment*, understand*able*, fly*ing*.

MORPHEMES AND PARTS OF SPEECH (DERIVATIONAL MORPHEMES)

As the following chart demonstrates, morphemes can change the part of speech to which a word belongs.

Morphemes can change

- nouns   to   adjectives

  girl   girl*ish*
  fury   furi*ous*
  Africa   Afric*an*
  picture   picture*sque*
  hate   hate*ful*
  metal   metall*ic*

- verbs   to   nouns

  refuse   refus*al*
  admit   admitt*ance*
  lead   lead*er*
  know   know*ledge*
  pacify   pacif*ist*
  bore   bore*dom*

- adjectives   to   adverbs

  quick   quick*ly*
  sick   sick*ly*

- nouns   to   verbs

  Pasteur   pasteur*ize*
  vaccine   vaccin*ate*
  loose   loose*n*

- adjectives   to   nouns

  short   short*ness*
  moral   moral*ity*
  mendacious   mendac*ity*

- verbs   to   adjectives

  adore   ador*able*
  create   creat*ive*
  sense   sens*ory*

INFLECTIONAL MORPHEMES

Inflectional morphemes do not change the parts of speech of the words they are attached to, but, rather, mark such grammatical functions as tense (paint the fence, paint*ed* the fence), number (one error, three error*s*), and agreement between subject and verb (*the child whine, the child whine*s*).

Morpheme	Function	Examples
-s	third person singular present	Joe eat*s* parsnips.
		He like*s* them.
-ed	past tense	Joe cook*ed* the parsnips yesterday.
-ed	past participle	Joe has cook*ed* many parsnips.
-ing	progressive	Joe is cook*ing* parsnips again.
-en	past participle	Joe has eat*en* parsnips again.
-'s	possessive	Joe*'s* parsnips taste good.
-er	comparative	Joe eats parsnips fast*er* than I do.
-est	superlative	Joe is the world's fast*est* parsnip eater.

If at the moment this list of inflectional morphemes seems a bit confusing, don't worry. As you go through the chapters on verbs and verbals, nouns and nominals, adjectives and adjectivals, and adverbs and adverbials, all will become perfectly clear.

CHAPTER REVIEW

- What are the three meanings of *lexicon*?
- Give examples of words borrowed from languages other than English.
- What is a compound? Give an example.
- What is an acronym? Give an example.
- What is a blend? Give an example.
- What is a back-formation? Give an example.
- Explain *morpheme*.
- Explain the difference between *bound* and *free* morphemes, and give examples.
- Explain *derivational morpheme*. Give three examples.
- Explain *inflectional morpheme*. Give three examples.

Basic Sentence Types

CHAPTER PREVIEW

The English language has eight basic sentence types. (In structuralist grammars, these sentences are called *kernels*.) In later chapters we will analyze the technical details of these eight types, but a general overview at the start is useful. The sentence types differ because in each, the verb acts as a pivot that requires or prohibits other structures in the sentence. The verb largely determines the structure of the sentence.

AN ILLUSTRATIVE LIST OF THE SENTENCE TYPES

As you examine the sentences in this list, pay attention to the verbs, for the verb determines what other elements the basic sentence can consist of. At this point, don't worry about the terminology. As you progress in the study of grammar, the terms will become familiar. Just focus on what goes with the verbs.

	NOUN PHRASE		NOUN PHRASE	
1.	The girl	*sees*	the tree.	

	NOUN PHRASE		NOUN PHRASE	NOUN PHRASE
2.	The professor	*gives*	the students	an assignment.

	NOUN		NOUN	NOUN PHRASE
3.	Milly	*calls*	Jane	a fool.

	NOUN		NOUN	ADJECTIVE
	Milly	*calls*	Jane	foolish.

	NOUN PHRASE	
4.	The man	*sleeps.*

	NOUN PHRASE		ADJECTIVE
5.	The man	*is*	nice.

	NOUN PHRASE		NOUN PHRASE
	The woman	*is*	a physician.

	NOUN PHRASE		ADVERB
6.	The meeting	*is*	here.

	NOUN PHRASE		PREPOSITIONAL PHRASE
	The meeting	*is*	at ten.

NOUN PHRASE		ADJECTIVE	
7. The dog	*becomes*	vicious.	

NOUN PHRASE		NOUN PHRASE	
The dog	*becomes*	a clown.	

NOUN PHRASE		ADJECTIVAL PHRASE	
8. The dog	*was*	afraid of the cat.	

NOUN PHRASE		ADJECTIVAL	CLAUSE
The dog	*was*	aware	that he was cold.

STRUCTURE OF THE BASIC SENTENCE TYPES

In the following explanation of basic sentence types, remember that the verb controls the structures that are possible in the predicate.

Transitive

1. Sentence with a transitive verb and an object.

   The easiest (but not entirely accurate) way to explain "transitive verb" is this: it transfers action from the subject to a noun phrase in the predicate. Some grammars say that a noun phrase in the predicate receives the action of the verb.

SUBJECT	PREDICATE
The boy	*sees* the girl. [In the predicate, *the girl* is a noun phrase functioning as the object.]

SUBJECT	PREDICATE
Dogs	*chase* cats. [In the predicate, *cats* is a noun phrase functioning as the object.]

2. Sentence with a transitive verb and a direct object (italicized) and an indirect object (underlined). Some verbs entail two noun phrases in the predicate of the sentence.

SUBJECT	PREDICATE
The professor	gives the students *an assignment.* [In the predicate, *the students* and *an assignment* are both noun phrases, but they function as indirect and direct objects, respectively.]

3. Sentence with a transitive verb and a direct object (italicized) and either a noun or an adjective as a complement (underlined).

SUBJECT	PREDICATE
Milly	calls *Jane* a fool. [*Jane* is the object and the noun phrase *a fool* is the complement.]

SUBJECT	PREDICATE
Milly	calls *Jane* foolish [adjective]. [*Jane* is the object and the adjective *foolish* is the complement.]

These verbs require a noun phrase or an adjective phrase to complete the structure of the predicate. The most common of the verbs that form this sentence type are *call, name, christen, elect, appoint.*

Intransitive

4. Sentence with an intransitive verb.

SUBJECT   PREDICATE
The man   sleeps.

When the verb is intransitive, no action is transferred to a noun phrase in the predicate. The verb can be modified, but it remains intransitive:

SUBJECT   PREDICATE
The man   sleeps soundly with the windows open.

Linking

5. Sentence with a *be* verb and a noun or adjective.

The verb *be* is often called a linking verb. It has various forms, such as *is, are, was, were,* and *been.*

SUBJECT   PREDICATE
That girl   is a *genius* [noun].

SUBJECT   PREDICATE
I   am *happy* [adjective].

SUBJECT   PREDICATE
That girl who won the spelling bee   is a *genius* [noun].

SUBJECT   PREDICATE
The boy   was *happy* [adjective] about the hot weather.

Some grammars do not list *be* as a verb at all, but place it in a separate category, usually called the *copula. Be* does not express an action (as does *walk*). In the sentences of patterns 5 and 6, *be* is the pivot word in the predicate.

6. Sentence with a *be* verb and an adverb of time or place or both.

Adverbs and adverb phrases denote, among other things, time and place.

SUBJECT   PREDICATE
The meeting   will be *at ten o'clock* [time].

SUBJECT   PREDICATE
The students   were *in the gymnasium* [place].

SUBJECT   PREDICATE
No one   will be *here* [place] *at noon* [time].

7. Sentence with a linking verb followed by a noun or an adjective.

Linking verbs are such words as *become* (*The dog becomes vicious*), *seem* (*The room seems hot*), and others. (In the following chapters, you will learn the details about linking verbs and how to differentiate them from other verb types.)

SUBJECT	PREDICATE
Ravel's music	becomes *a bore* [noun].

SUBJECT	PREDICATE
The idea	seems *stupid* [adjective].

8. Sentence with *be* verb or linking verb, an adjective, and either a prepositional phrase or a noun clause.

SUBJECT	PREDICATE
The dog	was *afraid of the cat* [adjective and prepositional phrase].

SUBJECT	PREDICATE
The actor	became *aware that he had forgotten his part* [adjective and noun clause].

Exercise 4.1

Classify the basic type of each of the following sentences.

1. Dick gave Jane a candy bar.
2. Spot is a mongrel.
3. Mother became angry.
4. Father was intolerant of laziness.
5. Jane kicked Dick.
6. Mother snores.
7. Spot was in the garage.
8. Mother called Father her honeybunch.
9. Everyone in the family became ill.
10. Lunch is at noon.

BASIC SENTENCE TYPES' RELATIONSHIP TO OTHER STRUCTURES

Speakers and writers of English use structures such as the following all the time. (In fact, people who cannot use these structures are severely limited in the ability to express their thoughts.) And, as will be obvious, these structures are related to (or derived from) the eight basic sentence types. In subsequent chapters, the structures illustrated here will be explained in detail; for now, the point is that the basic sentence types explain the grammar of nonsentence structures.

1. Sentence with a transitive verb and an object.

   The boy sees the girl.

   Derived structure:

   Seeing the girl, the boy hid behind a tree.

2. Sentence with a transitive verb and a direct object and an indirect object.

   The professor gives the students an assignment

   Derived structure:

   Having given the students an assignment, the professor dismissed the class.

3. Sentence with a transitive verb and a direct object and either a noun or an adjective as a complement.

   Milly calls Jane a fool.

   Milly calls Jane foolish.

   Derived structures:

   It is rude *for Milly to call Jane a fool.*

   For Milly to call Jane a fool is rude.

   Calling Jane foolish is a breach of etiquette.

4. Sentence with an intransitive verb.

   The man sleeps.

   Derived structure:

   When the man sleeps, the house is quiet.

5. Sentence with a *be* verb and a noun or adjective.

   That girl is a genius.

   I am happy.

   Derived structures:

   Being a genius, that girl won the scholarship.

   I need peace and quiet *to be happy.*

6. Sentence with a *be* verb and an adverb of time or place or both.

   The meeting will be at ten o'clock.

   The students were in the gymnasium.

   No one will be here at noon.

Derived structures:

Being at ten o'clock, the meeting was crowded.

Everyone approved of *the students' being in the gymnasium.*

I will try *to be here at noon.*

7. Sentence with a linking verb followed by a noun or an adjective.

   Ravel's music becomes a bore.

   The idea seems stupid.

Derived structures:

Ravel's music having become a bore, we played a Mozart CD.

Everyone hates *to seem stupid.*

8. Sentence with *be* verb or linking verb, an adjective, and either a prepositional phrase or a noun clause.

   The dog was afraid of the cat.

   The actor became aware that he had forgotten his part.

Derived structures:

The dog being afraid of the cat, Rover avoided Kitty.

Having become aware that to forget his part would ruin his career, the actor diligently memorized every line.

Exercise 4.2

In the following sentences, identify the types—1 through 8—of the italicized structures.

1. The boy wanted *to name his cat Cleopatio.*
2. *Having heard the alarm,* the students evacuated the building.
3. All of the neighbors realized that *the boy was a monster.*
4. By *being stubborn,* the girl got her way.
5. Everyone was amazed at *Alvin's being proud of his mistake.*
6. *Growing suspicious that the bank would fail,* the man withdrew all his money.
7. You can lose weight by *walking.*
8. *Giving your teachers respect* is a decent thing to do.
9. Thank you for *being here.*
10. William is happy *to be the leader.*

CHALLENGERS

In the following sentences, identify the types—1 through 8—of the italicized structures.

1. "If anything characterizes the culture of the seventies in America, it is an insistence on *preventing failures of communication.*" (Richard Dean Rosen)

2. "Music was invented *to confirm human loneliness.*" (Lawrence Durrell)

3. "*Having money* is rather like *being a blond.* It is more fun but not vital." (Mary Quant)

4. "*Being middle class* means always having to say you're sorry." (Tony Parsons)

5. "*Given the cultural barriers to intersex conversation,* the amazing thing is that we would even expect men and women to have anything to say to each other for more than ten minutes at a stretch." (Barbara Ehrenreich)

6. "Not only is it harder *to be a man,* it is also harder *to become one.*" (Ariana Huffington)

CHAPTER REVIEW

The purpose of this brief chapter has been to give you a general overview of the basic sentence patterns in English and the structures that are related to (or derived from) these basic patterns. The chapter is merely a prelude to the detailed explanations that will follow.

Verbs: Tense, Auxiliary Verbs, and Modals

CHAPTER PREVIEW

- Verbs can be defined notionally (on the basis of meaning), formally (on the basis of the changes they undergo when they are used), or functionally (on the basis of what they do in sentences).

- Traditional grammar lists six tenses: present (Father *works*), past (Father *worked*), future (Father *will work*), present perfect (Father *has worked*), past perfect or pluperfect (Father *had worked*), and future perfect (Father *will have worked*).

- The eight "basic" sentence patterns in English are determined by whether the verb is transitive (has one object or more than one: Jack sees *Jane;* Jack gives *Jane candy*), intransitive (no object: Spot barks), or linking (Dick *becomes* obstreperous).

- In the analysis presented in this book, there are only two tenses, present and past.

- Tense is a function of grammar and does not necessarily correspond with the idea of time. The following sentence is in present tense, but it talks about the future: *My sister graduates from med school next June.*

- The auxiliary verbs are *be, have,* and *do* and all of the modals. (The words *be, have,* and *do* are also main verbs.)

- The most common modals or modal auxiliaries are *can, could, may, might, must, shall, will, would,* and *ought.*

Here is a fact about knowledge: that which you use repeatedly becomes part of your repertory at hand; that which you do not use frequently is often not readily available, and you must refresh your memory. Throughout this book, you will be applying basic concepts again and again, and as you do so, you will make them readily available.

We feel that rote memorization is not productive. In subsequent chapters when you encounter problems regarding such matters as tense and modals, you should refer back to this chapter and to Chapters 6 and 7 for help. Ultimately, the system will be part of your analytical tool kit, at hand whenever you need it.

VERBS

This chapter and the next two are the most important ones for your understanding of grammar. If you understand verbs, you will be ready to deal with sentences (Dick knows Jane), clauses (Jane knows *that Dick guzzles Pepsi*), and reduced clauses (*Wanting peace and quiet,* Father spends his evenings in the basement). Verbs are the pivots that determine the organization of the rest of the sentence.

Of course, in many ways you already know all there is to know about verbs. You use them constantly in all of their various forms; you understand them when others use them. Thus, like almost everything in the study of grammar, an explanation of verbs is simply making explicit what you already know intuitively. One might say that you don't know what you "know" about verbs, and this chapter will enable you to know much of what you already "know."

DEFINITION OF VERBS

Notional Definition

A notional definition is one based on meaning. If you have studied traditional grammar,[1] you are probably already familiar with the most common notional definition: a verb names an action or a state of being.

Action: Spot *barks.*

State of being: Spot *becomes* vicious.

This definition can, however, lead to confusion; for example, in the following sentence, *desertion* names an action (the act of deserting), but, as your own intuitions about language tell you, it is not a verb:

The general's *desertion* caused a scandal.

In this sentence, the verb is *caused; desertion* is a noun. And in the following sentence, *weary* seems to name a state of being (tiredness, lack of energy); but it is not a verb, in this sentence, at least:

The professor grows *weary.*

The main verb in this sentence is *grows; weary* is an adjective.

So the notional definition of verb is inadequate; it does not give criteria for differentiating verbs from other parts of speech.

Formal Definition

Formal definition avoids the logical contradictions of the notional definition. On the basis of form, how do we know that a word is a verb?

---

[1] See Chapter 1 for discussion of traditional grammar.

1. Present and past tense: In the present tense, the third person singular form of a verb (when the subject is *he, she,* or *it*) ends with the *-s* inflectional suffix:

    He walk*s* to school.

    In the past tense, regular verbs end in *-ed*:

    He walk*ed* to school.

    Some irregular verbs change vowels (and consonants):

    They t*aught* math.

    and some do not change their form in the past tense:

    They *hit* the pillow an hour ago.

2. Present participle: Verbs can take the *-ing* present participial suffix (sing*ing*, eat*ing*, sleep*ing*):

    Dairies are pasteuriz*ing* milk every day.

3. Past participle: Verbs have a past participial form, commonly indicated by the *-ed* suffix (has walk*ed*), by the *-en* suffix (had tak*en*), or by a change in spelling and pronunciation (*fight*/has *fought, fly*/has *flown*).

4. Verb suffix: Some verbs have the derivational suffix *-ize* (critic*ize*, dogmat*ize*, emphas*ize*, familiar*ize*, global*ize*, homogen*ize*). Of course, not all verbs have such a suffix.

Formal Features of Verbs

- *-s* suffix in present tense
- Present participle form (ending in *-ing*)
- Past participle form (suffixes *-ed* or *-en* or spelling change)
- Suffix *-ize*

Principal Parts of Verbs

In identifying verbs, it is helpful to know that every verb has five principal parts. Here is an illustration with a regular verb.

Infinitive (or base form)

to walk: He likes *to walk* to school.

walk: He can *walk* to school.

Present tense

walk: I *walk* every morning.

walks: She *walks* in the evening.

Past tense

walked: They *walked* around the block.

Present participle (with some form of *be*)

walking: I am/was *walking* in the park.

You are/were *walking* on the treadmill.

Dick is/was *walking* Spot.

Past participle (with some form of *have*)

walked: Dick has *walked* into the wall.

The girls have *walked* out the door.

The children had *walked* on their toys.

given: The boys had *given* the girls a party.

sung: The choir has *sung* the hymn.

Forms of TO BE

PRESENT TENSE	PAST TENSE
Singular	Singular
I am	I was
you are	you were
(s)he/it is	(s)he/it was
Plural	Plural
we are	we were
you are	you were
they are	they were
PRESENT PARTICIPLE	PAST PARTICIPLE
being	been

Functional Definition

While formal tests for verbs are more reliable than notional ones, they are hardly fail-safe. For example, the word *interesting* ends in -*ing*, but in the following sentence it is an adjective, not a verb: *The interesting book grabs students' attention.*

Another way to determine whether a word is a verb is to see if it acts like a verb. Does it do verb work in a sentence? To tell whether a word is a verb, you may need to use more than one test.

1. Many verbs can be made into commands or imperatives.

   Jane *sees* Dick's error. [declarative]

   See Dick's error! [imperative]

2. Verbs can be negated.

   Jane has *given* Dick a warning. [positive]

   Jane has *not given* Dick a warning. [negative]

3. Verbs fill slots in pattern sentences.

   They _____ happy.

   They must _____ (it).

This last criterion needs a bit of explanation. Many verbs will fill the empty slot in *They _____ happy.*

   They *become* happy.

   They *seem* happy.

   They *remain* happy.

Verbs that cannot fill the slot in *They _____ happy* can fill the slot in *They must _____ (it).*

   They must *study*.

   They must *know* it.

   They must *sing*.

   They must *sing* it.

   They must *go*.

It is worth pausing a moment to demonstrate that nonverbs cannot fill the slots in the sentence frames:

   *They *spaghetti* happy.

   *They must *beautiful* it.

   *They *quickly* angry.

   *They *extremely*.

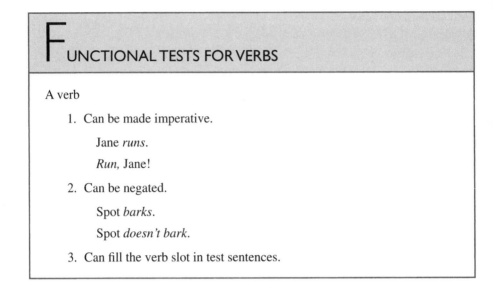

FUNCTIONAL TESTS FOR VERBS

A verb

1. Can be made imperative.

   Jane *runs.*

   Run, Jane!

2. Can be negated.

   Spot *barks.*

   Spot *doesn't bark.*

3. Can fill the verb slot in test sentences.

The test frames, useful in themselves, illustrate a point about grammatical analysis: to find out what's what, it is always useful to make substitutions and to change the forms of sentences. First, hypothesize about what a particular form is or what function it is fulfilling. For example, take the sentence *I chelated the metal.* I do not know exactly what *chelated* means, but I can hypothesize that *chelated* is a verb because of the *-ed* ending. However, as an additional test to see whether *chelated* is a verb, I can substitute another transitive verb in the *chelated* slot: *I melted the metal.* This substitution provides evidence that *chelated* is a verb. Throughout the following chapters, you will be learning about and using such analytical techniques.

FOR DISCUSSION

A dialect is a form of language spoken by a distinct group of people, defined either regionally or socially. The well-known Boston dialect (e.g., the pronunciation /cah/ for *car*) is defined regionally; on the other hand, "Spanglish," spoken by many Latinos, is defined socially. Of course, it is axiomatic that *everyone speaks a dialect,* for a dialect is nothing more than the version of language spoken by the group of which one is a member.

However, each speaker of a dialect has his or her own usages and pronunciations, which constitute an individual version of the dialect. This individual version of a dialect is called an *idiolect.* So everyone speaks a dialect *and* his or her own version of that dialect, an idiolect.

Speakers of a language often differ in the verb forms they use. For example, some people would say, "He has ran the race" while others would say "He has run the race." As you probably recognize, language usage, in this case choice of verb, may indicate the social group the speaker belongs to.

African American Vernacular English (AAVE), for example, is a dialect of English spoken by many African American people, at least some of the time. For example, in AAVE it is grammatical to say all three of the following sentences:

She happy.

She be happy.

She is happy.

Even though the first has no verb, it is grammatical in AAVE. The second sentence means that she is a happy person; happiness is a characteristic of her personality (similar to the verb *ser* in Spanish). The third sentence means that she is happy now. (See Chapter 17 for a longer discussion of AAVE.)

What attitudes in mainstream culture have you noticed toward AAVE? How about the media's treatment of AAVE? Is AAVE widely understood to be a dialect of English?

MORE FUNCTIONAL TESTS FOR VERBS

These sentence slots also help us test to whether a word is a verb.

1. If a verb can fit into the following pattern, the verb is transitive:

   I must _____ it. (I must *learn* it.)

2. If a verb fits into the following pattern, it is intransitive:

   I must _____. (I must *wait*.)

3. If a verb fits into the following pattern, it is a linking verb:

   I _____ weary. (I *become* weary. I *grow* weary.)

Many verbs fit more than one of the patterns, so that depending on how they are being used, we can say that they are transitive, intransitive, or linking.

I *get* an award. [transitive]

I *get* angry. [linking]

I *sing*. [intransitive]

I *sing* a song. [transitive]

USING GRAMMAR: LIE AND LAY

Perhaps no verbs in English are more frequently confused than the intransitive *lie* and the transitive *lay*.

> They must *lie* (on a bed of nails).

> They must *lay* it on the table.

Notice that *They must lay it on the table* can be changed thus: *It must be laid on the table by them.* The first sentence, with the intransitive *lie,* cannot be thus changed.

The source of the confusion probably lies in the overlap in their principal parts. These are as follows:

Base	Lie	Lay
With he/she/it in present	lies	lays
Past	lay	laid
Past participle	lain	laid
Pres participle	lying`	laying

The past and past participle forms of *lie* look as if they might belong to *lay.*

Exercise 5.1

A. Find the verbs in the following sentences. Use as many formal criteria as needed to verify your choices. *Note:* There may be more than one verb in some sentences, and look out for infinitives (such as *to choose*).

Examples

1. The monkey climbed up the tree.

   climbed [past tense, suffix *-ed*]

2. The monkey climbs up the tree.

   climbs [singular]

3. The monkey did not climb up the tree.

   did not climb [negative]

1. Boys laugh.
2. Girls tease boys.
3. Children become pests.
4. Girls and boys don't eat candy.
5. Most of us realize that art imitates life.
6. "In 1995, Dupage County Judge Ronald Mehling freed Rolando Cruz on the basis of a DNA test and evidence of prosecutorial misconduct." (*Lifelines*)
7. "The administration discriminates against fraternities and sororities." (Student)
8. "He who despairs over an event is a coward, but he who holds hope for the human condition is a fool." (Albert Camus)
9. "A grouch escapes so many little annoyances that it almost pays to be one." (Kin Hubbard)

B. Using the sentence frames, determine whether each of the following verbs is transitive, intransitive, or linking. Which of them can have more than one function?

act	lament
broil	manipulate
cheat	notice
dodge	operate
emphasize	perpetuate
feel	remain
grow	seem
harass	testify
interrupt	undo
jerk	verify
kick	weaken

Before we go on to other concerns, we repeat an important idea: you already know the features and functions of verbs; otherwise you would not be able to speak grammatical[2] English. The explanations above have two purposes: (1) to make you aware of what you already know and (2) to give you a vocabulary so that you can discuss what you know about verbs.

---

[2] Remember the definition of "grammatical" from Chapter 2. A grammatical sentence is one that a native speaker would utter or write. This concept is so important that we urge you to review it (pages 16–19).

FOR DISCUSSION: VERB TYPES AND MEANING

We can class verbs according to the kinds of meaning they convey.

- Durative verbs express actions that occur over a period of time: *work* is one example, and *learn* is another. Give two or three more examples of durative verbs.
- Punctual verbs express brief, quick actions: *jump, jerk, hop*. Give two or three more examples of punctual verbs.
- Stative verbs express a state rather than an action: *believe, dread, understand*. Give two or three more example of stative verbs.

THE VERB AND THE CONJUNCTION *AND*

The word *and* is a conjunction, the most common conjunction, in fact. The word *and* can be used to join basic sentences so that we end up with sentences that look like these:

> The dog was afraid of the cat, *and* the cat was afraid of the mouse. [conjunction of sentences]
>
> Dick *and* Jane are afraid of dogs, cats, *and* mice. [conjunctions of nouns]
>
> Dick is afraid of small *and* harmless dogs. [conjunction of adjectives]
>
> Jane constantly *and* insistently claims that small dogs are vicious. [conjunction of adverbs]

When sentences are combined, it is often necessary to substitute or delete structures within the two sentences. Let's illustrate this point:

> ?Dick likes cod liver oil, and Dick enjoys parsnips.

If both the first and the second Dick are the same person, the writer or speaker would normally substitute *he* for the second Dick:

> *Dick* likes cod liver oil, and *he* enjoys parsnips.

Otherwise, hearers or readers either are confused or assume that the sentence refers to two different people, $Dick_1$ and $Dick_2$. In other words, the grammar of English provides a way of solving such problems: substitution.

The following sentence will probably seem odd to you:

> ?Jane often plays soccer, and Jane often plays softball.

These ideas would more usually be expressed as

> Jane often plays soccer and softball.

with the redundant words *Jane often plays* in the second clause deleted.

Deletion occurs in other structures as well. In the second sentence below, the word *that* is deleted:

Mother knows *that* Father dislikes avocados.

Mother knows Father dislikes avocados.

Either sentence is perfectly grammatical, and both are acceptable at all levels of usage.

TENSE

Traditional Names for Tenses

Many grammar books name six tenses:

- Present: Mother pets Spot. You pet Spot.
- Past: Mother petted Spot.
- Future: Mother will pet Spot.
- Present perfect: Mother has petted Spot.
- Past perfect (pluperfect): Mother had petted Spot.
- Future perfect: Mother will have petted Spot.

The analysis that follows will be quite different from this. The way in which we explain the various forms of verbs and verb groups is more penetrating and more logical than the traditional analysis—and much easier to understand.

Tense and Time

English has only two tenses: present (PRES) and PAST. We might call these "simple tenses." We recognize PRES because in third person singular (with the pronouns *she, he,* and *it* and with singular nouns), the verb takes an *-s* suffix:

- First person singular: I like turnips.
- Second person singular: You like turnips.
- Third person singular: She like*s* turnips./He like*s* liver.
- First person plural: We like turnips.
- Second person plural: You like turnips.
- Third person plural: They like turnips.

And we see that in Standard English dialect, only third person singular takes the *-s*:

*Children enjoys popsicles.

*We cooks spaghetti on Fridays.

*You sounds happy today.

As we have already seen, in PAST tense, verbs take the *-ed* suffix (walk, walk*ed*) or show tense through a vowel change (technically known as *ablaut* (swim, swam; fall, fell; fight, fought)), and some do not change in PAST (hit, hit).

It is important to distinguish between the grammatical concept tense and the idea of time. We might say that tense is a formal aspect of sentences and clauses, whereas time is a concept about the way the world works. Let's look at an example sentence: *Sheri eats grapefruit.* Tense in this sentence is PRES, but the sentence does not mean that Sheri is eating grapefruit at this moment, rather that she usually eats grapefruit. If we want to express the idea that Sheri at this very moment is indulging in grapefruit, the sentence will take this form, which is not the simple present tense: *Sheri is eating grapefruit.*

For another example of the difference between the formal feature tense and the concept of time, consider the sentence *The semester starts tomorrow.* We know that *starts* is in the present tense (because of the -*s* suffix), but the sentence is referring to a time in the future.

The point here is that ideas and relationships of time are not always realized through tense alone.

So in the analysis that we are developing, English has only two tenses: PRES and PAST.

FOR DISCUSSION: TENSES AND INTENTIONS

Suppose a student addresses *one* of the following requests to a professor, and the professor addresses *one* of them to a student. In your opinion, which is which? Explain. Here's a hint: one of them sounds more like a direct order than the other, and one of them sounds more polite. Why should that be?

1. I *want* to see you after class.
2. I *wanted* to see you after class.

USING GRAMMAR: VERBS AND THEIR SUBJECTS

In formal usage, verbs must agree with their subjects. Agreement means simply that singular subjects must have singular verbs, and plural subjects must have plural verbs.

Subject	Verb	
The *crows*	caw	loudly every morning.
The *change* in fares	makes	traveling expensive.

When phrases intervene between the verb and its subject, writers and speakers sometimes make the verb agree with the nearest noun, not with the true subject:

Formal: The *walls,* as well as the floor, *need* painting.

Informal: The walls, as well as the floor, *needs* painting.

Formal: A *change* in their attitudes toward indeterminate sentences *is* necessary.

Informal: A change in their attitudes toward indeterminate sentences *are* necessary.

The so-called indefinite pronouns (such as *none, some,* and *any*) sometimes cause problems. In the most formal usage, these are treated as singular, not plural. Thus,

Formal: *None* of the problems *is* difficult.

Informal: *None* of the problems *are* difficult.

Correlatives (either . . . or, neither . . . nor) can lead writers and speakers astray. If the nouns following *either* and *or* are singular, the verb will be singular:

Formal: Either *prison* or *probation deters* criminals.

Informal: Either *prison* or *probation deter* criminals.

Formal: Neither *exercise* nor *diet substitutes* for good genes.

Informal: Neither *exercise* nor *diet substitute* for good genes.

However, if one of the nouns following the correlatives is plural and one is singular, problems arise, and the best solution is to rewrite.

Problematic: Either the *tests* or the *computer are* faulty. Either the *tests* or the *computer is* faulty.

Rewritten: Either the *tests are* faulty, or the *computer is.*

$\bigcup$ SING GRAMMAR: VERBS AND NOUNS

Nouns can be transformed into verbs: the noun *city* becomes the verb *citify.*

Fred lives in the *city.*

Two weeks in New York will *citify* Farmer Jones.

Verbs can be transformed into nouns: the verb *operate* becomes the noun *operation.*

Engineers *operate* trains.

The *operation* of trains takes skill.

Here is a sentence from the *Los Angeles Times* of April 20, 2002: "Finance minister says an upswing in U.S. growth would help accelerate expansion." Now note what happens when the verb *accelerate* is nominalized: "Finance minister says an upswing in U.S. growth would help the acceleration of expansion." Which version do you like better? Why?

AUXILIARY VERBS AND MODALS

To account for verb forms such as the one in *Sheri is eating grapefruit,* we need to consider auxiliary verbs. In sentences like this one, the verb is actually a group of words, a *verb group;* that is, a verb may consist of a main verb and an auxiliary verb, as in *Sheri is eating* grapefruit. Verbs and verb groups are italicized in the examples that follow.

I *enjoy* grammar.

I *needed* a new car.

Do you *enjoy* grammar?

I *do* not *want* a bagel for breakfast.

I *can go* with you to the movies.

I *am singing* on Saturday evening.

You *have won* the prize.

In these examples, we see *do, can, am* (*be*), and *have* used as auxiliary verbs.
    Let's look more closely at these auxiliaries.

Do

As the following sentences illustrate, *do* can function both as a main verb and as an auxiliary.

Jane *does* the dishes./Jane *does do* the dishes.

Jane *did* the dishes./Jane *did do* the dishes.

As an auxiliary, *do* carries emphasis in present and past tenses.

Father to Dick: Do your lessons!

Dick to Father: I *did* do my lessons (with heavy emphasis on *did*).

Auxiliary *do* also carries tense in so-called yes/no questions, questions that can be answered simply with "yes" or "no." For example, in *Mother wants Dick to mow the lawn,* the verb *want* carries PRES, as evidenced by the morpheme *-s*, indicating PRES in third person. In the yes/no version of this sentence, *do* carries the interrogative force: <u>*Does*</u> *Mother want Dick to mow the lawn?* The *-s* suffix indicates that *does* carries tense (PRES) in the sentence.

> The cowboy plays the guitar.
>
> *Does* the cowboy play the guitar?
>
> What *does* the cowboy play?

Exercise 5.2

Which of the following instances of *do* are verbs, and which are AUX?

1. Good students do their lessons every day.
2. Bad students did have problems in school.
3. Mediocre students have done their lessons in a slipshod way.
4. The teacher did have both good and bad students.
5. The valedictorian did practice her speech.
6. The salutatorian didn't forget his mortarboard.
7. Many graduates did have excellent records.
8. Some will have been doing menial work.
9. Lunch might have been done by noon.
10. Did all the graduates have their diplomas?

Modals

Modals are auxiliary verbs. The most common modals or modal auxiliaries are *can, could, may, might, must, shall, will, would,* and *ought.* The modals have three characteristics:

1. They have a single form, not adding *-s* in the third person singular.

> She *can* ride broncos.
>
> He *may* leave early.
>
> *It *wills* not make a lot of noise.

2. They are never used alone, but always appear in conjunction with verbs (except in answers to questions: Q. Will Mother go to Provo? A. She *may.*)

	MODAL	VERB	
Dick	should	stop	complaining.
Jane	might	take	swimming lessons.
*Spot	would		every night.

3. While verbs have forms with *-ing* (danc*ing*, look*ing*), modals do not: *Mother might*ing* bake brownies.

M ODAL AUXILIARIES

can, could, may, might, must, shall, will, would, ought

- Have a single form, not adding *-s* in third person
- Are never used alone
- Do not have forms with *-ing*

F OR DISCUSSION: THE FUNCTIONS OF MODALS

In their function, modals fall into two rough categories: belief modals (to express belief or probability) and social modals (to give advice or tell others what they should or must do).

BELIEF MODALS

John *will* be at the meeting tomorrow. [strong belief in the veracity of the statement]

John *should* be at the meeting tomorrow. [less assurance of the veracity of the statement: "John probably will be at the meeting tomorrow." (paraphrased)]

John *may/might/could* be at the meeting tomorrow. [less assurance that John will appear]

SOCIAL MODALS

Wife to husband: "If I were you, I *would* get some exercise every day."

Employee to boss: "Our Philboid Studge cereal *might* sell better if it contained more raisins."

Boss to employee: "Next quarter, you *must* sell more Philboid Studge."

If you were to ask your mother, friend, boss, or instructor for a ride, which of the following modals would you use: *will, could, would, might*? How would you phrase your requests, and how would you be polite with your words?

Irregular and Periphrastic Modals

Irregular Modals

Irregular modals consist of more than one word:

We *had better* get out of here.

We *ought to* leave soon.

We *would rather* not stay.

Note that the AUX *had* in the first example sentence is not really in past tense; it is an invariant form, as the following example demonstrates:

*We *have* better get out of here.

Periphrastic Modals

Periphrastic modals, like irregular modals, consist of more than one word: *have to, have got to, be supposed to, be able to,* and *be allowed to.* Unlike irregular modals, periphrastic modals do change form:

We *have to* go now, and *he has to* go, too. In fact, we *were supposed to* leave quite a while ago.

The forms *has* and *were* show that periphrastic modals can be marked for tense.

As the following sentences demonstrate, periphrastic modals can occur with "real" modals when we want to express more than one modal meaning:

I *may be able to* meet you for dinner. [Compare: I *may* meet you for dinner.]

Goodness gracious! I *would have to* fall asleep just when the show was getting interesting. [Compare: I *would* fall asleep just when the show was getting interesting.]

Modals and Tense

Historically, some modal auxiliaries, like verbs, referred to past time, and some grammars still talk about the tense of a modal. We agree with Geoffrey Leech's argument that "past" and "present" (tense) are misleading terms for modals.[3] This book's analysis of tense and modals reflects contemporary usage of these forms. For example, *can* was the present tense and *could* was past tense. But over time, *could* lost its past meaning and now signifies something like "be able (under certain circumstances)": *I could sing a hymn if I didn't have a sore throat.* Similarly, *might* is the historical past tense of *may,* but now expresses degree of probability:

Dick *may* pass his arithmetic test. [more likely]

Dick *might* pass his arithmetic test. [less likely]

---

[3] Geoffrey Leech, *Meaning and the English Verb* (London, Longman, 1987), 67.

The final two auxiliaries *have* and *be* will be considered in the next chapter as we take up the forms of the verb called the *perfect* and *progressive aspects.*

F OR DISCUSSION: TIME AND TIME WORDS

Notice the verb group *could dance* in the following two sentences:

In 1988 I *could dance* the night away.

I *could dance* the night away.

What is the difference in meaning in the two sentences? What is the source of the difference in meaning? What time does the second sentence refer to?

Recapitulation

From the analysis in this chapter, we can derive an important rule about sentences: Sentences have either tense (TN) or modal (MOD).[4]

Children *giggle.* (PRES)

Dick *giggled.* (PAST)

Children *might* giggle. (MOD)

Tense and modal are part of the auxiliary (AUX). The whole AUX consists of the features that allow us to construct sentences such as the following:

The children *are giggling.*

The children *might have been giggling.*

In the next two chapters, we will complete the analysis of AUX, but for the moment the principle that sentences have either tense or modal is very important. We can state this idea with a handy formula:

AUX → [TN, MOD]

The brackets [] simply mean "one or the other." (And remember that → means "consists of" or "is made up of.")

Using the same notational scheme, we can also define tense and modal:

TN → [PRES, PAST] [meaning that tense is either present or past]

MOD → [can, could, may, might, must, shall, should, will, would, ought] [meaning that the modal is one and only one of the words listed]

---

[4] To reiterate, here we rely on Geoffrey Leech's argument that there is not much point in considering the modal as having tense.

Exercise 5.3

A. *Mother can surf like a pro* looks like a sentence, sounds like a sentence, smells like a sentence, and *is* a sentence because, among other attributes, it has MOD (*can*) and a VERB (*surf*). But *Father sulking in the basement* doesn't look like a sentence or sound like a sentence, and in fact it is *not* a sentence because it has neither MOD nor TN. Which of the following are sentences, and which are not? Explain the basis for your decisions.

1. Dick ran home after school.

2. Jane going to the store.

3. Spot to bark at the mail carrier.

4. Having a good meal with my friends on my birthday.

5. Father can polish the car.

6. Jane being a good girl usually.

7. Dick will help with the dishes.

8. Jane to plant a garden in the backyard.

9. Mother and Father were thinking about a vacation in Florida.

10. Dick, Jane, and Spot having gone to the park.

B. Find the regular, irregular, and periphrastic modals in the following sentences. Are they belief or social uses of modals?

1. The children can clean up after supper.

2. Dick is able to run the dishwasher.

3. Jane will have to wash the crystal.

4. "It would be paradise to get away to a cheery island cottage like this!" (*Casual Living,* Summer 2002)

5. "Man is a credulous animal and must believe *something;* in the absence of good grounds for belief, he will be satisfied with bad ones." (Bertrand Russell)

6. "I'm not afraid of death but I am afraid of dying. Pain can be alleviated by morphine but the pain of social ostracism cannot be taken away." (Derek Jarman)

7. "I doubt that the Trojans will be able to dominate the PAC 10 next year." (Student)

> 8. "When we visit with our grandson, we have got to be careful of the language we use." (Writing workshop participant)
>
> 9. "When FBI and immigration agents arrested Zacarias Moussaoui at his motel in suburban Minneapolis on Aug. 16, they suspected he might be a potential airline hijacker." (*Los Angeles Times*, March 30, 2002).
>
> 10. When ought we to expect the results of the mammogram?

PASSAGES FOR ANALYSIS

A. In *Brothers and Keepers,* John Edgar Wideman tells of a visit to the prison in which his brother was an inmate. Find the verbs in this passage. What tense are they in? What is the relationship between tense and time in this passage?

> We visit you in prison. Here we come. The whole family. Judy, Dan, Jake, Jamila. Our nuclear unit and Mom and whoever else we can fit into the Volvo station wagon. We try to arrive at the prison as early as possible, but with five in our crew competing for time and space in Mom's tiny bathroom in the house on Tokay, and slow-as-molasses nieces Monique and Tameka to pick up in East Liberty after we're all ready, we're lucky if we set off before noon. But here we come.[5]

B. In the following passage from *Wild Decembers* by Edna O'Brien, incomplete sentences (or fragments) are punctuated to look like sentences. What is missing from the fragments. Rewrite the fragments to make complete sentences. In your opinion, which of the two versions is more effective? Why?

> In the street levity, expectation. In the lanes, kids with old curtains and straw hats in hiding, to scare the grown-ups. New blouses hauled out of carrier bags. Satin with little pearl buttons that come undone. Platform sole to kick out the beat. Mothers ironing white shirts for their wild colonial boys. Streamers, pale primrose, pale pink, flung up to the rafters. Noreen on a ladder tacking their scalloped ends to the cornice, a stout arm, her full breasts heaving.[6]

---

[5] Used by permission of the author.

[6] Edna O'Brien, *Wild Decembers* (Boston: Houghton Mifflin, 1999). Copyright © 1999 by Edna O'Brien. Reprinted by permission of the publisher. All rights reserved.

Using Grammar: Switching Tenses

Grammar handbooks and writing textbooks admonish writers not to switch tenses within paragraphs. Sometimes, however, a writer's meaning necessitates a switch in tense. In fact, handbooks would do better to remind writers that when a tense shift is necessary, a time word or time phrase is equally important to keep the reader following the text. For example:

> Critics believe that *Guernica* is one of Picasso's greatest works. *Guernica* depicts the devastation done to the Basque town of Guernica during the Spanish Civil War. Picasso *painted* this masterpiece *in 1937,* and *since this time* the Basque people *have hoped* that the painting could reside in the Basque region of Spain.

This paragraph begins in the present tense, changes to past tense and then to present perfect aspect. Each of these shifts is accompanied by a time phrase that eliminates confusion.

CHAPTER REVIEW

In your own words, explain the following:

- Notional definition of verbs
- Formal definition of verbs
- Functional definition of verbs
- Principal parts of verbs
- Basic sentence types
- Transitive and intransitive verbs
- Linking verbs
- Tense
- Auxiliary verb *do*
- Modal auxiliary
- Irregular modals
- Periphrastic modals
- Belief function of modals
- Social function of modals

Verbs: Perfect and Progressive Aspect

CHAPTER PREVIEW

- The chapter analyzes sentences in present perfect aspect (e.g., George has watched a movie), past perfect aspect (George had watched a movie), present progressive aspect (George is watching a movie), past progressive aspect (George was watching a movie), present perfect progressive aspect (George has been watching a movie), and past perfect progressive aspect (George had been watching a movie).

- The auxiliary rule for sentences in active voice is developed.

    Active voice: Bryce eats pickles.

    Passive voice: Pickles are eaten by Bryce.

- Nonfinite verb forms (such as *to go, going,* and *gone*) are introduced.

ASPECT

The nature of the action that the verb or verb group is conveying is its aspect. For instance, in the sentence *The orchestra <u>had been practicing</u> Beethoven's Fifth,* the practicing is completed; but in the sentence *The orchestra <u>has been practicing</u> Beethoven's Fifth,* the practicing is still going on. In *The dog barks,* the barking may or may not be occurring now, but in *The dog is barking,* the barking is occurring in real time.

Perfect Aspect (HAVE + EN)

What are the components of the verb group in the following sentence?

  The teacher *has given* Dick a scolding.

The complete verb group consists of *have + given. Have* is an auxiliary verb, and in this sentence it is in the present tense. *Given* is the past participle of *give.* Any verb that has the auxiliary *have* (or *has* or *had*) and the past participle of the main verb is in the perfect aspect.

  In the sentence *I have ridden my bicycle,* the auxiliary verb (*have*) is in the present tense, and the main verb is a past participle (*ridden*). We say, then, that the verb is in the present perfect aspect. In contrast, in *I had ridden my bicycle,* the auxiliary verb (*had*) is in the past tense and *ridden* is a past participle; therefore, the verb is in the past perfect aspect. What we see here is that the AUX carries the tense in these verb groups. In our discussions of the perfect aspect, we will let EN stand for the past participle because often the past participle ends with *-en*: give/given, take/taken, prove/proven. Sometimes, however, the past tense form and the past participle are identical. For example, in the sentence *I walked to the store,* the word *walked* is past tense. However, in the sentence *I have walked to the store,* the word *walked* is the past participle. In *I thought you were there,* the verb *think* is in the past tense; in *I had thought you were there,* the verb *thought* is the past participle of *think.*

Any sentence (or clause) that has HAVE + EN (i.e., *have* + a past participle) is in the perfect aspect, and we now have a rule that will account for sentences such as the following:

Dick has missed his ballet lesson.

PRES + HAVE + EN + *miss* (present tense of *have* plus the past participial form of *miss*)[1]

Jane had joined the wrestling team.

PAST + HAVE + EN + *join* (past tense of *have* plus past participial form of *join*)

Notice that PAST controls HAVE, putting it in the past tense, and EN controls the verb *join,* making it a past participle. If we were to read the sequence in ordinary language, we would say "the past tense of *have* (*had*) and the past participle of *join* (*joined*)." In other words, PAST + HAVE = HAD; EN + JOIN = JOINED.

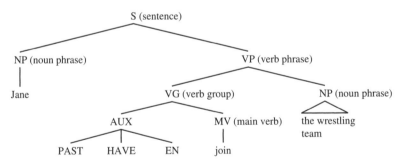

Figure 6.1 Branching tree diagram of *Jane had joined the wrestling team.* Interpretation: PAST TENSE OF *HAVE* = HAD; PAST PARTICIPLE OF *JOIN* = JOINED. That EN, the symbol for the past participle, precedes the verb causes some confusion. However, it is always associated with *have.* And it can always be interpreted as "past participle of" the verb. Thus, for example, *EN swim* can read as "the past participle of swim," which, of course is *swum* (e.g., *Gertrude has swum the English Channel*). Grouping the elements of the noun phrase *the wrestling team* under a triangle is a convenience. It means that at this point we are not concerned with the structure of the noun phrase.

---

[1] That EN, the symbol for the past participle, precedes the verb may seem confusing, since with the actual past participle the *morpheme* is at the end of the word (e.g., *eat, eaten*). However, in our notational system, the EN symbol just signals that the verb will be in the past participial form. Thus "EN + *drive*" can be read as "the past participle of *drive,* which is *driven,*" and "EN + *talk*" can be read as "the past participle of *talk,* which is *talked.*"

THE RULE FOR PERFECT ASPECT WITH TENSE

PERFECT ASPECT = TENSE + HAVE + EN

TENSE = [PRESENT, PAST]

EN = PAST PARTICIPLE

FOR DISCUSSION: PERFECT ASPECT

Take a look at the following sentences:

1. The Smiths *have traveled* extensively in Asia.
2. The Smiths *traveled* extensively in Asia.
3. The Smiths *traveled* to Asia in 1998.

Number 1 (present perfect aspect) implies that the Smiths might well travel in Asia again. Number 2 (past tense), however, implies that the Smiths' travels in Asia are a thing of the past. Number 3 (past tense with a specific date) implies that the Smiths visited Asia only once. In light of these data about the meanings of aspect and tense, why is the following sentence ungrammatical?

4. *The Smiths *have traveled* to Japan in 1998.

Exercise 6.1

Some of the following sentences are in present perfect aspect, some are in past perfect aspect, and some are in neither. Identify the sentences in perfect aspect (either present or past), and analyze their auxiliary structures.

Examples
  a. Dick has eaten his breakfast.

   Present perfect aspect

   PRES + HAVE + EN [present tense of *have* and past participial form of *eat*]

b. Jane had completed her homework.

Past perfect aspect

PAST + HAVE + EN (past tense of *have* and past participial form of *complete*)

c. Mother built the tool shed.

The sentence is in simple past tense.

1. Only one student has failed the course.
2. The teachers had prepared the lessons.
3. Someone is playing the oboe.
4. Has Father written the letter?
5. Spot hasn't bitten the mail carrier for weeks.
6. Who was trying to get into the room?

CHALLENGERS

1. Why is sentence a acceptable while sentence b is not? What makes sentence b different from sentence a? How would we rephrase sentence b to make it acceptable?

   a. Jodie Foster has won two Academy Awards.

   b. Bette Davis has won two Academy Awards.

2. What is the difference between the Impressionist exhibit at the time that sentence a is said and at the time sentence b is said? How do you know this?

   a. Have you been to the Impressionist exhibit?

   b. Did you go to the Impressionist exhibit?

We can also have sentences such as this:

Father could have seen the ballgame.

In this sentence we have a modal and the elements of the perfect aspect but no tense in the auxiliary verbs.

COULD + HAVE + EN + (the verb *see*) [the modal *could* plus *have* plus the past participial form of *see*]

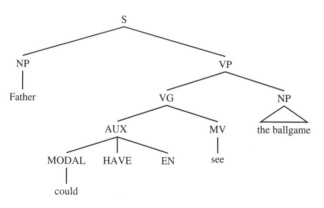

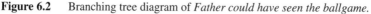

Figure 6.2   Branching tree diagram of *Father could have seen the ballgame.*

Further examples:

> Mother might have lost her temper.
>
> MIGHT + HAVE + EN + (the verb *lose*) [the modal *might* plus *have* plus the past participle of *lose,* which is *lost*)
>
> The family should have had Spot trained.
>
> SHOULD + HAVE + EN + (the verb *have*) [the modal *should* plus *have* plus the past participle of *have,* which is *had*]

And one more example, this one from the writings of Thomas Carlyle:

> "Lord Bacon *could* as easily *have created* the planets as he *could have written* Hamlet.*"*

The verb group in the first clause consists of MODAL + HAVE + EN (+ *create*). In the second clause: MODAL + HAVE + EN (+ *write*).

T HE RULE FOR PERFECT ASPECT WITH EITHER TENSE OR MODAL

PERFECT = [TENSE, MODAL] + HAVE + EN

TENSE = [PRESENT, PAST]

MODAL = [can, could, may, might, must, shall, will, would, ought]

Progressive Aspect (BE + ING)

The progressive aspect is formed with *be* as an auxiliary verb followed by the present participle (sing*ing,* sneez*ing,* sipp*ing*). As EN is the symbol for past participle, let ING be the symbol for present participle.

Let's begin examining the progressive by reviewing what *be* does as a verb and as an auxiliary:

The verb *be* has two functions:

1. as the main word in the predicate (VP)

   Dick *is* sullen.

   He *was* late for his violin lesson.

   They *were* disgusted.

   The family had *been* in Florida.

2. as an auxiliary verb

   Norma *is* singing a song.

   You *are* losing your mind.

   The members of the choir *are* practicing.

   Ana *was* writing her thesis.

   His friends *were* planning a party for his birthday.

Or *be* can function as the helper *and* the main verb. Sentences like the following are common:

	HELPING VERB	MAIN VERB	
Dick	is	being	obstinate.
The parents	are	being	lax.

In the sentences below we see again that the AUX carries tense unless the first element is a modal:

She *is* walking to school. [present progressive]

She *was* walking to school. [past progressive]

She could *be* driving to school. [modal + progressive]

THE RULE FOR THE PROGRESSIVE ASPECT WITH TENSE OR MODAL

PROGRESSIVE = [TENSE, MODAL] + BE + ING

TENSE = [PRESENT, PAST]

MODAL = [can, could, may, might, must, shall, will, would, ought]

F OR DISCUSSION: PROGRESSIVE ASPECT

In the following two sentences, what is the difference in the information given about the son's residency in Palmdale?

1. My son *lives* in Palmdale.
2. My son is *living* in Palmdale.

Exercise 6.2

Some of the following sentences are in progressive aspect, and some are not. Which ones are in progressive?

1. Vegetables are nutritious.
2. Fruit is getting expensive.
3. Could this winter be colder than usual?
4. Might the price of gasoline be coming down?
5. No one should be watching television for more than one hour per day.
6. If you are wise, you should be planning for the future.

Perfect Progressive Aspect

Any sentence that has BE + ING (e.g., a form of the verb *be* plus a present participle) is in the progressive:

Chantalle *is studying* religion.

Many *were discovering* the joys of cooking.

and any sentence that has HAVE + EN is in the perfect:

Clarence *has taken* his vitamins.

Connie *had written* a letter.

When these forms are combined, the sentence is in the perfect progressive:

Mother had been reading the newspaper.

PAST + HAVE + EN + BE + ING (+ verb)

In other words, the sentence is *perfect* because it has HAVE + EN and *progressive* because it has BE + ING:

PAST + HAVE = past tense of *have,* which is *had*

EN + BE = past participle of *be,* which is *been*

ING (+ verb) = present participle of verb *read,* which is *reading*

The following sentence has a MODAL plus HAVE plus EN plus BE plus ING (modal plus *have* plus the past participle of *be* plus the present participle of *mourn*):

Jane may have been mourning the death of her pet lizard.

[MODAL + HAVE + EN + BE + ING (+ *mourn*)]

Charles Lamb wrote the following sentence (from which we have have omitted a few words):

"He *was attending* parties . . . when he *should have been attending* on us."

AUX in the first clause of this sentence is

PAST tense of BE [*was*] and the morpheme, which signals that the verb will be a present participle [*attending*]: PAST + BE + ING

and in the second clause

MOD [*should*], HAVE, the past participial morpheme [signaling that *be* will appear as *been*], and the present participial morpheme [which results in *attending*]: MOD + HAVE + EN + BE + ING

THE RULE FOR PERFECT PROGRESSIVE WITH TENSE OR MODAL

PERF PROGR = [TENSE, MODAL] + HAVE + EN + BE + ING

TENSE = [PRESENT, PAST]

MODAL = [can, could, may, might, must, shall, will, would, ought]

Exercise 6.3

1. Write an original sentence in perfect progressive aspect.

2. Explain why the following sentences are or are not in perfect progressive aspect:

   a. The concert will be starting in five minutes.

   b. The audience must have been anticipating the delay.

CHALLENGERS

1. Write an original *negative* sentence in perfect progressive aspect.
2. Write a yes/no question in perfect progressive aspect.

THE AUX RULE

We have now completed the basic rule describing the auxiliary system:

AUX = [TN, MOD] (HAVE + EN) (BE + ING)

It's very much worth mentioning that this rule, in its elegance, is easier to grasp and remember than it would be if it were written out in natural language:

> The auxiliary consists of either tense or a modal auxiliary. *Have* and the past participle morpheme are optional, as are *be* and the present participial morpheme.

And it's also very much worthwhile to consider the explanatory power the rule gives us. With it, we can analyze sentences and clauses with AUX made up of

PRES: Dick teases Jane.

PAST: Dick teased Jane.

MOD: Dick will tease Jane.

PRES + HAVE + EN: Dick has teased Jane.

PAST + HAVE + EN: Dick had teased Jane.

MOD + HAVE + EN: Dick would have teased Jane.

PRES + BE + ING: Dick is teasing Jane.

PAST + BE + ING: Dick was teasing Jane.

MOD + BE + ING: Dick should be teasing Jane.

PRES + HAVE + EN + BE + ING: Dick has been teasing Jane.

PAST + HAVE + EN + BE + ING: Dick had been teasing Jane.

MOD + HAVE + EN + BE + ING: Dick might have been teasing Jane.

THE AUX RULE

AUX → [TN, MOD] (HAVE + EN) (BE + ING)

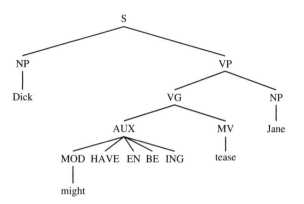

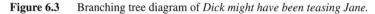

Figure 6.3 Branching tree diagram of *Dick might have been teasing Jane.*

Exercise 6.4

Analyze AUX in the following sentences.

Examples

Students love exams.

AUX = PRES

Professors flunked students.

AUX = PAST

The dean could have reprimanded the professor.

AUX = MODAL + HAVE + EN

The president might have been exerting her authority.

AUX = MODAL + HAVE + EN + BE + ING

1. Jane might give Spot a bath.
2. Spot has scratched at fleas all day.
3. "Here even the law of the jungle has broken down." (Walid Jumblatt)
4. "Even a paranoid can have enemies." (Henry Kissinger)
5. "It's not true I had nothing on. I had the radio on." (Marilyn Monroe).
6. "Violence has been Nicaragua's most important export to the world." (Ronald Reagan)

7. "My husband and I had been thinking about a trip around the world." (Writing workshop participant)

8. "The great nations have always acted like gangsters, and the small nations like prostitutes." (Stanley Kubrick)

9. "I wasn't thinking, I wasn't planning, I was just doing. I'm just saying murder vents rage. The murders are without reason." (Gary Gilmore)

CHALLENGERS

1. Many writing or grammar guidebooks suggest that writers eliminate forms of the verb *to be* whenever possible because it is a "weak" verb. Look at guidebooks and see what they say. Take a piece of your own prose and apply the suggestions you find in one or more guidebooks. Compare the two versions. Which do you think is better and why? Take a piece of published prose and examine it for *be* verbs. Apply the guidebooks' suggestions and then compare the original with the altered version.

2. Rewrite the guidelines for using forms of *to be* in your own words. Improve on them if possible.

VERB GROUPS AND THE SENTENCE

One way to describe the relationship between verbs and sentences is to say that every sentence has at least one verb with either TN (tense) or MOD (modal). Look at the following sentences as examples. Each of them has a modal or tense in the auxiliary or main verb if there is no auxiliary:

I *can make* ice cream. [modal]

The chairperson *asked* me to change the brochure. [past]

My friend *could have been* a winner. [modal and perfect]

We *have gone* to the moon and back. [present perfect]

You *are joking*! [present progressive]

Those soccer players *have been practicing* all night. [present perfect progressive]

In contrast, these groups of words are not sentences because they do not have a verb with tense or modal:

Cats crying at night. [present participle with no auxiliary]

The paper written over three days. [past participle with no auxiliary]

Exercise 6.5

We've been moving rapidly, so let's pause to consolidate the ideas so far. Using the notational system that we've developed, analyze AUX in the following sentences.

Examples
> Spot can walk on his hind legs.
>
> MOD (can)
>
> Dick flies model airplanes in the park.
>
> PRES

1. Mother likes horror films.
2. Father may stop playing golf.
3. Dick and Jane often torment Spot.
4. Jane's room sometimes can become a mess.
5. On Sunday afternoon, the family members played Monopoly.
6. Dick bought a skateboard.
7. Jane sleeps in class.
8. Mother can read the newspaper.
9. Father might have walked to work.
10. Spot was sleeping on the couch.
11. "U.S. officials will examine states' efforts on children's health coverage in the wake of welfare reform." (*Los Angeles Times*)
12. "I would die for my country, but I could never let my country die for me." (Neil Kinnock)
13. "The team had been winning in the first three quarters." (Student)

14. "Up to this point, the system prompt has shown the current drive and directory in abbreviated form. . . ." (*Running MS-DOS*)

15. "Ever since Descartes, La Mettrie, and others explicitly called man a machine, the metaphor has been a dominant one in educational thinking." (Wayne C. Booth)

FINITE AND NONFINITE VERB FORMS

So far we have been concentrating on finite verbs, which have either tense or a modal and are the head of a verb phrase or predicate in a sentence.

When present or past participles are used without auxiliary verbs, they are called *nonfinite verbs.*

Infinitives (*to* + V) are also nonfinite verbs.

The kid *flying* a kite is happy. [present participle]

Gone with the wind, the kite was lost. [past participle]

Alvin likes *to watch* the grass grow. [infinitive]

These verb forms have neither tense nor modals. The nonfinite verb forms have functions that we will examine as we go through this book. They might, for example, function as nominals (i.e., in place of nouns)

Counterfeiters make money. [noun]

Counterfeiting makes money. [present participle]

To counterfeit makes money. [infinitive]

or adjectivals

The *old* counterfeiter made money. [adjective]

The *aging* counterfeiter made money. [present participle]

PASSAGES FOR ANALYSIS

1. Find the verb groups and identify tense and aspect in the following passage by Jean Stafford.

My companions had all been illustrious in the world of *belle lettres,* architecture, painting, music, the natural and physical sciences, jurisprudence, medicine, and high finance. We had eaten ambrosia and drunk nectar in the smartest possible restaurants or in the dining rooms of splendidly appointed houses or apartments where Cézannes and Corots hung, where Aubussons and Sarouks lay and Chippendale and Queen Anne stood. These interiors reminded me of others I had seen or read about and I was happy to share my memories with my interlocutor—not, of course, that he was getting a word in edgewise.[2]

2. In the following passages, written by students who are not native speakers of English, find the verb groups and rewrite the sentences so that the use of tense and aspect is grammatical. Also, when appropriate, change the wording of the passages. For example, "doing fishing" is not idiomatic English; the passage might read, "First I put up a tent and then went fishing" or "First I put up a tent and then fished."

a. "I have fun on a camping trip. I have a lot of things in my bag, a fishing rod, a pot and pan, some food, a sleeping bag, etc. I reached the sea. First I put up a tent and I am doing fishing. I eat dinner and catch fish in my hands. People are enjoying together. Then we gathering firewood. At night we light firewood and we are singing and dancing. We keeping in mind good memories. When I was tired of life, it give me energy to live actively, so a travel is good for me."

b. "One sunny day it happened. A young man is skateboarding in the park of the city. He isn't cool. First he is skateboarding on the ground. There are some couples around him. Next he was challenging to skate on the ramp. He was smiling when he loose is balance. He fall into one man who has stern face. Young man is worrying and scaring to crash into him. Was he all right? I leave this story to your imagination."

CHAPTER REVIEW

In your own words, explain the following:

- Perfect aspect
- Progressive aspect
- Perfect progressive aspect
- The AUX rule
- Finite verb forms
- Nonfinite verb forms

---

[2] *New York Times* (June 8, 1974).

C H A P T E R

7

Negative, Interrogative, Imperative, Passive

CHAPTER PREVIEW

- Sentences can be classified according to what their verbs entail (require)—for example, objects (Horses eat *oats*), no objects (Horses gallop), complements (Horses seem *placid*).

- A basic sentence such as *Students study art* can be made into a negative (Students *do not* study art), yes/no and *wh-* questions (*Do* students study art?/*What* do students study?), imperatives or commands (*Study* art!), and passive voice (Art *is studied* by students).

- The auxiliary verb *do* carries tense in some negative and interrogative sentences. (*Did* the students graduate? I *do* not like green eggs and ham.)

- In explaining the relationship among basic sentences and their negative, interrogative, imperative, and passive counterparts, we can use the formula explained in Chapter 2: deletion, substitution, addition, and movement.

- In passive, the object is moved to the subject position, and the verb group includes *be* + past participle: BE + EN.

- The AUX rule, expanded to include passive, is AUX → [TN, MOD] (HAVE + EN) (BE + ING) (BE + EN).

REVIEW OF CHAPTERS 4 AND 5

In Chapter 4, we surveyed the eight basic sentence types; in Chapter 5, we analyzed the verb group. Our understanding of the sentence types and the verb groups helps us to understand interrogatives (Who stole the paper clip?), negatives (Someone did not steal the paper clip), imperatives (Steal the paper clip!), and passives (The paper clip was stolen).

These basic sentences are declarative. That is, sentences express affirmative propositions. Here is a list of sentence types.

A. Transitive

  1. The girl *sees* the tree.

     V + direct object

  2. The professor *gives* **the students** an assignment.

     V + **indirect object** + direct object

  3. Milly *calls* Jane **a fool**.

     V + direct object + **objective complement** (NP)

     Milly *calls* Jane **foolish**.

     V + direct object + **objective complement** (ADJ)

B. Intransitive

  4. The man sleeps.

C. Linking

  5. The man is nice.

     The woman is a physician.

  6. The meeting is here.

     The meeting is at ten.

  7. The dog becomes vicious.

     The dog becomes a clown.

  8. The dog was afraid of the cat.

     The dog was aware that its nose was cold.

These sentences can be changed (or "transformed" in the terminology of some grammarians) to questions, negative sentences, imperatives (sometimes called commands), and passive voice. Many of these changes require the use of auxiliary verbs: *do, have, be,* and the modals. The changes are brought about by deletion, addition, movement, and substitution of structures within the sentence.

However, you should not assume that when you speak or write, you somehow start with basic sentences and then transform them. When we speak of "transformations," we are not talking about the mental operation of generating language structures. The point is that negative sentences, questions, imperatives (commands), and passives are systematically related to their basic counterparts.

NEGATIVE

With Auxiliaries

As you recall, the auxiliaries are *do, have, be,* and modals. To form a negative sentence, the negative *not* is inserted after any of these auxiliaries and before the main verb.

The farmer *does* plant beans./The farmer *does not* plant beans.

The farmer *has* planted beans./The farmer *has not* planted beans.

The farmer *is* planting beans./The farmer *is not* planting beans.

The farmer *will* plant beans./The farmer *will not* plant beans.

Without Auxiliaries: Transitive and Nontransitive Verbs

If the verb group contains none of the auxiliaries (i.e., if AUX = TN), the tense-carrying *do* is inserted, followed by the negative *not*.

Carol sings ballads./Carol *does not* sing ballads.

Carol sang./Carol *did not* sing.

Without Auxiliaries: Be

If AUX consists only of TN, and the main verb is a form of *be,* negative *not* follows the main verb.

The herd *was* restless./The herd *was not* restless.

Jonathan *is* the hero of the day./Jonathan *is not* the hero of the day.

The cowboys *were* ravenous./The cowboys *were not* ravenous.

Negative

WITH AUXILIARIES
If the verb group in the sentence has any of the auxiliaries, the negative *not* is inserted after them and before the main verb.

The farmer *will* plant beans./The farmer *will not* plant beans.

WITHOUT AUXILIARIES: TRANSITIVE AND NONTRANSITIVE VERBS
If the verb group contains none of the auxiliaries (i.e., if AUX = TN), the tense-carrying *do* is inserted, followed by the negative *not*.

The farmer planted beans./The farmer *did not* plant beans.

WITHOUT AUXILIARIES: BE
If AUX consists only of TN, and the main verb is a form of *be,* negative *not* follows the main verb.

The farmer *is* diligent./The farmer *is not* diligent.

USING GRAMMAR: CONTRACTIONS

Often the negative word *not* and the auxiliary verb are contracted (cannot/can't, will not/won't, do not/don't). In many formal situations contractions are not appropriate. Business correspondence to an unknown person, contracts, and other legal papers are examples of formal contexts in which most writers do not use contractions. On the other hand in speech, contractions are the norm, even in very formal circumstances. To say, "I do not eat meat" or "She did not give me the money" (rather than "I don't eat meat" and "She didn't give me the money") emphasizes the negative and perhaps even expresses anger or irritation.

USING GRAMMAR: NO DOUBLE NEGATIVES

"This rule [that proscribes the double negative] originates with the sixteenth-century poet, Sir Philip Sidney, who states in his poem 'Astrophel and Stella' that two negatives cancel each other out and make a positive."[1] The rule was taken up by grammarian Robert Lowth in the eighteenth century, but in fact, two negatives do not always cancel each other out. For example, the sentence *I can't drive to the store no more* means *I can't drive to the store* (and not *I can drive to the store*). The sentence *I can't drive to the store no more* would be inappropriate in formal situations.

FOR DISCUSSION

"What has been termed 'correct English' is nothing other than the blatant legitimation of the white middle-class code," says Dale Spender.[2] Think about "correct English" and the example of the double negatives above. Do you agree with Spender? Why or why not?

---

[1] Kathryn Riley and Frank Parker, *English Grammar* (Boston: Allyn & Bacon, 1998), 39.

[2] Dale Spender, *Man Made Language* (London: Routledge, 1985).

Exercise 7.1

Change the negative sentences to positive, and change the positive sentences to negative.

1. Dick does not hate Jane.

2. Jane admires Dick.

3. Mother will tolerate Father.

4. Father has not fed Spot.

5. The family were angry at their neighbors.

6. "Men of my age live in a continual state of desperation." (Trevor McDonald)

7. "Marxism is not scientific; at the best, it has scientific prejudices." (Albert Camus)

8. "Humour is by far the most significant activity of the human brain." (Edward De Bono)

9. "A man knows when he is growing old because he begins to look like his father." (Gabriel Garcia Marquez)

INTERROGATIVE

With the interrogative transformation, we are changing not only the structure of the sentence but also what the speaker wants the sentence to do. We are no longer asserting that something is true, but instead we are asking. Basically there are two types of questions: yes/no questions and *wh-* (or constituent) questions.

Yes/No Questions

As the name implies, yes/no questions can be answered with a simple "yes" or "no."

Sentences with Auxiliaries *Do,* Modal, *Have, Be*

In each of the sentences below, the yes/no question is formed by inverting an auxiliary verb (underlined) and the subject (italicized).

The *nurse* <u>did</u> take care of his patient./<u>Did</u> the *nurse* take care of his patient?

The *nurse* <u>will</u> take care of his patient./<u>Will</u> the *nurse* take care of his patient?

The *nurse* <u>has</u> taken care of his patient./<u>Has</u> the *nurse* taken care of his patient?

The *nurse* <u>was</u> taking care of his patient./<u>Was</u> the *nurse* taking care of his patient?

Sentences in Which AUX Is Only TN

In these sentences, the tense-carrying *do* is placed before the subject. In the declarative version of the following sentence, the verb carries tense:

The doctor *prescribed* aspirin.

In the yes/no interrogative version, *do* (underlined) carries tense:

<u>Did</u> the doctor *prescribe* aspirin?

The following are some additional examples:

The doctor *smiles.*/<u>Does</u> the doctor *smile?*

The doctor *gives* Dick good advice./<u>Does</u> the doctor *give* Dick good advice?

Sentences with *Be* as Main Verb

In these sentences, the yes/no question is formed by inverting the subject (italicized) and verb (underlined).

The *woman* <u>is</u> a masseuse./<u>Is</u> the *woman* a masseuse?

The *men* <u>were</u> happy./<u>Were</u> the *men* happy?

Forming Yes/No Interrogatives

Yes/no questions are formed by movement or addition.

a. Movement consists of inversion of the auxiliary and the subject.

b. Addition means adding the auxiliary *do* when no other auxiliary is present and the main verb is not *be*. The auxiliary *do* will assume or carry the tense of the main verb in the declarative sentence.

Wh- Questions

Wh- questions use words such as *who, whom, where, when,* and *how* to form the interrogative. Here is a slow-motion version of the relationship between a declarative sentence and its *wh-* question counterpart.

1. An interrogative word is substituted for the NP in question.

The girl sees *the tree.*/The girl sees *what?*

The girl sees the tree./*Who* sees the tree?

2. If the NP in question is *not* the subject, it is moved to the front of the sentence.

> The girl sees *the tree.*/*What the girl sees?
>
> *The girl* sees the tree./*Who* sees the tree?

3. Tense-carrying *do* is inserted between the interrogative word and the subject of the sentence.

> The girl sees *the tree.*/*What* <u>does</u> the girl see?

In step 1 of the example, the *wh-* word (*what*) substitutes for the object in the declarative sentence. But this substitution is not enough to make a grammatical question. Two more steps are necessary. The *wh-* word must move to the beginning of the question, and the subject and auxiliary must invert. Here, the addition of the auxiliary *do* is necessary to support the question formation because there is no other auxiliary. The operations of substitution, movement, and addition are necessary for the transformation of this declarative sentence into a *wh-* question.

The following examples will make you aware of what you already know about the relationship between *wh-* interrogatives and their declarative counterparts.

1. When: The girl can see the tree *at night.* (*When can* the girl see the tree?) [Since the sentence has the modal *can,* tense-carrying *do* is unnecessary.]

2. Where: The girl sees the tree *in the park.* (*Where does* the girl see the tree?) [Since the sentence does not have any of the auxiliaries (*do,* MOD, *have, be*), tense-carrying *do* is necessary.]

3. How: The girl has seen the tree *clearly.* (*How has* the girl seen the tree?) [The AUX *have* carries tense and is moved to a position between the *wh-* word and the subject of the sentence.]

4. Why: The girl has seen the tree clearly *because she wears glasses.* (*Why has* the girl seen the tree clearly?)

Forming WH- Interrogatives

1. Substitution of a *wh-* word for a part of the declarative sentence. If the *wh-* word is substituting for the subject of the sentence, then steps 2 and 3 are not necessary. Substitution is the only operation required.

2. Movement of the *wh-* word to the beginning of the sentence.

3. Movement of subject and auxiliary verb—inversion (and addition of tense-carrying *do* if there is no modal or other auxiliary verb in the declarative sentence).

Exercise 7.2

Change each of these declarative sentences to a yes/no question and then to a *wh-* question. Name the operations you used to make the change (movement, substitution, and addition).

1. Carlos is the best student in the class.
2. In Spain dinner is eaten at nine or ten o'clock.
3. In the summer I can read to my heart's content.
4. Dick and Jane have been swimming in the ocean.
5. My friends traveled to Morocco to a music festival.

CHALLENGER

Dick and Jane have been wondering about their dog Spot.

If you make a *wh-* question about the dog Spot, you are left with a preposition at the end of the question. Does that preposition bother you? Does the question seem awkward with a preposition at the end? How would you form the question to avoid the preposition at the end of the sentence? The word *whom* (rather than *who*) is technically correct after a preposition because *whom* is the object form. Does it seem strange to use *whom* to refer to a dog? Does the question seem to be very formal? Would you ever use a question formed in this manner? In what situations or contexts?

Exercise 7.3

ESL students frequently have trouble with English negatives and with question formation. Here are examples of mistakes they sometime make. Do you understand what these students are trying to say? What would you ask them to be sure you understand? Then describe the error and try to explain the correct rule—as simply as possible for the student.

1. Where he goed?
2. I no understand the question.
3. You will going with me?
4. What we are doing next?
5. The teacher no explaining the lesson again?

F OR DISCUSSION: INTERROGATIVES AND SPEECH ACTS

Frequently questions are not really meant as questions at all. That is, the intended speech act is not interrogative. The speech act may actually be a request for someone to do something. For example:

> Do you have the time? (Tell me the time.)
>
> Are you hungry? (Let's go eat now.)
>
> Is it hot in here? (Turn on the air conditioner.)
>
> Is that music too loud for you? (Turn down the music.)

Can you give other examples? When are you direct in your speech acts, and when do you imply what you want through a question?

IMPERATIVES

The imperative changes the speech act from a declarative to a request/command. Changing a declarative sentence to imperative requires deleting the subject and changing the verb form to a bare infinitive, by deleting any endings from the verb (infinitive = *to* + V; bare infinitive = V). The strength of the imperative depends on words like "please," the tone of the speaker's voice, and the context of the situation.

Declarative	Imperative
I feed the cat every day.	Feed the cat every day.
He should practice piano.	Practice piano.
They are strong.	Be strong.

PASSIVE VOICE

Changing a sentence into passive voice will not change the speech act. Instead, passive voice changes the emphasis from the doer of the action to the receiver of the action. Usually the doer of the action is the subject of the sentence. In a passive voice sentence, the subject function is held by the object, which is usually the receiver of the action. Passive voice may also be used to eliminate the doer of the action from the sentence. Here are some examples of active sentences changed to passive:

> Active: The mail carrier will deliver the mail today.
>
> Passive: The mail will be delivered today (by the mail carrier).
>
> Active: I cooked dinner for my friends.
>
> Passive: Dinner was cooked for my friends (by me).

In changing a sentence from active to passive voice, the NP that functions as the object is moved to the subject function and position. The subject is either deleted or moved into a phrase beginning with *by* following the verb group.

What this means is that only transitive sentences can have passive versions. Another way to say this is that only transitive verbs can be transformed into the passive.

Active: They must do it.

Passive: It must be done (by them).

The passive voice also requires a change in the verb group itself. The subject changes, and the verb changes in form too. *Be* is the auxiliary for the passive voice. The auxiliary is followed by the past participle. Here is another way to state the rule for the transformation of the verb to passive voice: Passive adds BE + EN (past participle) to the formula for the auxiliary.

Active: Jane teased Dick.

Passive: Dick was teased by Jane.

Figure 7.1 is the active version: *Mother hides the cookies*. Figure 7.2 is the passive version: *The cookies are hidden by mother*.

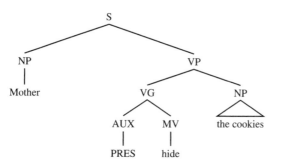

Figure 7.1   Branching tree diagram of *Mother hides the cookies*.

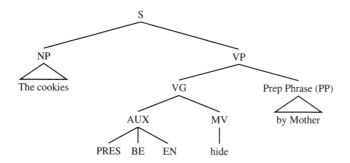

Figure 7.2   Branching tree diagram of *The cookies are hidden by mother*.

So we can now state the complete AUX rule.

AUX → [TN, MOD] (HAVE + EN) (BE + ING) (BE + EN)

Sentence in which AUX = PAST: *Jane teased Dick.*

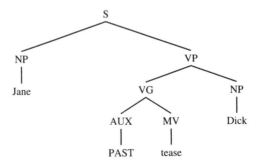

Figure 7.3   Branching tree diagram of *Jane teased Dick.*

Sentence in which AUX → PRES + BE + EN: *Dick is teased by Jane.*

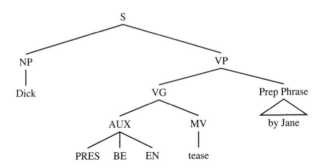

Figure 7.4   Branching tree diagram of *Dick is teased by Jane.*

Passive voice can occur in present and past tense, with modals, and with the perfect and progressive aspects. Examine the following examples.

• Present

Active: Father *steals* paper clips.

AUX → PRES

Passive: Paper clips *are stolen* by Father.

AUX → PRES + BE + EN

• Past

Active: Mother *watched* TV all day.

AUX → PAST

Passive: TV *was watched* all day by Mother.

AUX → PAST + BE + EN

- Modal

    Active: Dick *will eat* too much candy.

    AUX → MOD

    Passive: Too much candy *will be eaten* by Dick.

    AUX → MOD + BE + EN

- Present perfect

    Active: Jane *has used* too much perfume.

    AUX → PRES + HAVE + EN

    Passive: Too much perfume *has been used* by Jane.

    AUX → PRES + HAVE + BE + EN

- Past perfect

    Active: The children *had wanted* new squirt guns.

    AUX → PAST + HAVE + EN

    Passive: New squirt guns *had been wanted* by the children.

    AUX → PAST + HAVE + EN + BE + EN

- Modal + perfect

    Active: Spot *will have ruined* the carpet once more.

    AUX → MOD + HAVE + EN

    Passive: Once more the carpet *will have been ruined* by Spot.

    AUX → MOD + HAVE + EN + BE + EN

- Progressive

    Active: Mother *is buying* frozen dinners.

    AUX → PRES + BE + ING

    Passive: Frozen dinners *are being bought* by Mother.

    AUX → PRES + BE + ING + BE + EN

- Future perfect aspect

    Active: Mother *will have bought* frozen dinners.

    AUX → MODAL + HAVE + EN

    Passive: Frozen dinners *will have been bought* by Mother.

    AUX → MODAL + HAVE + EN + BE + EN

Exercise 7.4

A. In the following sentences, find the verb groups and identify their parts. A reminder: AUX may include MOD, TN (PRES or PAST), aspect (HAVE + EN, BE + ING), and passive (BE + EN). The sentences that consist of more than one clause will, of course, have more than one verb group.

Example

The passenger *had been informed* that he *would be taken* to the airport by limousine.

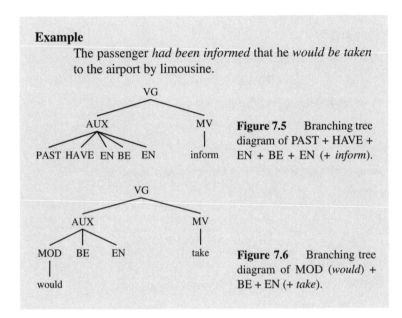

Figure 7.5 Branching tree diagram of PAST + HAVE + EN + BE + EN (+ *inform*).

Figure 7.6 Branching tree diagram of MOD (*would*) + BE + EN (+ *take*).

1. Wisdom exceeds riches in worth.

2. "Children in high risk populations should be tested for tuberculosis in the first year." (*Los Angeles Times*)

3. The dean told us that Murgatroyd had been thrown out last semester.

4. If your wild oats were sown when you were young, you will be eating oatmeal when you are old.

5. She is considered the most brilliant student in the class.

6. No one accepted Helen's explanation.

7. Little by little, Herman was intimidated by his cat.

8. "At the peak of his career (he won 26 and 27 games his last two seasons), Sandy Koufax was forced into premature retirement because of a chronic arm ailment." (*Los Angeles Times*)

B. In the following, if a sentence is passive, change it to active. If it is active, change it to passive—unless the change would be so awkward that no one would ever use the passive version of the sentence. Some of the sentences in the exercise cannot be changed because their verbs are not transitive.

Examples

> Jane actually hated Dick. [active]
>
> Dick was actually hated by Jane. [passive]
>
> Spot was often thrown out of the house by Mother. [passive]
>
> Mother often threw Spot out of the house. [active]
>
> "He who despises himself esteems himself as a self-despiser." (Nietzsche) [active]
>
> He who is despised by himself is esteemed by himself as a self-despiser. [passive]

1. The police questioned the suspect.
2. The suspect was intimidated by the police.
3. The riot had been led by the chairperson of the party.
4. "Even paranoids have real enemies." (Delmore Schwartz)
5. College students often study before tests.
6. "To love oneself is the beginning of a lifelong romance." (Oscar Wilde)
7. "Most people would die sooner than think; in fact, they do so." (Bertrand Russell)
8. "Whereas thou hast been forsaken and hated . . . I will make thee an eternal excellency, a joy of many generations." (Isaiah 60:15)
9. "The devil is an optimist if he thinks he can make people meaner." (Ambrose Bierce)
10. "Life is divided into the horrible and the miserable." (Woody Allen)
11. "I regard golf as an expensive way of playing marbles." (G. K. Chesterton)
12. "I was voted pill of the year by the Pharmaceutical Society." (Oscar Levant)
13. "Most meals consisted of lots of fresh vegetables and fruits along with small portions of meat or fish." (Donna Deane, *Los Angeles Times*)

FOR DISCUSSION

Computer grammar checkers will ask you to change the passive voice to active voice. Grammar handbooks also issue warnings about the passive voice. Here is one such warning from the *Bedford Handbook:* "Active verbs express meaning more emphatically and vigorously than their weaker counterparts—forms of be or verbs in the passive voice. . . . Verbs in the passive voice lack strength because their subjects receive the action instead of doing it."[3]

On the next page, this handbook goes on to say that "the passive voice is appropriate when you wish to emphasize the receiver of the action or to minimize the importance of the actor."

When is passive voice not only appropriate but necessary? Can you think of instances when you would need to use the passive? Why has passive gotten such a bad reputation?

STATIVE PASSIVE

Sometimes the past participle of passive voice seems to function as an adjective, modifying (adding more meaning to) the subject NP, rather than as a verb. For example, consider this sentence: *The door is closed.* The word *closed* seems to describe a quality of the door.

Now compare these sentences:

1. The dinner is ready.

2. The door is closed.

3. The pizza is delivered (by the college student).

The past participle *closed* seems to operate more like *ready* (an adjective) in sentence 1 than like *delivered* (a past participle) in sentence 3.

PASSAGE FOR ANALYSIS

In the following passage from *Whistling of Birds* by D. H. Lawrence, there is one true passive. Find it, and explain why the author might have used passive rather than active voice. How about interrogatives? Why do you think the author uses them? Does the passage contain stative passives? If so, identify them. Are there any negatives? How about imperatives?

> The frost held for many weeks, until the birds were dying rapidly. Everywhere in the fields and under the hedges lay the ragged remains of lapwings, starlings, thrushes,

---

[3] Diane Hacker, *Bedford Handbook* (Boston: Bedford/St. Martin's, 2002), 165.

redwings, innumerable ragged bloody cloaks of birds, when the flesh was eaten by invisible beasts of prey.

Then, quite suddenly, one morning the change came. The wind went to the south, came off the sea warm and soothing. In the afternoon there were little gleams of sunshine, and the doves began, without interval, slowly and awkwardly to coo. The doves were cooing, though with a laboured sound, as if they were still winter-stunned. Nevertheless, all the afternoon they continued their noise, in the mild air, before the frost had thawed off the road. At evening, the wind blew gently, still gathering a bruising quality of frost from the hard earth. Then, in the yellow-gleamy sunset, wild birds began to whistle faintly in the blackthorn thickets of the stream-bottom.

It was startling and almost frightening after the heavy silence of frost. How could they sing at once, when the ground was thickly strewn with the torn carcasses of birds? Yet out of the evening came the uncertain, silvery sounds that made one's soul start alert, almost with fear. How could the little silver bugles sound the rally so swiftly, in the soft air, when the earth was yet bound? Yet the birds continued their whistling, rather dimly and brokenly, but throwing the threads of silver, germinating noise in the air.

It was almost a pain to realize, so swiftly, the new world. *Le monde est mort* [the world is dead]. *Vive le monde!* But the birds omitted even the first part of the announcement, their cry was only a faint, blind, fecund *vive!*

There is another world. The winter is gone. There is a new world of spring. The voice of the turtle[dove] is heard in the land. But the flesh shrinks from so sudden a transition. Surely the call is premature while the clods are still frozen, and the ground is littered with the remains of wings! Yet we have no choice. In the bottoms of impenetrable blackthorn, each evening and morning now, out flickers a whistling of birds.

CHAPTER REVIEW

- Explain the rules for negative and imperative formation and *wh-* and yes/no question formation.
- Explain how passive voice sentences are formed.
- Write a paragraph in which you use passive voice appropriately (or even necessarily). Explain why the passive voice is appropriate.

8

Nominals: Nouns and Noun Phrases, Nonfinite Verbs

CHAPTER PREVIEW

- Nouns are defined notionally, according to meaning; formally, according to such features as suffixes (e.g., with the suffix *-ation,* the verb *consider* becomes the noun *consideration*); and functionally, according to the ways in which they can be used in sentences, for example, as subject (*Hogs* eat slops) or as object (Farmers raise *hogs*).

- Nouns of two types are described: common (e.g., apple, bird, charcoal) and proper (e.g., Austria, Baptist, Carla).

- Nouns can be either singular (e.g., limit, mouse) or plural (e.g., limits, mice).

- Some nouns can normally be counted (e.g., one film, two films, three films) and some, depending on context, usually are considered noncount (e.g., rice, water).

- Nouns are the heads of noun phrases; *determiners* are optional elements of noun phrases (e.g., *the* lesson, *that* concerto, *these* tickets.) Adjectives, also optional elements of noun phrases, may be placed between the determiner and the noun (e.g., the *hard* lesson, that *beautiful* concerto, these *expensive* tickets).

- Present participles (gerunds) and infinitives can be used as nominals.

NOMINALS AND NOUN PHRASES

This chapter is the first of three dealing with nominals. The word *nominal* will be used for all structures that can function as subjects, objects (direct, indirect, objects of prepositions), and complements. In other words, a nominal is a noun or any word or phrase that can be substituted for a noun in function, the word *noun* denoting a form and *nominal* denoting a function. Take a close look at the following examples:

The wish	seems strange.
That	seems strange.
This	seems strange.

It	seems strange.
To like raw oysters	seems strange.
Studying grammar	seems strange.
That he resigned his job	seems strange.

Here we see a variety of forms functioning nominally as the subjects of the sentence: *to like* and *studying* are nonfinite verbs—that is, verbs without tense; *to like* is an infinitive; *studying* is a present participle; and *that he resigned his job* is a noun clause.

In this chapter we will focus on nouns. Nouns most often function as the main or *head* words in phrases (noun phrases, or NPs). For instance, in the sentence

Jane liked the big dog with the floppy ears.

dog is the noun head word, *the* is a definite article, *big* is an adjective modifying *dog,* and *with the floppy ears* is a prepositional phrase modifying *dog.* An NP functions as a unit; a single pronoun can be substituted for the whole NP. For example:

The brown car is broken.

It is broken.

DEFINING NOUNS

Notional Definition

In Chapter 5, we discussed the inadequacy of a notional definition of *verb:* "A verb names an action or a state of being." The most common notional definition of noun is that "A noun is the name of a person, place, or thing." Underlying such a definition is the assumption of our sense of a three-part universe: each entity, material or nonmaterial, falls into one of the three categories. Yet if we stop to think, our own experience falsifies such an artificial oversimplification. Is *love* a person? A place? A thing? How about idea? The traditional definition defies common sense and the way we perceive the world. George Curme, a noted grammarian, defined "noun" as "the name of a living being or lifeless thing," but that definition is even more problematic than the traditional "person, place, or thing." Are the nouns in the following sentence living beings or lifeless things, or is Curme's definition simply inadequate?

Brevity is the soul of *wit.*

Enough, then. Notional definitions simply lead us into a quagmire from which we can never escape.

Formal Definition

The formal definition of *noun* is more adequate than the notional definition. The formal definition has these four parts:

1. Nouns may be used as plurals.

   idea/idea*s*

child/child*ren*

alumnus/alumn*i*

2. Many nouns can take articles.

the idea

a child

an alumnus

3. Some nouns have nominal suffixes.

murder*er*	direc*tion*
act*or*	assist*ance*
agree*ment*	exist*ence*
good*ness*	fail*ure*
fix*ation*	appro*val*

4. Nouns can take the *-'s* suffix in the possessive.

murderer's weapon

actor's role

failure's consequences

If the noun is plural, an apostrophe indicates possessive.

two murderers' weapons

three actors' roles

If the noun has an irregular or so-called mutation plural (see below), *-'s* indicates possessive.

children's game

oxen's yoke

alumni's reunion

the feet's agony

FORMAL DEFINITION OF NOUN

- Plural: girl/girls, child/children
- Articles: *the* aardvark, *a* lion
- Suffixes: modern/modern*ity*, quick/quick*ness*
- Possessive (genitive): a man*'s* coat, several teacher*s'* lessons

USING GRAMMAR: THE APOSTROPHE

Some grammatical problems seem to be merely annoyances; yet sometimes "correct" usage makes the difference between effective and ineffective communication. One such problem is the placement of the apostrophe, which depends on whether the noun that is doing the possessing is singular or plural (regular or irregular) and whether it ends in -*s*. Here is a brief rundown of standard usage.

- Singular noun

   The *girl's* books were on the table.

- Singular noun ending in -*s*

   Susan *Wells's* new book is brilliant.

- Irregular plural noun

   The *children's* books were on the table.

- Plural noun ending in -*s*

   The *witnesses'* testimony provided compelling evidence.

- Compound nouns with individual possession

   Jane *Austen's* and Charlotte *Brontë's* novels can be read from a feminist perspective.

- Compound nouns with joint possession

   Ginger Rogers and Fred *Astaire's* dances were smooth as silk.

Functional Definition

At this point in your study of grammar, nominal functions might seem overly difficult, but we ask you to think about what follows, for you will be introduced to sentence structures that we will be referring to again and again. We repeat this bit of advice: don't try to memorize these functional patterns; do spend some time thinking about and analyzing them. Ultimately, the function of nominals will become part of your conscious knowledge of grammar.

Nominals, including noun phrases, can function as subjects, direct objects, indirect objects, objects of prepositions, subjective complements, objective complements, appositives, or vocatives.

Subjects

The *mice* scurry.

The mice are performing the action of running.

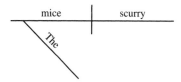

Figure 8.1   Reed-Kellogg diagram of *The mice scurry.* The vertical line separates the subject *mice* from the predicate *scurry.* Adjectives and articles are on slant lines under the nominals to which they relate.

The branching tree diagram is now becoming more common than the Reed-Kellogg diagram.

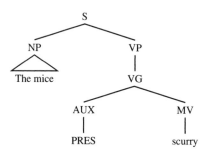

Figure 8.2   Branching tree diagram of *The mice scurry.* The triangle indicates a phrase that the diagram does not analyze.

Direct Objects

Apes eat *grapes.*

1. The grapes are the receivers of the action.

2. A sentence with a direct object can always be made passive: *Grapes are eaten by apes.*

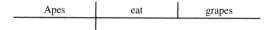

Figure 8.3   Reed-Kellogg diagram of *Apes eat grapes.* The vertical line that does not cut through the horizontal line sets off the direct object of the verb (*grapes*).

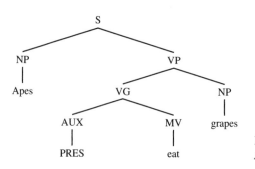

Figure 8.4   Branching tree diagram of *Apes eat grapes.*

Indirect Objects

Professors give *students* grades.

1. The verb *give* has two objects: *students* [indirect] and *grades* [direct].

2. Either of these can become the subject of a passive sentence: *Students are given grades by professors* and *Grades are given to students by professors.* In the active sentence, *professors* is the subject of the verb *give.* In one passive version, the indirect object *students* becomes the subject of the verb group *are given,* and in the other passive version, the direct object *grades* becomes the subject.

A visual aid helps one understand the function of indirect objects.

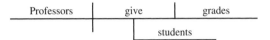

Figure 8.5 Reed-Kellogg diagram of *Professors give students grades.* The right-angle below the verb shows the indirect object relationship in the sentence.

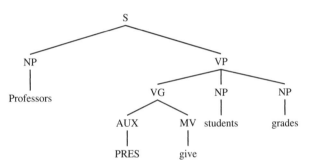

Figure 8.6 Branching tree diagram of *Professors give students grades.*

Objects of Prepositions

Professors often stray from *the subject.*

Prepositions are words like *to, from, into, over, under.* Nouns that follow prepositions are their objects. (Chapter 15 contains a list of prepositions and explains their functions.)

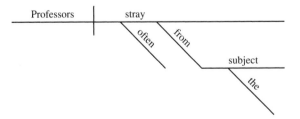

Figure 8.7 Reed-Kellogg diagram of *Professors often stray from the subject.* The adverb *often* is on the slant line under the verb that it modifies. The preposition *from* is on the slant line under the verb, and its object *subject* is on the straight line. The article is on the slant line under *subject.*

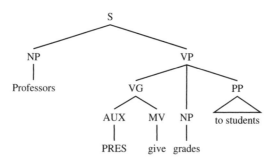

Figure 8.8 Branching tree diagram of *Professors give grades to students*. In the branching tree diagram, PP means, of course, "prepositional phrase."

Subjective Complements

Scouts are *leaders*.

Verbs like *are, become,* and *turn* (in certain constructions) are called *linking verbs.* The nouns that follow them add meaning to or clarify the subjects:

Children become *adults*.

Patriots sometimes turn *traitors*.

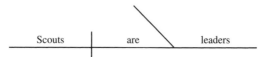

Figure 8.9 Reed-Kellogg diagram of *Scouts are leaders*. The backward-slanting line indicates that *leaders* is a subjective complement.

Since a branching tree diagram is not particularly helpful with subjective complements, we will not include one here.

Objective Complements

Pastors call lying a *sin*.

1. The objective complement adds meaning or clarification to the direct object. In the sentence above, *lying* is the direct object, and *a sin* modifies it or adds meaning to it.

2. Remember that in sentences with direct (italicized) and indirect (underlined) objects, either one can become the subject in passive:

   Mother loaned <u>Mr. Jones</u> a *mop*./<u>Mr. Jones</u> was loaned a *mop* by Mother./ *mop* was loaned to <u>Mr. Jones</u> by Mother.

In sentences with objective complements, only the direct object can become the subject in passive:

		DIRECT OBJECT	OBJECTIVE COMPLEMENT	
Pastors	call	lying	a sin.	

		OBJECTIVE COMPLEMENT	
SUBJECT			
Lying	is called	a sin	by pastors.

*A sin is called lying by pastors.

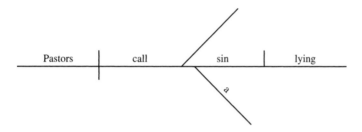

Figure 8.10   Reed-Kellogg diagram of *Pastors call lying a sin*. The forward-slanting line after the verb indicates that *a sin* is the objective complement, modifying the direct object.

Appositives

My professor *the genius* lost my paper.

1. The appositive renames the noun with which it is associated.
2. Either one can be deleted without creating an ungrammatical structure:

   The professor lost my paper./The genius lost my paper.

Nominals can be in either loose apposition

John, *the famous baptist,* baptized Jesus.

"The school system, *custodian of print culture,* has no place for the rugged individual." (Marshall McLuhan)

or close apposition

John *the Baptist* baptized Jesus.

Sometimes the distinction between loose and close apposition is, however, splitting hairs. Clearly, in the sentence *My uncle, Clayton Fike, is an air traffic controller,* the name *Clayton Fike* is added information, not identifying a specific uncle among several, but *my uncle Clayton* is singling out one uncle from at least two.

My uncle Clayton was an air traffic controller, my uncle Charles was a plumber, and my uncle Jack was a railroad brakeman.

Figure 8.11   Reed-Kellogg diagram of *My professor the genius lost my paper*. The appositive nominal (the genius) is in parentheses.

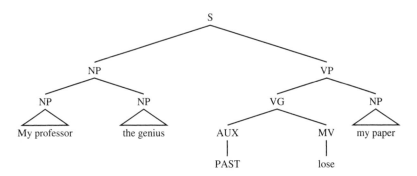

Figure 8.12   Branching tree diagram of *My professor the genius lost my paper*. The left branch clearly shows that two noun phrases occupy the subject position.

Vocatives (Also Called "Direct Address")

> *Professor,* please return my paper.

Vocatives name the person spoken to.

At this point, don't try to memorize all of these grammatical terms; in due time, we will take a close look at varieties of sentences. Right now, it's important that you begin to think about structures and their components.

FUNCTIONS OF NOMINALS

- Subject: *Fools* rush in mindlessly.
- Direct object: Wise people dislike *fools*.
- Indirect object: Wise people give *fools* the cold shoulder.
- Object of preposition: Wise people do not talk to *fools*.
- Subjective complement: Some learned people are *fools*.
- Objective complement: Wise people call smokers *fools*.
- Appositive: Those shoppers, the *fools,* pay a high price for brand names.
- Vocative: *Fools,* you should not watch TV all day.

U SING GRAMMAR: MEDIA

The word *medium* is an interesting example of language in transition. (The noun *medium* is derived from the Latin *medius,* meaning "middle.") The plural form *media* is now widely used as a singular.

> "The advertising *media* in this country continually *informs* the American male of his need for indispensable signs of his virility." (Frances M. Beal, 1970)

> "The *media transforms* the great silence of things into its opposite." (Michel de Certeau, 1974)

> "The *media overestimates* its own importance." (Mark E. Smith, 1990)

Formerly, standard usage was *medium is* and *media are* or *mediums are.*

> "[T]he mass *media are* nearly universal. . . ." (C. Wright Mills, 1951)

> "The *medium is* the message." (Marshall McLuhan, 1964)

As you read the newspaper or listen to news reports in TV or radio, note instances of *media* used as a singular, and bring these examples for class discussion. Currently, it seems that *media* as a singular is acceptable at all levels of usage.

Exercise 8.1

Identify the nouns in the following sentences, and list some of the formal features that validate your choices.

Example
> In considering impeachment, the senators discussed the president's actions.

> • *impeachment*
>
> > has the noun suffix *-ment*
> >
> > can be preceded by an article: *the* impeachment
> >
> > can be pluralized: impeachment*s*
> >
> > can take the possessive suffix: impeachment*'s* outcome

- *senators*

  has the article *the*

  is plural

  has noun suffix *-or*

  can take the possessive suffix: the senator*s'* votes

- *president's*

  has the possessive suffix *-'s*

  is preceded by the article *the*

  can be pluralized: president*s* of the world's democracies

- *actions*

  is plural

  can be preceded by *the* or *an*

  has the noun suffix *-ion*

  can be possessive: the action*'s* outcomes

1. Dogs eat steak.

2. The cat yowled.

3. An apple in the morning is healthy.

4. "Insanity is doing the same thing over and over again, but expecting different results." (Rita Mae Brown)

5. "He looks like a man who has just swallowed an entire human being." (Truman Capote on William S. Paley)

6. "It is not the office of the novelist to show us how to behave ourselves; it is not the business of fiction to teach us anything." (Agnes Repplier)

7. "The art of advertisement—untruthfulness combined with repetition." (Freya Stark)

8. "For rain it hath a friendly sound / To one who's six feet underground; / And scarce the friendly voice or face, / A grave is such a quiet place." (Edna St. Vincent Millay)

9. "Satire is a sort of glass, wherein beholders do generally discover everybody's face but their own." (Jonathan Swift)

10. "Scandal is gossip made tedious by morality." (Oscar Wilde)

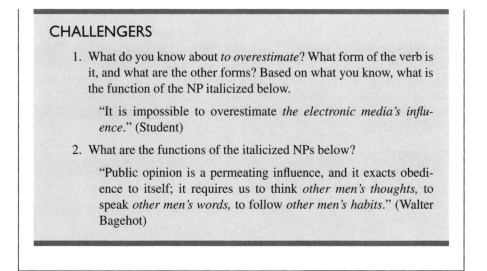

CHALLENGERS

1. What do you know about *to overestimate*? What form of the verb is it, and what are the other forms? Based on what you know, what is the function of the NP italicized below.

   "It is impossible to overestimate *the electronic media's influence*." (Student)

2. What are the functions of the italicized NPs below?

   "Public opinion is a permeating influence, and it exacts obedience to itself; it requires us to think *other men's thoughts*, to speak *other men's words*, to follow *other men's habits*." (Walter Bagehot)

COMMON AND PROPER NOUNS

We have considered nouns from the standpoint of forms and of functions. Nouns can be subdivided into two categories: common and proper. The distinctions between common and proper nouns are neither formal nor functional but are based on meaning and convention. For instance, if we take the noun *California* to be the name of a particular place, we capitalize. And such honorifics as *Dr., Mrs.,* and *Jr.* are conventionally capitalized as in Dr. Jones, Mrs. Smith, and Paul Olson, Jr.

Proper Nouns

Proper nouns denote, or give the names of, specific places or persons. For example, *Susan is taking a course called Wildlife Biology.* Here the word *Susan* is capitalized because it is a woman's name and because it is the first word in a sentence. The words *Wildlife Biology* are capitalized because they are the name of a specific course.

U SING GRAMMAR: CAPITALIZATION

Capitalizing correctly can be one of those "litmus test" errors for your readers. In other words, if you capitalize correctly, they assume you are generally competent. However, if you do not capitalize correctly, your reader may think that you are incompetent and poorly educated. For these reasons it is important to pay attention to these rules:

> ## CAPITALIZE
> months, days, holidays (Christmas), religions (Seventh Day Adventist), names of deities (Jesus Christ), sacred books (the Qur'an), particular countries (Thailand), cities (Bangkok), places (the Midwest), people (Martin Luther King, Jr.), Mother and Father when used as names, political parties (the Green Party), historical periods and events (the Age of Enlightenment, the Great Depression), languages (Swahili), nationalities (Spanish, English), specific courses in school (Economics 101)
>
> ## DO NOT CAPITALIZE
> seasons (summer), centuries (the nineteenth century), numbers (two thousand), names of general school subjects (biology, math), times (two o'clock)

Common Nouns

Nouns that are not proper nouns are called *common nouns*. Most of the time common nouns are not capitalized, but occasionally they are if they are derived from a proper noun and refer to a category of people, places, or time periods. Here is an example:

> Wilfred thinks he is a *Shakespeare* in the making.

In this example, the word *Shakespeare* is a common noun because it does not designate a specific person; instead it refers to a category of people.

In the following sentence, the difference between the proper noun *Chicago* and the common noun *city* is obvious.

> *Chicago* is the windy *city*.

Chicago refers to a particular place, and *city* denotes a category. But what about the following?

> Salt Lake City is a western *Chicago,* a bustling rail center and the hog butcher to the Intermountain area.

In this sentence, *Chicago* denotes a category of places, not a particular city in Illinois.

PROPER NOUNS

- Are not made plural
- Do not take the indefinite article *a(n)*
- Cannot be replaced by phrases

FOR DISCUSSION: USE OF TITLES

Proper nouns and titles (Dr., Professor, Reverend) are part of an intricate language game. In medical offices, for instance, the staff normally refers to the physician as "Doctor," but addresses patients by their first names: a nurse announces, "Norma, Dr. Pandit will see you now." (Of course, Norma might well have a doctorate herself, though not in medicine.)

In some contexts, the use of only a last name denotes a power relationship. A plant foreman to a line worker, "Smith, I'm going to transfer you to the widget section." Smith answers, "Yes, Mr. Jones."

How does the use of titles and names in your college reveal power relationships?

SINGULAR AND PLURAL (NUMBER)

In modern English, nouns have only two numbers: singular and plural.

-(e)s

The most common way of indicating number is through addition of the suffix -(e)s:

girl/girls

birch/birches

Words ending in -y (such as *baby, lady, fury*) usually substitute *i* for *y* and add -es:

babies

ladies

furies

When the *y* is preceded by a vowel, the change is not made:

forays

boys

bays

Some words ending in *f* change the *f* to *v*:

thief/thieves

half/halves

calf/calves

In the spoken language, the -*s* plural has three pronunciations, depending on the last set of consonants in the word. Pronounce the following words, and notice the differences in the sounds of plural suffixes:

/s/	/z/	/iz/
rats	pads	churches
caps	cabs	boxes
picks	pigs	misses

Irregular (Mutation) Plurals

Plurals such as *feet, geese, teeth,* and *men,* which come about through vowel change, are holdovers from Old and Middle English. The plural *women* is an interesting case of language change. In Middle English, the word had two forms, *womman,* with the plural *wommen,* and *wimman,* with the plural *wimmen.* Our singular comes from the first form (Middle English *womman* = Modern English *woman*), and our plural from the second (Middle English *wimmen* = Modern English *women*).

The -(e)*n* Plural

The -(*e*)*n* plural was common in Middle English, but only one example has come into Modern English: *oxen.* Modern English *children* and *brethren* are actually double plurals. In Old English the plural of *cild* /chilled/ was *cildru* for males and *cildra* for females; in Middle English the -(*e*)*n* plural was added, resulting in the modern English *children.* The same process resulted in *brethren.*

You already know that some words have the same form in singular and plural:

one sheep/twenty sheep

a deer/several deer.

Plurals from Languages Other than English

Some plurals in English give evidence of the contribution made to English by other languages.

Language	Plural	Examples
Latin	-ae	alumna/alumnae
		larva/larvae
		nebula/nebulae
		vertebra/vertebrae
	-i	alumnus/alumni
		fungus/fungi
		terminus/termini
	-a	memorandum/memoranda
		medium/media
		datum/data

(Continued)

Language	Plural	Examples
(Latin)	-es	basis/bases
		thesis/theses
		vortex/vortices
Greek	-a	criterion/criteria
		phenomenon/phenomena
	-mata	stigma/stigmata
		stemma/stemmata
French	-x	beau/beaux
		trousseau/trousseaux
Italian	-i	bandit/banditti
Hebrew	-im	cherub/cherubim

PLURALIZATION

- Addition of suffix -(e)*s*: book*s*, ranch*es*
- Change in vowels: f*oo*t/f*ee*t, m*a*n/m*e*n
- Plurals from other languages: alumn*a*/alumn*ae*, stigm*a*/stigm*ata*, b*eau*/b*eaux*

Exercise 8.2

What are the plurals of the following nouns? If you are in doubt, check your dictionary.

alumnus	journey	stimulus
bacterium	klatch	thesis
cero	lex	usury
deli	medium	vivarium
entelechy	nibs	warmonger
fleur-de-lis	oligarchy	xanthochroi
guaranty	patois	yucca
housewife	quarry	zero
illuvium	rebozo	

COUNT AND NONCOUNT NOUNS

Some nouns can be modified by a *cardinal number* (one, two, a thousand, etc.).

> one apple
>
> two peaches
>
> a thousand cherries

Some nouns, on the other hand, cannot normally be counted. For example, in the following, *rice* is a noncount noun:

> We had Chinese food for supper. The *rice* was mushy.

In the passage

> We had Chinese food for supper. *The two rices* were mushy.

the implication is that the meal included two separate varieties of rice. (Interestingly, the spell checker in my Microsoft Word program does not recognize *rices* as valid; hence the program underlines the word in red.)

Another way of explaining the distinction between count and noncount nouns is this: noncounts have no plural forms. Patrick Henry said, "Give me liberty, or give me death." How would the meaning be changed if he had said, "Give me liberties, or give me death"? (For an answer to this question, look up the word "liberties" in your dictionary.)

DETERMINER

Up to this point we have been discussing single-word noun phrases. Often noun phrases consist of head nouns and determiners, qualifiers that precede the head noun and any adjectives modifying the noun. The most common determiners are the definite article *the* (DEF) and the indefinite (nondefinite) article *a(n)* (NONDEF). The definite article (DEF) denotes a specific entity:

> *The* wind whines through *the* trees.
>
> *The* fear of things unknown makes *the* children tremble.
>
> *The* fog rises from *the* swamp.

The nondefinite article (NONDEF) does not denote a specific entity:

> *A* strange sound catches their attention.
>
> *An* owl hoots.

Furthermore, we know that other sorts of words (from other word classes) can also be part of the noun word group:

> *Those* people complain loudly. [*Those* is a demonstrative adjective: DEM.]

Our people never whine. [*Our* is a possessive adjective: POS.]

Some people are never happy. [*Some* is an indefinite adjective: INDEF.]

Second guesses are often wrong. [*Second* is an ordinal number: ORD.]

Three people booed loudly. [*Three* is a cardinal number: CARD.]

In addition, nouns are not always modified by ART, DEM, or POS, and in our notational system, we can use the null symbol (∅) to show this absence:

∅ Blood is thicker than ∅ water.

Nouns that are not preceded by any determiner, like those preceded by *a(n)*, have a general reference, not a specific, and we can indicate this meaning with the null symbol:

∅ Fear grips the children.

∅ Terrors await them in the woods.

In fact, the null symbol (which, of course, doesn't appear in actual texts, only in our notation) denotes the same kind of generality conveyed by *a* and *an*. Thus, we can classify null symbol as NONDEF.

And we can indicate that a noun can be modified by ART, POS, or DEM, but that they cannot co-occur:

DET → [ART, POS, DEM] . . .

The rule is saying, of course, that DET will contain *either* ART *or* POS *or* DEM.

Now we must account for determiners like the following:

NONDEF   INDEF
A   few seconds of silence followed the wailing.

POS   INDEF
Their   many sins weighed heavily on them.

DEM   INDEF
Those   few moments seemed an eternity.

INDEF
Some creatures rustled the dry leaves.

*The some apples tasted delicious.

*Those any children were hilarious.

We see, then, that some of the indefinite adjectives can follow ART, DEM, or POS. We can expand our rule:

DET → [ART, POS, DEM] (INDEF)

From the following example sentences, we can derive the conclusion to our rule for DET:

DEF   ORD
The   first law is self-preservation.

DEM   ORD
That   second idea is better than the first.

POS   ORD
Your   third attempt might be successful.

CARD
One   bad apple ruins the barrel.

DEF   ORD CARD
The   first three apples were rotten.

DEM   ORD CARD
That   second twelve donuts is freshest

POS   ORD CARD
Your   third five minutes have expired.

An ordinal number (first, second, third . . .), a cardinal number (one, two, three . . .), or an ordinal number and a cardinal number (e.g., third five) may follow ART, DEM, or POS. Thus, we can derive the complete rule for DET.

THE DETERMINER RULE

DET → [ART, DEM, POS] (INDEF: many, few, fewer, less, little, several, every) (ORD) (CARD)

ART → [DEF, NONDEF]

DEF → the

NONDEF → [a(n), ∅]

DEM → [this, that, these, those]

POS → [my, our, his, her, its, their, your]

INDEF → [some, many, few, fewer, less, any, enough, little, much, several, more, all, both, every, each, either, neither, none]

ORD → [first, second, third, . . .]

CARD → [one, two, three, . . .]

Exercise 8.3

A. Using the rules given in the box above, generate different determiners for each of the following nouns:

apple	elation
bananas	frugality
Congress	generations
dipsomania	

B. Find the determiners in the following sentences. If the determiners are ungrammatical, rewrite them to make them grammatical.

> **Examples**
> The some first peaches of the season were ripe.
>
> *The some first* is an ungrammatical determiner.
>
> Rewrite: *The first* peaches of the season . . .
>
> Rewrite: *Some first* peaches of the season . . .
>
> The first twenty persons of the hundred contestants received booby prizes.
>
> *The first twenty* and *the hundred* are the determiners. They are grammatical.

1. Take the money and run.

2. Take the first money you see, and run.

3. After you take that money, see if you can find second a source.

4. The your ideas are for the birds.

5. What might you think of making the guest house into a bed-and-breakfast?

6. Before investing in those junk bonds, you should consult the some specialist in second mortgages.

7. The many thousands of tourists who flock to Rome often travel on the Metro.

8. "Most people get a fair amount of fun out of their lives, but on balance life is suffering, and only the very young or the very foolish imagine otherwise." (George Orwell)

9. "Few pleasures there are indeed without an after-touch of pain, but that is the preservation which keeps them sweet." (Helen Keller)

10. "I've been told that since the beginning of civilization, millions and millions of laws have not improved on the Ten Commandments one bit." (Ronald Reagan)

NOMINALS—NONFINITE VERBS: PRESENT PARTICIPLES/GERUNDS AND INFINITIVES

So far in this chapter we have been dealing with nouns. However, forms other than nouns can fulfill nominal functions. As a group, these forms, as we have seen, can be called *nominals*.

When a present participle does not have an auxiliary verb, it may function nominally. Present participles that function nominally are called *gerunds*. Here are some examples

Gerunds

- Gerund functioning as the subject

  Swimming in the river is dangerous.

- Gerund functioning as the object

  I enjoy *reading*.

- Gerund functioning as the object of a preposition

  I am thinking about *traveling* to Spain.

- Gerund functioning as the complement with *be* verb

  Your job is *cooking*.

In the sentence *My favorite pastime is playing chess,* the gerund *playing* is the head of the nominal phrase *playing chess,* which functions as the complement of *is* (*be*). The noun *chess* is the object of the gerund because the gerund is in some senses still a verb and can have objects and modifiers.

Infinitives

Infinitives can also function as nominals, and they too can take objects and modifiers.

- Infinitive functioning as the complement of *is*

  His job is *to cook* dinner.

- Infinitive functioning as the subject

  To swim in the ocean is a great pleasure.

- Infinitive functioning as the object

  I wanted *to read* that novel immediately.

Note that in each of these sentences the infinitive has either an object or a modifier.

FOR DISCUSSION: NOMINALIZATION

Consider this quotation about the relationship of language forms to our ideas about the way things are and the way things ought to be. "Linguistic style simultaneously expresses and constructs an ideology."[1] Analyzing this quotation, we can translate the word *ideology* to mean belief system or world view. Roger Fowler, the source of the quotation, goes on to argue that nominalization or turning a verb into a noun is "treacherous":

> Nominalization permits deletion of reference to the persons responsible for and affected by the processes described by the verb; Nominalization can depersonalize, depopulate.

Fowler also claims that nominalization can transform processes and actions into things and objects, hiding how events happen and making them appear completely stable and even inevitable.

What do you think of Fowler's argument? Look for samples of prose with a large number of nominalizations and examine his claims in light of the text(s) that you find. (See Exercise 8.4.)

Exercise 8.4

A. In the following sentences find nonfinite verbs (infinitives and participle/ gerunds) functioning nominally. Be specific about how the nonfinite verb is functioning (subject, object, complement).

1. Jane enjoys watching television.
2. Dick wants to succeed.

---

[1] Roger Fowler, *Literature as Social Discourse* (Bloomington: Indiana University Press, 1981), 29.

3. Studying Latin improves the mind.

4. To make a billion dollars takes luck.

5. Are you afraid of wrestling alligators?

6. "Of course, resolving the Palestinian issue at this point through a separation of the two peoples into distinct states will be hard. . . . We might all need to brace for further violence before that happens." (Helena Cobban, *Christian Science Monitor,* February 9, 2001)

7. "If keeping a lid on what Gore says in class offers me the chance to hear some inside information, I'll gladly keep quiet." (Michael Arnone, *Christian Science Monitor,* February 9, 2001)

B. Find three sentences using infinitives nominally and three using gerunds. Bring them to class to share.

PASSAGES FOR ANALYSIS

A. In the following passage from *Refuge* by Terry Tempest Williams,

1. Find the proper nouns. How many are there? What is the basis for your identification of the proper nouns?

2. Do any of the words end in a typical noun suffix? If so, which one or ones?

We checked into the Stateline Casino for the night. Wendover, Nevada, is to Salt Lake City what Las Vegas is to Los Angeles. Mother and I were given complimentary tickets redeemable for ten dollars worth of nickels. Mother agreed a night in front of a slot machine would be more entertaining than a movie. After settling into our room, we descended upon the casino.

We let our eyes adjust to the neon-induced darkness, the black walls and gilded ceilings, the chaos of blips and bloops from the adjacent video arcade, and the constant ringing of bells, falling of coins, and ebullient cries of winners.

We sat at two adjacent red stools and began inserting nickels and pulling down levers. Almost instantly, Mother began winning—cherries, bells, single bars, and doubles. I inched my stool closer to the machine. Things started picking up. I didn't take my eyes off the flashing cherries. Fast and furious, we pulled the levers— simultaneously. Mother winning. Me winning. Nickels were hitting our silver trays like heavy rain. By now, my left foot was up on the counter between our two machines for leverage. Five nickels in, pull the arm down; spin, spin, spin, bar, bar, bar; nickels rain down.[2]

---

[2] Terry Tempest Williams, *Refuge: An Unnatural History of Family and Place* (New York: Pantheon, 1991), 127–128.

FOR DISCUSSION: VERBLESS SENTENCES AND OTHER STYLISTIC DEVICES

1. In the passage from *Refuge*, the author includes some structures that are punctuated like sentences but have no verbs or verb groups. Locate these structures, and explain why you think they are or are not effective *stylistically*?

2. Are there any other structures that you find unusual? Which are they? Why do you consider them unusual? Are they effective stylistically?

B. Many nonnative speakers have trouble with the uses of articles in English. The following examples of writing by people who are struggling to put together the rule system reveal how learners will construct temporary rules—which may or may not be correct. That is, these "interlanguage" rules differ from those used by native speakers of the language. Try to state what rules these learners are using for articles; then try to explain to the learners how to use articles in these passages. (See the companion website for a more complete discussion of interlanguage.)

1. "Is it possible for robot to have power? intelligence? style? Perhaps the answer is yes because the humans are developing RCS's [Robot Controlled Spacecraft's] faculties with a design base on the extensive study of human motion. The RCS currently walks, climbs stairs, and turns a corner with ease. It also carried the loads, pushes carts and makes a U-turn all the while maintaining a remarkable sense of the balance. RCS is designed to work in harmony with the humans."

2. "Ancient Maya occupied vast geographic area in Central and South America into part of the Mexico, Honduras and El Salvador. Maya civilization produced awe-inspiring temple and pyramids, highly correct calendars, and a complex social and political order. Now the archaeologists digs are uncovering temple, plaza and other stone buildings and the thatched-roof huts. Maya's building made without metal tools. Also, Maya was surrounded by jungles, but they traded with distant people. Ancient people have higher skill we cannot imagine."

CHALLENGER

Look for structures that have been nominalized—that is, changed from a verb into a noun form—or for words that, unchanged, can serve as either nouns or verbs. (For example, *computer* from *compute* and *teacher* from *teach, failure* from *fail, proposition* from *propose,* or *build,* as in Dick and Jane *build* the doghouse and Arnold Schwarzenegger has a good *build.*) Find the nouns and ask yourself whether they are in some sense derived from verbs. In other words, have they been nominalized?

1. "Flag burning as a form of symbolic speech is protected by the Constitution and has historically been used as a protest. While some argue that it is a desecration of American patriotism, I argue that it is a protest of political ills. Supreme Court decisions and historical events are support for my case." (Student)

2. "Even in the freest countries our property is subject to the control and disposal of our partners, to whom the laws have given a sovereign authority." (Abigail Adams)

CHAPTER REVIEW

Explain the following:

- The meaning of *nominal.*
- Notional definition of *nouns.*
- Formal definition of *nouns.*
- Functional definition of *nouns.*
- "Common" and "proper" nouns.
- The three categories of pluralization. Give examples.
- "Count" and "noncount" nouns. Give examples.
- The determiner rule: DET = [ART, DEM, POS] (INDEF) (ORD) (CARD). Give an example of each category (e.g., DEM = *that*).
- Nonfinite verbs. Give an example of each used in a sentence.

Nominals: Pronouns

CHAPTER PREVIEW

- Pronouns (e.g., *I, you, them, that*) are nominals; they have nominal functions. They take their meaning from other nominal words, phrases, or clauses, which are called their *antecedents*.

- There are several categories of pronouns: personal (e.g., *I, you*), compound personal (e.g., *herself, themselves*), reciprocal (e.g., *each other*), demonstrative (*this, that, these, those*), interrogative (e.g., *what?, which?*), indefinite (e.g., *some, many*), and relative (e.g., *who, whom*).

- A few pronouns are simply "slot fillers" and have only a syntactic value. In "*It* is raining," the pronoun has no semantic value but does fill our expectations about the structure of English.

So then, we turn to a survey of the varieties of pronouns. Don't try to memorize all of this information, but use the chapter as a reference source.

Personal Pronouns

	Subjective	Possessive	Objective
First Person Singular	I	mine	me
First Person Plural	we	ours	us
Second Person Singular	you	yours	you
Second Person Plural	you	yours	you
Third Person Singular	he, she, it	his, hers, its	him, her, it
Third Person Plural	they	theirs	them

FOR DISCUSSION: THOU, THEE, THY, THINE

Thou, thee, thy, and *thine* are familiar to readers of the King James Version of the Bible.

Thou is the subjective case ("*Thou* shalt have none other gods before me"), and *thee* is the objective case ("Keep the sabbath day to sanctify it, as the Lord thy God hath commanded *thee*"). *Thy* and *thine* are not pronouns, but possessive adjectives (see pp. 110–113; "Honor *thy* father and *thy* mother"). *Thine* is often used before nouns that begin with a vowel ("*thine* ox and *thine* ass").

These pronouns and possessive adjectives are still in daily use by members of the Society of Friends (i.e., Quakers). Why do you think the members of this group still use these archaic forms?

CASES

As the table above indicates, *subjective, possessive,* and *objective* name the forms of personal pronouns. The term case applies to how forms change depending on their functions. Using first person as our example, we can run through the functions of these cases.

- Subject

    I enjoy Offenbach's music.

- Subjective complement

    The caller is *I.*

The possessive (genitive) form *mine* functions as subject, direct object, indirect object, objective complement, and subjective complement:

- Subject

    Mine is the hat with the ostrich plume.

- Direct object

    Phil likes *mine* better than his own.

- Indirect object

    Your Cajun pasta is good, but give *mine* a try.

- Object of preposition

    What do you think of *mine*?

- Objective complement

    If you want to, you can call the hat *mine.*

- Subjective complement

    The hat is *mine.*

And the objective case form *me* functions as direct object, indirect object, and object of preposition.

- Direct object

    The professor dislikes *me.*

- Indirect object

    The professor gave *me* an F on my paper.

- Object of preposition

    The professor gave some advice to *me.*

The personal pronouns *thou, thee,* and *ye* are now used almost exclusively in the context of religious discourse and scripture.

U SING GRAMMAR

Think about this situation. An English professor comes home from his office. As he enters the front door, his wife calls, "Who's there?" Is the best answer "It is I" or "It's me"? If he answers, "It is I," might his wife think that he's making a joke or being a wise guy?

Or this situation. In his office on campus, the English professor picks up the telephone and hears the following: "May I speak with Professor Smith?" Should he answer "This is him" or "This is he"? Why?

Exercise 9.1

1. Identify the personal pronouns in the following sentences.

    a. I like crisp, tart apples.

    b. Please give me a beautiful Jonathan.

    c. Do you have an apple tree in your backyard?

    d. She has an orchard but doesn't tend it.

    e. Please give us a ripe apple.

    f. When apples are ripe, we pick them.

2. Identify the personal pronouns in the following passages. What is the case of each, *subjective, possessive,* or *objective?* Don't confuse the determiners with personal pronouns.

   a. "The mouth organ man said, 'It don't matter if you're looking for Chicago or Detroit or Orlando or Oklahoma City, I rode the rails to all of them. You might think or you might hear that things are better just down the line, but they're singing the same sad song all over this country. Believe me, being on the road is no good. If you two boys are from Flint, this is the right Hooverville for you.'" (Christopher Paul Curtis, *Bud, Not Buddy,* 68)

   b. "When I got next to him, I could see that it was just rocks he was pushing around. Finally he grunted a couple of times and started to bend over but his big belly got in the way and wouldn't let his arms reach to the ground. After a bunch more grunts, he said, 'Make yourself useful, boy, come and hand me this one.'" (Curtis, *Bud, Not Buddy,* 207)

3. Identify the personal pronouns and the determiners in the following passages. Specify the cases of the personal pronouns. Look for slot-filler uses of *it*—that is, uses of *it* without a direct antecedent.

   a. "I was well on my way to forming my present attitude toward politics as it is practiced in the United States; it is a beautiful fraud that has been imposed on the people for years, whose practitioners exchange gilded promises for the most valuable things their victims own, their votes." (Shirley Chisholm)

   b. "I am quite aware that owing to some of its scenes *Ulysses* is a rather strong draught to ask some sensitive, though normal, persons to take. But my considered opinion, after long reflection, is that whilst in many places the effect of *Ulysses* on the reader is somewhat emetic, nowhere does it tend to be an aphrodisiac. *Ulysses* may, therefore, be admitted into the United States." (Judge John M. Woolsey)

   c. "Flag burning as a form of symbolic speech is protected by the Constitution and has historically been used to protest policy. While some argue that it is a desecration of American patriotism, I argue that it is a way of protesting political ills, using Supreme Court decisions and historical events to support my case." (Student)

   d. "Patriotism in the female sex is the most disinterested of all virtues. Excluded from honors and from offices, we cannot attach ourselves to the State or Government from having held a place of eminence. Even in the freest countries our property is subject to the control and disposal of our partners, to whom the laws have given a sovereign authority. Deprived of a voice in legislation, obliged to submit to those laws which are imposed upon us, is it not sufficient to make us indifferent to the public welfare? Yet all history and every age exhibit instances of patriotic virtue in the female sex; which considering our situation equals the most heroic of yours." (Abigail Adams)

e. "I remember that a wise friend of mine did usually say, 'That which is everybody's business is nobody's business.'" (Izaak Walton)

CHALLENGER

In 1600, according to the English language historian Elizabeth Traugott,[1] the form *It is me* was acceptable, if not required. However, by 1800 the rule seems to have settled down and come to require the subjective form after *be*, as in *It is I*. What would the reasoning be for a rule that requires *It is me* and conversely for one that requires *It is I*?

USING GRAMMAR: CASES

In informal situations, and particularly in speech as opposed to writing, personal pronouns are often used for emphasis:

Me, I like kimchi.

You, you don't understand the problem.

Them, they always come late.

It is not uncommon for speakers and writers to use the subjective case (he, I) when the objective case (him, me) would be preferred (e.g., in writings for college classes or in talks with professors):

Jim and I talked with Professor Smurthwaite. He gave *he* and *I* help with our project. [Formal usage: He gave *him* and *me* help with our project.]

Keep alert for such usages. Take notes on what is said and to whom for class discussion. Be sure to explain the situation (e.g., a bull session in the student union, an oral report in class, a piece of writing for a class) and the participants in the conversation or the audience for the writing or report.

---

[1] Elizabeth Traugott, *A History of English Syntax* (New York: Holt, 1972), 126.

USING GRAMMAR: SEXISM

Two or three decades ago, *he* and *his* were used in the general sense of "human being, male or female," but that situation has changed. Writers and speakers now avoid sexist language.

Sexist: As for complaints, every student on campus has *his*.

Revised: As for complaints, every student on the campus has *his or hers*.

Many editors ask their authors to alternate masculine and feminine pronouns when these refer to general classes such as professors or plumbers.

The easiest and perhaps most widely accepted way of avoiding sexist language is to pluralize:

Sexist: Every man has the right to pursue life, liberty, and justice.

Revised: All people have the right to pursue life, liberty, and justice.

COMPOUND PERSONAL PRONOUNS

The compound personal pronouns are *myself, ourselves, yourself, yourselves, himself, herself, itself, themselves,* and *oneself.*

Some examples:

Jane hated *herself* for having helped Dick with the dishes.

"I celebrate *myself,* and sing *myself,* / And what I assume you shall assume." (Walt Whitman)

"Morality is not properly the doctrine of how we may make *ourselves* happy, but how we may make *ourselves* worthy of happiness." (Immanuel Kant)

"If you must hold *yourself* up to your children as an object lesson (which is not necessary), hold *yourself* up as a warning and not as an example." (George Bernard Shaw)

"What are you laughing at? You are laughing at *yourselves!*" (Nikolai Gogol)

"What is life? It is the flash of a firefly in the night. It is the breath of a buffalo in the wintertime. It is the little shadow which runs across the grass and loses *itself* in the sunset." (Crowfoot's last words, 1890)

"Intellectuals can tell *themselves* anything, sell *themselves* any bill of goods, which is why they are so often patsies for the ruling classes in nineteenth-century France and England, or twentieth-century Russia and America." (Lillian Hellman)

"When one is a stranger to *oneself* then one is estranged from others too." (Anne Morrow Lindbergh)

Exercise 9.2

You should be gaining the ability to analyze words, phrases, clauses, and sentences. Therefore, you are ready to begin finding grammatical principles on your own without much prompting from us, and that being the case, what principles about compound personal pronouns can you derive from the following examples?

1. Jane saw *herself* in the mirror.
2. *Jane saw in the mirror *herself*.
3. Dick *himself* solved the puzzle.
4. Dick solved the puzzle *himself*.
5. The children enjoyed *themselves* at the park.
6. *The children enjoyed at the park *themselves*.
7. The children *themselves* started the fire in the garage.
8. The children started the fire in the garage *themselves*.
9. Mother and Father *themselves* built the house for Spot.
10. Mother and Father built the house for Spot *themselves*.
11. Mother and Father built the house for Spot.
12. The children admired *themselves* for being good.
13. *The children admired for being good *themselves*.
14. *The children admired for being good.

From these examples, we conclude the following:

1. Some compound personal pronouns cannot be deleted from their sentences.

   Students pride *themselves* on writing brilliant essays.

   *Students pride on writing brilliant essays.

2. Some compound personal pronouns cannot be moved in their sentences.

   The professor made *herself* prepare for class.

   *The professor made prepare for class *herself*.

Compound personal pronouns that fulfill both conditions 1 and 2—that is, they cannot be deleted and they cannot be moved—are *reflexive*.

From the examples, we draw two additional conclusions:

3. Some compound personal pronouns can be deleted from their sentences.

   The dean *himself* spoke to the basket-weaving class.

   The dean spoke to the basket weaving class.

4. Some compound personal pronouns can be moved about in their sentences:

The president *herself* raised funds for the new building.

The president raised funds for the new building *herself.*

Compound personal pronouns that fulfill conditions 3 and 4—that is, they can be deleted and they can be moved about in their sentences—are *intensifiers.*

Pause for a moment to let us restate an important principle: you do not need a linguist or a grammar book to discover, through your own intuitive knowledge of English, such principles as the differences between reflexives and intensifiers. One of the major goals of this book is to give you the ability to analyze language. In a sense, all we are doing is helping you discover features and forms and giving you names for what you discover.

USING GRAMMAR: COMPOUND PERSONAL PRONOUNS

Compound personal pronouns are often used as personal pronouns. In most contexts, the compound personal pronoun is less acceptable than the personal pronoun, except, of course, when the compound is used as a reflexive or intensifier. For example,

Margaret and *myself* wrote the screenplay.

is less acceptable than the alternative with the personal pronoun:

Margaret and *I* wrote the screenplay.

Sometimes, the compound personal pronoun seems to be the only choice. For example,

The dean requested that complaints about student behavior be referred to the Disciplinary Committee rather than to *himself.*

In spoken English, one sometimes hears *hisself* in place of *himself.* This usage would not occur in formal speech or writing.

Informal: Dick made the pie *hisself.*

Formal: Dick made the pie *himself.*

Exercise 9.3

Reflexive pronouns cannot be deleted and are not movable; intensive pronouns can be deleted and are movable. Applying these tests, identify the reflexives and intensives in the following sentences.

1. Dick saw himself in the mirror.

2. The children themselves cooked supper.

3. I myself solved the crossword puzzle.

4. One should never doubt oneself.

5. The movie itself caused audiences to panic.

6. "True guilt is guilt at the obligation one owes to oneself to be oneself." (R. D. Laing)

7. "Beauty itself doth of itself persuade / The eyes of men without an orator." (Shakespeare)

8. "Pleasant it is, when over a great sea the winds trouble the waters, to gaze from shore upon another's tribulation: not because any man's troubles are a delectable joy, but because to perceive from what ills you are free yourself is pleasant." (Lucretius)

CHALLENGER

Identify the reflexives and intensives in the following passage.

"As for the aims and ideals of Marxism, there is one feature of them that is now rightly suspect. The taking-over by the state of the means of production and the dictatorship in the interests of the proletariat can by themselves never guarantee the happiness of anybody but the dictators themselves. Marx and Engels, coming out of authoritarian Germany, tended to imagine socialism in authoritarian terms; and Lenin and Trotsky after them, forced as they were to make a beginning among a people who had known nothing but autocracy, also emphasized this side of socialism and founded a dictatorship which perpetuated itself as an autocracy." (Edmund Wilson)

FOR DISCUSSION

Is the following sentence formal usage? How might it be rephrased?

Mother baked a cake for Mary and myself.

RECIPROCAL PRONOUNS

The reciprocal pronouns are *each other* and *one another,* and they function as

- Direct objects

   The children hated *each other.*

- Indirect objects

   They gave *one another* dirty looks.

- Objects of prepositions

   Mother and Father often listened to *each other.*

They cannot be pluralized (**each others,* **one anothers*), and they do not take articles (**the each other,* **a one another*); when they function as modifiers (adjectives), however, they can take the possessive (genitive) suffix - *'s*: *each other's Twinkies, one another's marbles.*

DEMONSTRATIVE PRONOUNS

The demonstrative pronouns are *this* and *that* in the singular and *these* and *those* in the plural. (A bit of perhaps unnecessary technical jargon: *this* and *these* are called *proximals* (denoting relative nearness) and *that* and *those* are called *distals* (denoting relative remoteness).

"*This* is the most magnificent movement of all!" (John Adams, on the Boston Tea Party)

"Liberty means responsibility; *that* is why most men dread it." (George Bernard Shaw)

"*These* were the swift to harry; / *These* the keen-scented; / *These* were the souls of blood." (Ezra Pound)

"Amusement is the happiness of *those* who cannot think." (Alexander Pope)

Once again, you can use your grammatical skills to discover an important fact about the demonstratives. What can you learn about how to tell the difference between determiners and pronouns through deletion and substitution in the following sentences?

> *This* book interests me.
>
> *The* book interests me.
>
> *This* interests me.
>
> *That* film bores me.
>
> *The* film bores me.
>
> *That* bores me.
>
> *These* questions puzzled Dick.
>
> *The* questions puzzled Dick.
>
> *Obscure* questions puzzled Dick.
>
> *These* puzzled Dick.
>
> *Those* chores annoyed Jane.
>
> *The* chores annoyed Jane.
>
> *Messy* chores annoyed Jane.
>
> *Those* annoyed Jane.

From these examples, we learn that, depending on their use in sentences, the forms *this, that, these,* and *those* must fall into one of two categories, being either a nominal or a determiner. The determiner is always followed by a noun (with optional adjective in between).

> *These* are ripe. [nominal function as subject]
>
> *These* grapes are ripe. [determiner precedes noun in NP]

As nominals, the demonstratives function like nouns, as

- Subjects

   This seems ideal for my purposes.

- Direct objects

   Jane deeply resented *that.*

- Indirect objects

   Father gave *these* a quick once-over.

- Subjective complements

   Mother's favorites are *those.*

- Objective complements

    Did Dick call Jane *that*?

- Objects of prepositions

    Who thought of *these*?

Exercise 9.4

Find the demonstrative pronouns in the following sentences. Be sure to differentiate determiners (such as *Those oysters were spoiled*), which are not pronouns, from nominals (such as *Those were spoiled*), which are pronouns.

1. These seem to be riper than those.
2. We gave this reason for our tardiness.
3. That just won't suffice.
4. Who would believe that alibi?
5. Those cost a good deal more than these.
6. "Anybody who doesn't like this book is healthy." (Groucho Marx, on a book by Oscar Levant)
7. "These are the gardens of the desert, these / The unshorn fields, boundless and beautiful, / For which the speech of England has no name— / The prairies." (William Cullen Bryant)
8. "I refer those actions which work out the good of the agent to courage, and those which work out the good of others to nobility. Therefore temperance, sobriety, and presence of mind in danger, etc., are species of courage; but modesty, clemency, etc., are species of nobility." (Spinoza)

INTERROGATIVE PRONOUNS

Who stole the floppy disk?

Whom did Spot bite?

Which did Dick steal?

What did Mother say?

Whoever in the world would believe that tale?

Whomever did you plan that caper with?

Whichever was most expensive, the VW or the Beamer?

Whatever were you thinking when you bought that wreck?

When they introduce questions, *who, whom, which, what, whoever, whomever, whichever,* and *whatever* are called *interrogative pronouns*. However, when these eight words occur in other structures, they are not interrogatives.

INDEFINITE PRONOUNS

Indefinite pronouns do not refer to a specific noun. Unlike other pronouns, indefinites never have antecedents. The followings shows indefinite pronouns in context:

> "*Anyone* can be heroic from time to time, but a gentleman is *something* you have to be all the time." (Luigi Pirandello)

> "Make yourself necessary to *somebody*." (Ralph Waldo Emerson)

> "*Nothing* worth doing is completed in our lifetime; therefore, we must be saved by hope." (Reinhold Niebuhr)

> "In men whom men condemn as ill / I find so *much* of goodness still, / In men whom men pronounce divine / I find so *much* of sin and blot, / I do not dare to draw a line / Between the two, where God has not." (Joaquin Miller)

It is important to distinguish indefinite pronouns from these forms used as determiners. Note how the following examples work:

1. I wish I had lots of money, but I don't have *any*. (In this sentence, *any* is an indefinite pronoun.)
2. I don't have *any* money. (In this sentence, *any* is a determiner, modifying the noun *money*.)

In 1, we can substitute other nominals for *any*:

	a cent.
	wealth.
I don't have	means.
	liquidity.
	millions.

In 2, we can substitute *the* for *any*:

I don't have *the* money.

Indefinite pronouns that function as pronouns and as determiners are *any, some, none, all, another, both, each, either, enough, few, less, little, many, more, much, neither, one,* and *several*.

Pronoun	Determiner
Do you have *any*?	Do you have *any* money?
All love this country.	*All* patriots love this country.
Neither is possible.	*Neither* choice is possible.

Indefinite pronouns that function only as pronouns are *anyone, anything, anybody, someone, something, somebody, no one, nobody, nothing, everyone, everybody,* and *everything.*

> Can *anyone* help me?

> *Everyone* likes Molly.

> Jake seems to know *everything.*

IT AS SLOT FILLER

In some cases the pronoun *it* does not have an antecedent. It is simply a "slot filler." That is, it fills the subject slot and has no semantic value. The sentence *It is raining* illustrates this use of *it.*

Exercise 9.5

In the following sentences, identify the indefinite pronouns. Some of these forms are used as determiners. Explain how you know the difference between the indefinite pronouns and determiners.

1. Dick wants money and fame, and he has neither.

2. Jane had many wishes, but few were fulfilled.

3. "If you can't annoy somebody, there's little point in writing." (Kingsley Amis)

4. "I do not like work, even when someone else does it." (Mark Twain)

5. "Wife: one who is sorry she did it, but would undoubtedly do it again." (H. L. Mencken)

6. "Television is a device that permits people who haven't anything to do to watch people who can't do anything." (Fred Allen)

7. "Everything ends this way in France—everything. Weddings, christenings, duels, burials, swindlings, diplomatic affairs—everything is a pretext for a good dinner." (Jean Anouilh)

8. "Hermaphrodite . . . animal or plant with both female and male reproductive systems, producing both eggs and sperm." (*The Concise Columbia Encyclopedia*)

9. "There is something to be said for growing old. Not much, but something." (Laura Black)

10. "Let every nation know, whether it wishes us well or ill, that we shall pay any price, bear any burden, meet any hardship, support any friend, oppose any foe to assure the survival and the success of liberty." (John F. Kennedy)

RELATIVE PRONOUNS

The relative pronouns *who, whom, that, which, whoever, whomever,* and *whichever* are not only interrogatives; they are also pronouns that begin relative or adjective clauses. They have an antecedent from which they take their meaning. For example, in the sentence *The soccer game that we attended was very exciting,* the relative pronoun *that* takes its meaning from the noun phrase *the soccer game.* We will explore these pronouns in detail in Chapter 12 on adjectival clauses.

U SING GRAMMAR: WHO AND WHOM

In contemporary usage, *who* is beginning to serve both subjective and objective functions. *Whom,* however, is used for the objective case in formal speech and writing.

> Informal: Bob knows *who* you gave it to.
>
> *Who* did you buy the printer from?
>
> Formal: Bob knows *whom* you gave it to.
>
> From *whom* did you buy the printer?

Have you been aware of this distinction in usage? Do you think that most of your classmates and professors (other than English professors) would notice the deviation from formal usage?

Do you think that within a few decades, *who* will be the only form, and *whom* will be as much a thing of the past as *thee* and *thou.*

U SING GRAMMAR: AGREEMENT

In formal usage, pronouns must agree with their antecedents (i.e., with the words or phrases they refer to and from which they gain their meaning).

When the antecedent is a compound as in *Dick and Jane* or *both Dick and Jane,* the pronoun should be plural:

> *Dick and Jane* realized *they* were in trouble.

When the two parts of the compound name the same entity, the pronoun is singular:

> *My favorite teacher and wisest counselor* gives *her* advice freely.

When the parts of the antecedent name an entity that is thought of as a whole, the pronoun can be singular:

I like *ham and eggs*. *It* is the perfect breakfast.

When the antecedent is a collective noun (such as *family, committee, staff*), the pronoun can be either singular or plural, depending on the viewpoint of the speaker or writer:

The family vacationed in Nevada each year. *They* enjoyed the wide open spaces.

The committee voted to disband, since *it* had accomplished nothing.

Indefinite pronouns sometimes cause agreement problems. In formal English, *another, anybody, anyone, anything, each, either, everybody, everyone, everything, neither, nobody, none, nothing, one, somebody, someone,* and *something* are singular.

Each should bring *his* or *her* own chess set.

Everyone in the classes *is* studying for the final.

Some indefinite pronouns can be either singular or plural, depending on grammatical context:

Enough of the members *are* [plural] here to start the meeting.

Enough of the stew *is* [singular] left for tomorrow night.

Some of the customers are satisfied, but *plenty* are [plural] complaining.

Plenty of the caviar *is* [singular] left.

USING GRAMMAR: REFERENCE OF PRONOUNS

As you know, pronouns gain their meaning from the words to which they refer: their antecedents. If readers have trouble identifying antecedents, reference is faulty. Here are three common reference problems and their solutions:

1. Hidden or unstated antecedent: supply an antecedent.

    Unclear: On July 24, 1847, the Mormons entered Salt Lake Valley, *which* Utahns celebrate every year.

    Clear: On July 24, 1847, the Mormons entered Salt Lake Valley, *an event which* Utahns celebrate every year.

2. Two possible antecedents: revise to eliminate the ambiguity.

> Unclear: Jane told Mother *she* had forgotten to feed Spot. [Who had forgotten to feed Spot, Jane or Mother?]
>
> Clear: Jane had forgotten to feed Spot and told Mother.
>
> Clear: *Mother* had forgotten to feed Spot, and Jane told *her* so.

3. Implied, unstated antecedent: supply the antecedent.

> Unclear: Thai food is very popular in Los Angeles. *They* have started restaurants in all parts of the area.
>
> Clear: Thai food is very popular in Los Angeles. *The Thais* have started restaurants in all parts of the area.

Pronouns

PERSONAL PRONOUNS

	Subjective	Possessive	Objective
First Person Singular	I	mine	me
First Person Plural	we	ours	us
Second Person Singular	you	yours	you
Second Person Plural	you	yours	you
Third Person Singular	he, she, it	his, hers, its	him, her, it
Third Person Plural	they	theirs	them

COMPOUND PERSONAL PRONOUNS
myself, ourselves, yourself, yourselves, himself, herself, themselves, oneself

RECIPROCAL PRONOUNS
each other, one another

DEMONSTRATIVE PRONOUNS
this, that, these, those

INTERROGATIVE PRONOUNS
who, whom, which, what, whoever, whomever, whichever, whatever

> ### INDEFINITE PRONOUNS
> any, anyone, anything, anybody, some, someone, something, somebody, no, no one, none, nobody, nothing, every, everyone, everybody, everything, all, another, both, each, either, enough, few, less, little, many, more, much, neither, one, several
>
> ### RELATIVE PRONOUNS
> who, whom, which, that, whoever, whomever, whichever

PASSAGE FOR ANALYSIS

In the following passage by Jonathan Mirsky,

1. Find the personal pronouns (if there are any). Identify them as first, second, or third person, and specify their case (subjective, possessive, or objective).

2. Find the compound personal pronouns (if there are any). Are they intensive or reflexive? How do you know?

3. Find the reciprocal pronouns (if there are any).

4. Find the demonstrative pronouns (if there are any). Do not confuse them with demonstrative adjectives.

5. Find the interrogative pronouns (if there are any).

6. Find the indefinite pronouns (if there are any).

The only Tibetan lama most Westerners knew of until recently was the fourteenth Dalai Lama, the genial Nobel Prize winner and symbol of the Tibet that was. But now newspaper readers also know about the kidnapping within Tibet in 1995 of the six-year-old eleventh Panchen Lama, the region's second-highest-ranking religious leader, and the flight into India last January of the fourteen-year-old seventeenth Karmapa Lama, on whom Beijing had pinned its hopes of legitimizing Chinese rule in Tibet.

Even the word "lama" itself is misunderstood. In Tibetan it means guru or teacher; it can also mean incarnation. A person may be both or only one. "Lama Buddhism," a term which has come to mean Tibetan-style Buddhism, has no meaning in Tibetan. Incarnations have existed in Tibet since the thirteenth century. The most famous are the Dalai Lamas; the Karmapas arose several centuries earlier. Many other Tibetans are said to be incarnations of long-dead lamas of lower status.[2]

---

[2] Jonathan Mirsky, "A Lamas' Who's Who," *The New York Review of Books,* April 17, 2000, 15. Reprinted by permission. © 2000 The New York Review of Books.

CHAPTER REVIEW

- What are the three case forms of the first person singular personal pronoun?

- Use each of the three cases in a sentence.

- Explain *compound personal pronouns* as reflexives and as intensifiers. In sentences, give an example of each function.

- What are reciprocal pronouns? Write a sentence that contains a reciprocal pronoun?

- Use two different demonstrative pronouns in one sentence.

- Use three interrogative pronouns in sentences.

- Use four indefinite pronouns in sentences.

Nominals: Noun Clauses

CHAPTER PREVIEW

• Like a sentence, a clause is a structural unit. It has a noun phrase and a verb phrase (in traditional terminology, a subject and a predicate).

Sentence

NOUN PHRASE (SUBJECT)	VERB PHRASE (PREDICATE)
Music lovers	enjoy Mahler's symphonies.

Clause (object of the verb *know*)

	NOUN PHRASE (SUBJECT)	VERB PHRASE (PREDICATE)
We know that	*music lovers*	*enjoy Mahler's symphonies.*

• A sentence has at least one clause, but a clause is not a sentence if it is a dependent clause. A dependent clause is part of a sentence so it cannot stand alone as a sentence.

CLAUSE/SENTENCE	DEPENDENT CLAUSE
Most people enjoy music	if it is well performed.

Most people enjoy music.

*If it is well performed.

• Clauses that have nominal functions (subject, direct object, etc.) are noun clauses. *Dick attended the violin concert* is a sentence. It can also function as a nominal in another sentence: *Jane thought that Dick attended the violin concert.*

• Noun clauses are dependent (or subordinate) clauses. They fulfill nominal functions (subject, object, complement) in a sentence.

• Noun clauses can be part of other *clauses*:

Father knows that *the kids filch cookies*. [noun clause]

Father knows that *the kids filch whatever they can*. [noun clause within noun clause]

CLAUSES

We have talked about phrases and how they work in sentences. We will now introduce the clause as a unit of structure within the sentence. A clause has a subject and a verb. All sentences consist of at least one clause. This sentence, for example, has one clause: *She is a determined athlete.* Other sentences may have more than one clause and more than one subject and verb group: *I study grammar, and I love it.* Here the clauses are connected by *and.*

In this chapter we are going to study noun clauses, which are nominals functioning as subjects, objects, and complements. They are subordinate clauses in that they are units within sentences or other clauses.

NOUN CLAUSES

Because the following group of words has MOD (modal), a subject (NP), and a verb phrase (or, in traditional terms, a predicate), it is a sentence: *The boy might know the thief.* Because this next group of words has TENSE, NP (noun phrase), and VP (verb phrase), it is a sentence: *Someone stole the bubble gum.* [Just a reminder: every sentence has either MOD or TN, and AUX → [TN, MOD] (HAVE + EN) (BE + ING) (BE + EN).] With a small substitution and a deletion, we can insert one sentence into the other, thus: *The boy might know who stole the bubble gum.* The first element still has MOD, and the second has PAST. Thus *who stole the bubble gum* is a noun clause.

Noun clauses have the same functions as nouns and other nominals.

FUNCTIONS OF NOUN CLAUSES

SUBJECT

Noun: *Magic* baffles people.

Noun clause: *What Marilyn can do* baffles people.

DIRECT OBJECT

Noun: Shoppers seek *bargains.*

Noun clause: Shoppers seek *whatever costs least.*

INDIRECT OBJECT

Noun: Police give *speeders* citations.

Noun clause: Police give *whoever exceeds the speed limit* citations.

OBJECT OF PREPOSITION

Noun: The children laughed at the *clown*.

Noun clause: The children laughed at *what the clown did*.

SUBJECTIVE COMPLEMENT

Noun: The price of freedom is *vigilance*.

Noun clause: The price of freedom is *what vigilance can really mean*.

OBJECTIVE COMPLEMENT

Noun: The boss called Myrtle a *dud*.

Noun clause: The boss called Myrtle *whatever popped into his mind*.

APPOSITIVE

Noun: Our friend the *taxidermist* said he would prepare Spot.

Noun clause: Our friend, *who is a taxidermist,* said he would prepare Spot.

VOCATIVE

Noun: *Father,* please rescue Spot from the dogcatcher.

Noun clause: *Whoever has political influence,* please rescue Spot from the dogcatcher.

Whether a direct object, for instance, is a single noun (NP) or a clause, the function is the same. A single noun used as direct object becomes the subject in passive, and that is exactly the case with clauses:

Dick swiped *bubble gum./Bubble gum* was swiped by Dick.

Dick swiped *whatever pleased him./Whatever pleased him* was swiped by Dick.

Exercise 10.1

Find the noun clauses in the following sentences, and identify their function (subject, direct object, indirect object, object of preposition, subjective complement, objective complement, appositive, vocative). Remember that a clause has either TN or MOD.

> **Example**
> Irving believes that he can beat the odds.
>
> *That he can beat the odds* is a noun clause, the direct object of *believes*.

> a. A noun can be substituted for the clause: Irving believes the *alibi.*
>
> b. The sentence can be transformed into (an awkward) passive: *That he can beat the odds* is believed by Irving.

1. Wise people know that exercise is healthy.

2. That jogging improves cardiac function seems obvious.

3. The philanthropist gave whoever was needy financial help.

4. That the right will prevail is what I strongly believe.

5. "What our competitive and careerist knowledge industry has produced already hopelessly exceeds our ability to make general use of it." (Theodore Roszak)

6. "Don't forget that even our most obscene vices nearly always bear the seal of sullen greatness." (Gesualdo Bufalino)

7. "Everyone in the class waited for what seemed like hours." (Student)

8. "What is more important in a library than anything else—than everything else—is the fact that it exists." (Archibald MacLeish)

9. "For years I thought what was good for our country was good for General Motors and vice versa." (Charles E. Wilson)

INDEFINITE RELATIVES

Indefinite relative pronouns, adjectives, and adverbs establish the link between noun clauses and the sentences of which they are part.

Pronouns

Here is a sentence containing a noun clause with an indefinite relative pronoun as the link:

Dick knows <u>which</u> *is best for him.*

For the clause *which is best for him,* we can substitute a noun (with its determiner):

Dick knows *the ropes.*

Here is a sentence containing a noun clause with an indefinite relative adjective as the link:

Dick knows <u>which</u> *alibi is best for him.*

In this sentence, *which* is an adjective modifying the noun *alibi.*

Here is a sentence containing a noun clause with an indefinite relative adverb as the link:

Dick knows *where Jane hid the book.*

Indefinite relatives do not refer to other nominals in their sentences.

Definite relative pronouns, adjectives, and adverbs *do* refer to other nominals in their sentences, and the result is adjective clauses. (See Chapter 12 for adjective clauses.)

Noun clause introduced by indefinite relative pronoun: Father forgot *who had set the garage on fire.*

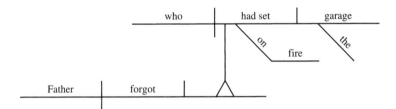

Figure 10.1   Reed-Kellogg diagram of *Father forgot who had set the garage on fire.* The noun clause (*who had set the garage on fire*) is on "stilts" in the direct object position and is diagrammed exactly as a sentence would be.

Adjective clause introduced by definite relative pronoun: Father forgot the child *who had set the garage on fire.*

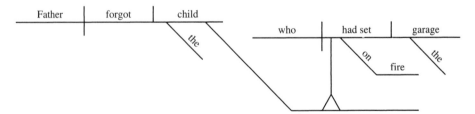

Figure 10.2   Reed-Kellogg diagram of *Father forgot the child who had set the garage on fire.* The adjective clause is on "stilts" in the conventional slant-line/straight-line structure that indicates adjectives.

Note that the definite relative pronoun *who* has an antecedent: *the child.* Indefinite relative pronouns do not have antecedents.

In Chapter 12, we will deal with definite relative pronouns, but in this chapter on nominals, we are concerned only with indefinite relatives since they are parts of noun clauses.

There are eleven and only eleven indefinite relative pronouns:

"_Who_ serves his country well has no need of ancestors." (Voltaire)

Someone's muddy footprints tracked across the kitchen floor, but Mother didn't know _whose_ they were.

Jane wondered _whom Dick had loaned his comic book._ (The more common form is either Jane wondered _to whom Dick had loaned his comic book_ or Jane wondered _whom Dick had loaned his comic book to._)

Of the two horror movies, Dick couldn't decide _which he should see._

Whoever attends concerts should not snore.

Be wary of _whosoever offers you something_ for nothing.

Choose _whichever seems to fit you best._

You want to buy an Audi, a Mercedes, or a BMW, but _whichsoever you choose_ will cost too much.

Wise people know _what they want._

Wise people often get _whatever they want._

Foolish people often get _whatsoever they deserve._

THE INDEFINITE RELATIVE PRONOUNS

who, whose, whom, which, whoever, whosoever, whichever, whichsover, what, whatever, whatsoever

As you have seen, some of the indefinite relatives are not commonly used, and it might be that you have never used _whatsoever_ or _whichsoever._

As the examples so far have shown, in their own clauses, indefinite relative pronouns function as

- Subjects

    What makes Lola happy might not be good for her.

- Direct objects

    Lola says _whatever she wants._ (Thinking about this sentence as two propositions helps to untangle the syntax:

Lola says *Something*.

She wants *whatever*.

In other words, the indefinite relative pronoun *whatever* is the direct object in its own clause.)

- Indirect objects

  Do you know <u>whom</u> *Lola gave her negligee*? (More commonly, Do you know to whom Lola gave her negligee?)

  Do you know *something*?

  Lola gave *whom* her negligee.

- Objects of prepositions

  You know *to* <u>whom</u> *Lola gave her negligee*.

  You know *something*.

  Lola gave her negligee to *whom*.

- Subjective complements

  Someone told us <u>what</u> *Lola is*.

  Someone told us *something*.

  Lola is *what*.

- Objective complements

  We know *that some brute called Lola* <u>whatever</u>.

  We know *something*.

  Some brute called Lola *whatever*.

Exercise 10.2

In the following sentences, find the indefinite relative pronouns. Since each indefinite relative is part of a noun clause, when you locate an indefinite relative, you will also have located a noun clause. By now you are probably ready to explain the function of nominals, so determine whether the noun clauses are subjects, direct objects, indirect objects, objects of prepositions, subjective complements, objective complements, appositives, or vocatives. In summary:

1. Locate the indefinite relative pronouns in the following sentences.

2. Identify their function in the noun clauses.

Examples

A. Everyone knew *who* had spilled the syrup.

Who is the indefinite relative.

The clause *who had spilled the syrup* is the direct object of the verb *knew*. (We can substitute a noun for the clause *Everyone knew the culprit*. The sentence can be changed to passive, indicating that the clause is a direct object: *Who had spilled the syrup was known by everyone.*)

B. *What* the family had decided puzzled the neighbors.

What is the indefinite relative.

The clause *What the family had decided* is the subject of the sentence.

C. "The only way to keep your health is to eat what you don't want, drink what you don't like, and do what you'd rather not." (Mark Twain)

What (you don't want) is the indefinite relative.

The clause is the direct object of the verbal *to eat*.

What (you don't like) is the indefinite relative.

The clause is the direct object of *drink*.

What (you'd rather not) is the indefinite relative with the verb *do* deleted.

The clause is the direct object of *do*.

1. The police know who kidnapped Jane.
2. Do you know whom they arrested?
3. Father told whoever would listen the story.
4. Experts understand what castor oil is.
5. Whatever you think about Marvin will probably be wrong.
6. There were several problems. Does anyone know which created all the commotion?
7. Jacquie fretted over what she would wear to the reception.
8. Fernando couldn't remember whom he had invited.
9. The problem of who should take the lead was solved by the toss of a coin.

10. Did you see to whom it was addressed?

11. "A husband is what's left of the lover once the nerve has been extracted." (Helen Rowland)

12. "I and my public understand each other very well: it does not hear what I say, and I don't say what it wants to hear." (Karl Kraus)

13. "What people call insincerity is simply a method by which we can multiply our personalities." (Oscar Wilde)

Indefinite Relative Adjectives

Adjectives modify nouns and other nominals: *ugly* weather, *proud* father, *morose* teacher. The forms of the indefinite relative adjectives are

The teacher found out *whose test had been stolen.*

The principal understood *which children had cheated.*

She would punish *whichever children were guilty.*

Do you know *what punishment she was contemplating?*

Whatever penalty she chooses will no doubt be fiendish.

By substituting other nominals, you can demonstrate that the clauses containing indefinite relative adjectives are noun clauses:

The teacher found out *the culprit.*

The principal understood *the kids.*

She would punish *the thieves.*

Do you know *the result.*

Her penalty will no doubt be fiendish.

THE INDEFINITE RELATIVE ADJECTIVES

whose, which, whichever, what, whatever

Indefinite Relative Adverbs

In Chapter 13, we will deal extensively with adverbs, which are words that relate to such concepts as place (e.g., *where*), time (e.g., *when*), reason (e.g., *why*) and manner (e.g., *how*). These adverbs can introduce noun clauses:

Where

> "*Where* I was born and *where* and *how* I have lived is unimportant. It is what I have done with *where* I have been that should be of interest." (Georgia O'Keeffe)

Two clauses are the subjects of the verb *is*: *Where I was born* and *where and how I lived*. In these clauses, the adverbs *where* and *how* modify the verb groups *was born* and *have lived*. In the second sentence, the clause *where I have been* is the object of the preposition *with,* and the adverb *where* completes the verb phrase *have been*.

When

> "When we start deceiving ourselves into thinking not that we want something or need something, not that it is a pragmatic necessity for us to have it, but that it is a moral imperative that we have it, then is *when* we join the fashionable madmen, and then is *when* the thin whine of hysteria is heard in the land, and then is *when* we are in bad trouble." (Joan Didion)[1]

The *when* with which the quotation begins is not an indefinite relative adverb, but a subordinating conjunction. (See Chapter 16.) The other three instances of *when* introduce noun clauses as subjective complements.

Why

> Do you know *why* Albert saved string?

> "I understand <u>why</u> *the saints were rarely married women*." (Anne Morrow Lindbergh)

How

> The instructions explained *how* the cabinet should be assembled.

> "Economics . . . the study of <u>how</u> *human beings allocate scarce resources to produce various commodities* and <u>how</u> *those goods are distributed for consumption among the people in society*." (*The Concise Columbia Encyclopedia*)

THE INDEFINITE RELATIVE ADVERBS

where, when, why, how

---

[1] Joan Didion, "On Morality," in *Slouching Toward Bethlehem* (New York: Farrar, Straus and Giroux, 1996). Copyright © 1966, 1968, renewed 1996 by Joan Didion. Reprinted by permission of the publisher.

Exercise 10.3

Find the indefinite relative adjectives and adverbs in the following sentences. Determine the function of the noun clauses in which they occur (subject, direct object, indirect object, object of preposition, objective complement, subjective complement, appositive).

1. Dick explained how he had avoided punishment.

2. Jane wanted to know whose bicycle Dick had wrecked.

3. Jane knew where Dick had hidden the bicycle.

4. When the bell rings is the time for Dick and Jane to go home.

5. Be very careful about what language you use.

6. Mother asked why the children were so late.

7. Give whatever job you undertake all of your effort.

8. Spot was heading for where he could hide from the kids.

9. "Morality is not properly the doctrine of how we may make ourselves happy, but how we may make ourselves worthy of happiness." (Immanuel Kant)

10. "I would much rather have men ask why I have no statue, than why I have one." (Marcus Porcius Cato, 234–149 BCE)

11. "As of January, 1988, hospitals are required by the Joint Commission on Accreditation of Health Care Organizations to have formal policies specifying when doctors and nurses can refrain from trying to resuscitate terminally ill patients." (*Ethics on Care of the Terminally Ill*)

12. "From where the sun now stands I will fight no more forever." (Chief Joseph of the Nez Percé, c. 1840–1904)

13. "Money is always dull, except when you haven't got any, and then it's terrifying." (Sheila Bishop)

WORDS USED TO INTRODUCE NOUN CLAUSES

That

In many sentences, the word *that* is not a demonstrative pronoun at all; rather, it introduces a noun clause. Our term for that use of *that* is "strategic *that*" because it allows the reader to sort out the information in the sentence. The more common term, however, is "expletive *that*."

We have seen that indefinite relative pronouns are always parts of clauses. Such is not the case with strategic *that*. Compare these two sentences:

1. I understood *what* you wanted.

2. I understood *that* you wanted the ice cream.

In sentence 1, *what* is the direct object of *wanted*. In sentence 2, *that* is not part of the clause, but merely helps the reader process the sentence. In fact, *that* can be deleted:

I understood you wanted the ice cream.

However, strategic *that* introducing a noun clause that is subject of the sentence cannot be deleted:

That Margaret could win the marathon inspires her students.

*Margaret could win the marathon inspires her students.

That any member of the fraternity would cheat on an exam seems unbelievable.

*Any member of the fraternity would cheat on an exam seems unbelievable.

To test for strategic *that,* try substituting *who* or *which*. If the substitution does *not* create an ungrammatical sentence, the *that* is a pronoun, not strategic *that*.

The fact *that* George Washington had false teeth amazes some people.

*The fact *which* George Washington had false teeth amazes some people. [Substituting *which* made the sentence ungrammatical. Therefore, *that* in the original is strategic *that*.]

The fact *that* we found in the encyclopedia dispelled our doubts.

The fact *which* we found in the encyclopedia dispelled our doubts. [With the substitution of *which,* the sentence does not become ungrammatical; thus, the *that* in the original is not strategic *that*.]

Whether and If

Other words used to introduce noun clauses are *whether* and *if*:

Tell me *whether I should take a class in basket weaving.*

Do you know *if the class will be offered next semester?*

These words are most commonly classed as conjunctions, but, as we shall see, they do not function like other conjunctions; thus, we prefer to put them in the same category as strategic *that*. The words *whether* and *if* do not fulfill functions (subject, object, etc.) for the structure of the clause itself, and thus they are much like strategic *that*.

Uses of That

You should distinguish among strategic *that,* demonstrative *that,* and relative *that*.

• Strategic *that*

I know *that* my Redeemer liveth.

I know my Redeemer liveth.

That my Redeemer liveth gives me hope.

*My Redeemer liveth gives me hope.

- Demonstrative *that* as determiner

    That book bores everyone. (Compare *The* book bores everyone.)

    Wilhelmina sat patiently through *that* soporific lecture.

- Demonstrative pronoun *that*

    No one pays attention. *That* annoys me.

- Relative *that*

    Novels *that* become best-sellers are often trashy.

(In Chapter 12, we will explain relative *that*.)

Exercise 10.4

In the following sentences, differentiate strategic *that* from demonstrative *that*.

1. That made me think that life is worth living.
2. Gourmets know that Julia Child wrote that cookbook.
3. "What is irritating about love is that it is a crime that requires an accomplice." (Charles Baudelaire)
4. "The reason that lovers never weary each other is because they are always talking about themselves." (François de la Rochefoucauld)
5. If you don't like that, lump it!
6. "The trouble with wedlock is that there's not enough wed and too much lock." (Christopher Morley)
7. "The main difference between men and woman is that men are lunatics and women are idiots." (Rebecca West)
8. "The trouble with Oakland is that when you get there, there isn't any there there." (Gertrude Stein)

CLAUSES WITHIN CLAUSES

The grammar of English (and, indeed, of all languages) allows speakers and writers to embed clauses within clauses. For example, the following sentence contains a noun clause as the direct object of the verb in another noun clause:

Grammarians know *that native speakers understand* <u>*which sentences are*</u> <u>*grammatical.*</u>

The clause *that native speakers understand* [something] is the direct object of the verb *know,* and the clause *which sentences are grammatical* is the direct object of the verb *understand.* We will use diagrams to represent the relationships among the clauses in the sentence.

| Grammarians know | that native speakers understand | which sentences are grammatical |

Figure 10.3 Constituent structure diagram of *Grammarians know that native speakers understand which sentences are grammatical.* This diagram shows the "nesting" of a clause within a sentence and the "nesting" of a clause within a clause.

Another graphic illustration of this embedding is the following branching tree diagram.

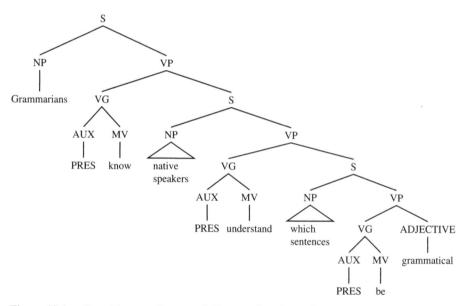

Figure 10.4 Branching tree diagram of *Grammarians know that native speakers understand which sentences are grammatical.* This diagram shows the hierarchy of embedding. Note that the object of the verb *know* (*native speakers understand which sentences are grammatical*) is represented by the S symbol, meaning that the clause has all the features of a sentence. (We could, of course, simply use the symbol C for clause; however, that representation is not part of the "language" that grammarians use when they do branching tree diagrams.) And the embedded clause *which sentences are grammatical,* object of the verb *understand,* is also represented by S (rather than by C or some other such symbol).

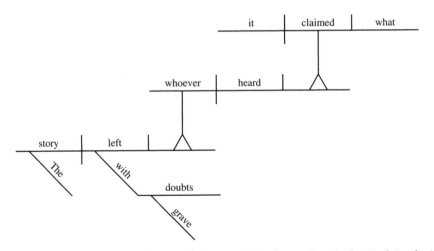

Figure 10.5 Reed-Kellogg diagram of *The story left whoever heard what it claimed with grave doubts.* In the Reed-Kellogg diagram, the clauses are put on "stilts" to show their relationships. The clause *whoever heard what it claimed* is the object of the verb *left,* and the clause *what it claimed* is the object of the verb *heard.*

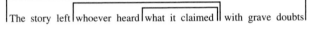

Figure 10.6 Constituent structure diagram of *The story left whoever heard what it claimed with grave doubts.*

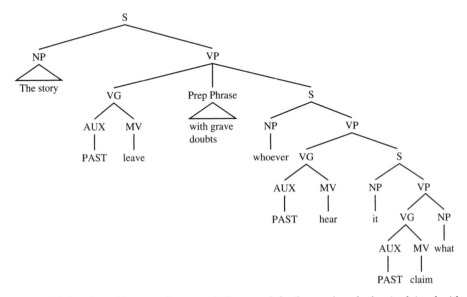

Figure 10.7 Branching tree diagram of *The story left whoever heard what it claimed with grave doubts.*

Here is another example of a noun clause embedded within a noun clause:

The story left *whoever heard <u>what it claimed</u>* with grave doubts.

In this sentence the noun clause *whoever heard what it claimed* is the object of the verb *left,* and the noun clause *what it claimed* is the object of the verb *heard.*

One more time it must said: if the diagrams help you understand the structure of sentences, use them as an aid to learning. After you have thought about the diagrams, if they seem to be hindrances, ignore them.

Exercise 10.5

Find the noun clauses and the noun clauses within noun clauses in the following sentences.

1. Autobiographers know that they cannot find out what their subjects have done every minute of every day.

2. Novelists can invent whatever they think their characters might do.

3. That historians don't believe Henry VIII gave his wives whatever they desired seems strange to me.

4. The diarist records what he thinks others shouldn't know.

5. This book left whoever read what it contains in a coma.

PASSAGE FOR ANALYSIS

First, read and enjoy the wit in the following brief selection by Zora Neale Hurston. Then find the noun clauses and identify their function.

> And now, I'm going to tell you why I decided to go to my native village first. I didn't go back there so that the home folks could make admiration over me because I had been up North to college and come back with a diploma and a Chevrolet. I knew they were not going to pay either one of these items too much mind. I was just Lucy Hurston's daughter, Zora, and even if I had—to use one of our down-home expressions—had a Kaiser baby,[2] and that's something that hasn't been done in this country yet, I'd still be just Zora to the neighbors. If I had exalted myself to impress the town, somebody would have sent me word in a match-box that I had been up North there and had rubbed the hair off of my head against some college wall, and then come back there with a lot of form and fashion and outside show to the world. But they'd stand flat-footed and tell me that they didn't have me, neither my sham polish, to study 'bout. And that would have been that.[3]

---

[2] That is, if she had had a baby fathered by Kaiser Wilhelm, the emperor of Germany.

[3] Zora Neale Hurston, *Mules and Men* (Harper Perennial Edition, 1990), 2. Copyright 1935 by Zora Neale Hurson; renewed © 1963 by John C. Hurston and Joel Hurston. Reprinted by permission of HarperCollins Publishers Inc.

CHAPTER REVIEW

- In what ways is a clause identical with a sentence?
- In what ways does a clause differ from a sentence?
- Write sentences in which noun clauses are used in each of their eight functions.
- Write sentences in which noun clauses are introduced by indefinite relative adjectives and by indefinite relative adverbs.
- Explain the difference between what we call strategic *that* and relative *that*. Write sentences that illustrate the difference.
- Write a sentence with a noun clause introduced by *whether*.
- Write a sentence with a noun clause introduced by *if*.
- Write a sentence in which one noun clause is embedded within another noun clause.

11

Adjectivals: Adjectives, Nouns, Prepositional Phrases

CHAPTER PREVIEW

- Adjectives are words like *good, bad, pretty, ugly, hot, cold.* Adjectives modify nouns:

  good coffee

  bad dude

  pretty gown

  ugly tie

  venial sins

  hot tamale

- Adjectives have three syntactic slots in sentences. They can be attributive, standing before the noun or nominal:

  The *ugly* shirt hung in the closet.

  They can be appositive, following the nominal that they modify:

  The shirt, *ugly* in the extreme, hung in the closet.

  They can be predicate:

  The shirt was *ugly.*

- Attributive adjectives are part of the noun phrase. They fit in between the determiner[1] and the noun: DET + (ADJECTIVE) + NOUN.

---

[1] Remember that the determiner can be null: ∅ (*the* good supper, ∅ good suppers). See pages 110–114.

DEFINITION OF ADJECTIVES

Notional Definition

The common definition is this: "an adjective modifies a noun." That, however, is not very helpful, for prepositional phrases, present and past participles, and clauses also modify nouns; in other words, these other grammatical units can function adjectivally.

> The woman *in white* stole the gem. [prepositional phrase]
>
> The woman *wearing white* stole the gem. [present participial phrase; also can be analyzed as a reduced adjective clause]
>
> The woman *who was wearing white* stole the gem. [clause]

Furthermore, what does "modify" mean in this context? Another definition states that "nouns name substances while adjectives name qualities," but that simply gets us into the tight loop of defining substances and qualities. Is *love* a substance or a quality? How about *woody* as in *a woody carrot*? As in the case of nouns, we are better off with formal and syntactic definitions.

Formal Definition

1. Nouns can be pluralized. Adjectives cannot:

   interesting problem

   interesting problem*s*

   *interestings problem

2. Adjectives can be compared.

Positive	Comparative	Superlative
fast	faster	fastest
good	better	best
fascinating	more fascinating	most fascinating

3. Adjectives can be modified by words like *very, simply, somewhat*:

   very serious

   simply gorgeous

   somewhat smutty

4. Most adjectives, but not all, have endings that mark their class:

   -*y*: muddy, chilly, ruddy

   -*ful*: soulful, faithful, sinful

   -*less*: soulless, faithless, sinless

-en: rotten, golden, wooden

-able: payable, chewable, renewable

-ive: decisive, excessive, constructive

-ous: vigorous, nervous, marvelous

-ish: skittish, selfish, English

-al: national, rational, cordial

-ic: civic, homeric, metric

-ary: revolutionary, contrary, secondary

-some: bothersome, worrisome, handsome

-ly: lonely, portly, friendly

A few of these suffixes occur with parts of speech other than adjectives:

lone*ly* place (adjective)

swift*ly* falling (adverb)

To differentiate the adjective *lonely* from the adverb *swiftly,* we can apply functional tests.

FORMAL DEFINITION OF ADJECTIVE

- Cannot be pluralized:

  good advice

  *goods advice

- Can be compared:

  good advice/*better* advice/*best* advice

  sane/saner/sanest

  intelligent/more intelligent/most intelligent

- Can be modified by words like *very*:

  very cold weather

- In some instances, takes adjectival suffixes (endings):

  happ*y*

  tooth*some*

U SING GRAMMAR: DOUBLE SUPERLATIVE

It is not uncommon to hear speakers use a double superlative: the *most fastest* runner, the *most best* way. Even triple superlatives crop up occasionally: the *most worstest* disease. (*Worst* is the superlative degree of *bad;* adding both *most* and the suffix *-est* makes the superlative triple.) We suspect that many instances of double and triple superlative are attempts by speakers to be mildly humorous. Of course, in formal language, these usages are taboo.

Functional Definition

Take a close look at the following sentences:

1. The nutty professor is nutty.
2. *The psychology professor is psychology.

Applying formal tests, we can determine that *nutty* is an adjective:

- It cannot be pluralized, so it is not a noun: *nutties.
- It can be compared: nutty, nuttier, nuttiest.
- It can be modified by adverbs: very nutty, utterly nutty.
- It has an adjective suffix: *-y*.

On the other hand, the formal test shows that *psychology* is a noun.

- It can be pluralized: psychologies.
- It can take an article: the psychology of adolescents.
- It takes the *-'s* suffix in the possessive: psychology's theories

From the contrast between *The nutty professor is nutty* and **The psychology professor* *is psychology*, we can derive a type of sentence that will enable us to differentiate adjectives from nouns.

F UNCTIONAL TEST FOR ADJECTIVES

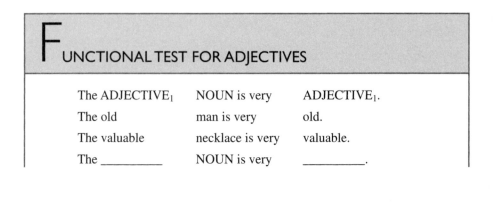

The ADJECTIVE$_1$	NOUN is very	ADJECTIVE$_1$.
The old	man is very	old.
The valuable	necklace is very	valuable.
The _____	NOUN is very	_____.

Words that can fill both of the slots without creating ungrammaticality are most likely adjectives.

> The *wealthy* woman is very *wealthy*.
> *The *repair* man is very *repair*.
> *The *sleeping* baby is very *sleeping*.

Exercise 11.1

Find the adjectives in the following sentences, and use the formal and syntactic tests to explain your choices.

> **Example**
> "Love is the white light of emotion." (Diane Ackerman)
>
> *White* is an adjective.
>
> It can be compared: *whiter, whitest*.
>
> It can be modified by an adverb: *very white*.
>
> It fits the adjective frame sentence: The *white* light is *very white*.

1. The angry cat is very angry.
2. Good can never come of bad deeds.
3. Thrifty makes the very best ice cream.
4. The heartless man took the pretty cat to the pound.
5. "The silence drew off, baring the pebbles and shells and all the tatty wreckage of my life. Then, at the rim of vision, it gathered itself, and in one sweeping tide, rushed me to sleep." (Sylvia Plath, *The Bell Jar*)
6. "We are an intelligent species and the use of our intelligence quite properly gives us pleasure. In this respect the brain is like a muscle. When it is in use we feel very good. Understanding is joyous." (Carl Sagan)
7. "Future shock: the shattering stress and disorientation that we induce in individuals by subjecting them to too much change in too short a time." (Alvin Toffler)
8. "I who have cursed / The drunken officer of British rule, how choose / Between this Africa and the English tongue I love?" (Derek Walcott)
9. "There is no Jewish blood in my veins, But I am / hated with a scabby hatred / By all the anti-Semites, / like a Jew." (Yevgeny Alexandrovich Yevtushenko)

10. "Private beneficence is totally inadequate to deal with the vast numbers of the city's disinherited." (Jane Addams)

11. "I wish that every human life might be pure transparent freedom." (Simone de Beauvoir)

12. "What is man, when you come to think upon him, but a minutely set, ingenious machine for turning with infinite artfulness, the red wine of Shiraz into urine?" (Isak Dinesen)

CHALLENGER

What problem or problems do you find in trying to define the adjectivals in the following sentence? Do the formal and functional tests apply?

"We are not engaged in domestic politics, in church building or in social uplift work, but we are engaged in nation building." (Marcus Garvey)

ADJECTIVES IN SENTENCES

As the following sentences illustrate, adjectives characteristically fill three slots.

The Attributive Position

An adjective in the attributive position is standing before the noun it modifies:

The *wealthy* man gave millions to the Fabian Society.

"He was a *wealthy* man, and kindly to his fellow men; for dwelling in a house by the side of the road, he used to entertain all comers." (Homer, *The Iliad*)

When the adjective is in the attributive slot, it is part of the noun phrase. The noun phrase, including any determiners and adjectives, functions as a unit. A pronoun would substitute for the entire noun phrase, including the determiners and adjectives. For example, in the sentence *The wealthy man gave millions to the Fabian Society,* the pronoun *he* would substitute for the entire noun phrase *the wealthy man.* Compare these two sentences, which illustrate the point:

He gave millions to the Fabian Society.

*The wealthy he gave millions to the Fabian Society.

The Appositive Position

An adjective in the appositive position is following or preceding the noun it modifies, a syntactic position traditionally called *appositive,* but not to be confused with nouns in apposition (see pages 101–102):

> The man, *wealthy* as Croesus, gave millions to the Fabian Society.
>
> *Wealthy* as Croesus, the man gave millions to the Fabian Society.

The appositive adjective is a clause from which the subject and verb have been deleted. *The man, who was wealthy as Croesus, gave millions to the Fabian Society* becomes *The man, wealthy as Croesus, gave millions to the Fabian Society.*

The Predicate Position

An adjective in the predicate position is following the verb:

> The man is *wealthy*. [subjective complement]
>
> "Early to bed and early to rise, makes a man healthy, *wealthy*, and wise." (Benjamin Franklin) [objective complement]
>
> "Early to rise and early to bed makes a male healthy and *wealthy* and dead." (James Thurber) [objective complement]

SYNTAX OF ADJECTIVES

ATTRIBUTIVE

> The *old and doddery* professor was also cantankerous.

APPOSITIVE

> The professor, *old and doddery*, was cantankerous.
>
> *Old and doddery*, the professor was cantankerous.

PREDICATE

> The professor was *old and doddery* and cantankerous.

USING GRAMMAR: TAUTOLOGY

Sometimes an adjective in combination with a noun gives information that is already part of the meaning of the noun. For instance, *dead corpse*. Since a corpse is, by definition, a dead body, addition of the adjective creates what is known as *tautology*—that is, needless repetition of an idea. Other examples of tautology: *rich billionaire, intelligent genius, spaghetti pasta*. Is *cheddar cheese* a tautological statement? After all, cheddar is cheese. Would you normally say, "With our apple pie we had cheddar cheese" or "With our apple pie we had cheddar"? In your opinion, is one of these uses less acceptable in formal language than the other?

Exercise 11.2

Find the adjectives in the following sentences and tell whether they are attributive, appositive, or predicate.

1. The old raccoon enjoyed ripe apples.

2. The possum, wary of the trap, sniffed at the smelly bait.

3. The skunk was clever.

4. "He was a short man, well below average, and he walked with his chin up, gazing about as though searching for his missing inches." (Helen Hudson)

5. "Afoot and light-hearted I take to the open road, / Healthy, free, the world before me, / The long brown path before me leading wherever I choose." (Walt Whitman)

6. "Home. It's being new and old all rolled into one. Measuring your new against old friends, old ways, old places. Knowing that as long as the old survives, you can keep changing as much as you want without the nightmare of waking up to a total stranger." (Gloria Naylor)

7. "We owe most of our great inventions and most of the achievements of genius to idleness—either enforced or voluntary. The human mind prefers to be spoon-fed with the thoughts of others, but deprived of such nourishment it will, reluctantly, begin to think for itself—and such thinking, remember, is original thinking and may have valuable results." (Agatha Christie)

8. "The imagination of a boy is healthy, and the mature imagination of a man is healthy; but there is a space of life between, in which the soul is in a ferment, the character undecided, the way of life uncertain, the ambition thicksighted: thence proceeds mawkishness, and the thousand bitters which those men I speak of must necessarily taste in going over the following pages." (John Keats)

OTHER ADJECTIVALS

Nouns

The following sentences demonstrate an important point about modification:

> The *strong* poison is very strong.
>
> The *rat* poison is very strong.

adjectives like *strong* can modify nouns, but nouns like *rat* can also modify other nouns—that is, nouns can function adjectivally. Nouns that modify other nouns do not work in the frame sentence for testing adjectives.

> The *glib* salesman is very glib.
>
> *The *book* salesman is very book.
>
> The *huge* supermarket is very huge.
>
> *The *computer* supermarket is very computer.

Exercise 11.3

In the following sentences, find nouns that modify other nouns.

1. The Norway rat carries plague.
2. In Vienna we bought sauerkraut at the vegetable shop.
3. The Marine lieutenant gave the Army general the report.
4. The ax murderer got a life sentence.

Nonfinite Verb Forms

Past and present participles are often used adjectivally.

Present Participles

> The *running* car left a trail of smoke in the air.
>
> I was awakened by the *howling* wind.

Present Participles in Phrases

> The car *running* on diesel fuel left a trail of smoke in the air.
>
> *Howling* around the house, the wind awakened me.

Past Participles

> The lawyer dreaded a *hung* jury.
>
> *Done* deals result from carelessness.

In *Goodfellas,* the character played by Joe Pesci thought he was a *made* man.

Throw away the *wilted* flowers.

Past Participles in Phrases

The judge dreaded a jury *hung* by one stubborn person.

Deals *done* in haste are often bad deals.

Infinitives

The way *to succeed* in school is *to study.*

My mother's advice *to save money* was wise.

Exercise 11.4

In the following sentences, find the nonfinite verb forms used adjectivally.

1. Everyone enjoyed the singing waiter.

2. The game played at night was boring.

3. "In this unbelievable universe in which we live there are no absolutes. Even parallel lines, reaching into infinity, meet somewhere yonder." (Pearl S. Buck)

4. "A celebrity is a person who works hard all his life to become known, then wears dark glasses to avoid being recognized." (Fred Allen)

Prepositional Phrases

Chapter 15 is a complete discussion of prepositions, but for the moment it is enough to say that prepositions are words like *in, to, over, under, of,* and *for.* Prepositional phrases are made of the head words, which are prepositions, and the noun phrases that follow them.

in the soup

to the concert

over the patio

under the bed

of my foot

for your health

Of course, you know what we're about to explain: prepositional phrases can modify nominals; hence, prepositional phrases can be adjectivals.

The beef *in the soup* was rubbery.

We awaited the overture *to the concert.*

The roof *over the patio* began to leak.

Do you ever vacuum the lint *under the bed?*

The ball *of my foot* was tender.

My suggestions *for your health* include eating an apple a day.

ADJECTIVALS

- Nouns:

  A *foot* doctor is a podiatrist.
- Present participles:

  Her *tinkling* laughter charmed everyone.
- Past participles:

  The *hardened* criminal was remorseless.
- Infinitives:

  The attempt *to reform* Dick was futile.
- Prepositional phrases:

  Follow the rule *of law.*

Exercise 11.5

In the following sentences, find the adjectivals, and if they are not prepositional phrases or nouns, tell whether they are attributive, appositive, or predicate.

1. Little mice nested in the barn.
2. Field mice nested in the barn.
3. Scurrying mice nested in the barn.
4. Rats, big as cats, crawled in the sewers.
5. Norway rats crawled in the sewers.
6. Rats, slinking around, crawled in the sewers.
7. "We do not have to visit a madhouse to find disordered minds; our planet is the mental institution of the universe." (Johann Wolfgang von Goethe)

8. "One reason the human race has such a low opinion of itself is that it gets so much of its wisdom from writers." (Wilfrid Sheed)

9. "Americans are like a rich farmer who wishes he knew how to give his son the hardships that made him rich." (Robert Frost)

10. "Americans are childish in many ways and about as subtle as a Wimpy burger; but in the long run it doesn't make any difference. They just turn on the power." (Tom Wolfe)

11. "Bonny isn't ordinary. She has a liquid, intellectual gaze, as if she's not a dog but a Democrat, interested, like Gabe and Len, in civil liberties." (Laura Cunningham)

12. "I learned that economics was not an exact science and that the most erudite men would analyze the economic ills of the world and derive a totally different conclusion." (Edith Summerskill)

13. "There is something about a home aquarium which sets my teeth on edge the moment I see it. Why anyone would want to live with a small container of stagnant water populated by a half-dead guppy is beyond me." (S. J. Perelman)

14. "I have learned silence from the talkative, toleration from the intolerant, and kindness from the unkind; yet strange, I am ungrateful to those teachers." (Kahlil Gibran)

15. "Only by pursuing the extremes in one's nature, with all its contradictions, appetites, aversions, rages, can one hope to understand a little—oh, I admit only a very little—of what life is about." (Françoise Sagan)

INTERROGATIVE ADJECTIVES

We retrace our course briefly, going back to interrogative pronouns.

What did Jane pull on Dick?

Dick and Jane each told a different story. *Whose* did Mother believe?

Which was more preposterous?

You guessed it! *What, whose,* and *which* can also be used as interrogative adjectives. These replace—or serve in lieu of—the determiner.

What trick did Jane pull on Dick?

Dick and Jane each told a different story. *Whose alibi* did mother believe?

Which excuse was more preposterous?

Whatever and *whichever* also occur as interrogative adjectives; however, these forms are becoming obsolete.

Whatever got into Dick? [pronoun]

Whatever craziness got into Dick? [adjective]

Whichever was the most popular? [pronoun]

Whichever program was the most popular? [adjective]

INTERROGATIVE ADJECTIVES

What choice do you have?

Whose invitation did you accept?

Which automobile gets the best gas mileage?

Whatever whim prompted Jane to buy a Barbie doll?

Whichever reason for tardiness is unacceptable?

Exercise 11.6

In the following sentences, find the interrogative pronouns and the interrogative adjectives.

1. Whose can I trust, your excuse or your wife's?
2. Whose excuse can I trust, yours or your wife's?
3. Which do you prefer, jail or a fine?
4. Which penalty do you prefer, jail or a fine?
5. What in the world did Oscar mean by that remark?
6. Whichever investment would you choose if you had millions of dollars?
7. Whatever foreign country would you most like to visit?
8. Whose attorneys are honest and reliable?
9. "What is our life but a succession of preludes to that unknown song whose first solemn note is sounded by death?" (Alphonse de Lamartine, 1790–1869)
10. "What contemptible scoundrel stole the cork from my lunch?" (W. C. Fields)

PASSAGES FOR ANALYSIS

In the following passages, find all adjectivals (including adjectives themselves, obviously). Some of the adjectivals in the passages are clauses. Ignore these for the present. In Chapter 12 we will analyze adjectival clauses.

1. "Black power . . . is a call for black people in this country to unite, to recognize their heritage, to build a sense of community. It is a call for black people to begin to define their own goals, to lead their own organizations and to support those organizations. It is a call to reject the racist institutions and values of this society." (Stokely Carmichael)

2. "Look in the mirror. The face that pins you with its double gaze reveals a chastening secret. You are looking into a predator's eyes. Most predators have eyes set right in the front of their heads, so they can use binocular vision to sight and track their prey. . . . Prey, on the other hand, have eyes on the sides of their heads, because what they really need is peripheral vision, so they can tell when something is sneaking up behind them. Something like us." (Diane Ackerman)

3. "The NAACP started with a lynching 100 years after the birth of Abraham Lincoln, and in the city, Springfield, Illinois, which was his long time residence. William English Walling, a white Southerner, dramatized the gruesome happening and a group of liberals formed a committee in New York, which I was invited to join. A conference was held in 1909.

   "This conference contained four groups: scientists who knew the race problem; philanthropists willing to help worthy causes; social workers ready to take up a new task of Abolition; and Negroes ready to join a new crusade for their emancipation. An impressive number of scientists and social workers attended; friends of wealthy philanthropists were present and many Negroes but few followers of Booker Washington. In the end, Trotter, the most radical Negro leader, and Mrs. Ida Wells Barnett who was leading an anti-lynching crusade, refused to join the new organization, being distrustful of white leadership. I myself and most of the Niagara Movement group[2] were willing to join. The National Association for the Advancement of Colored People was formed, which without formal merger absorbed practically the whole membership of the Niagara Movement. With some hesitation I was asked to join the organization as Director of Publications and Research." (W. E. B. DuBois)[3]

---

[2] From 1905 through 1910, the Niagara Movement, a group of black intellectuals, called for full political, civil, and social rights. The Niagara Movement was the forerunner of the NAACP (National Association for the Advancement of Colored People).

[3] W. E. B. DuBois, *The Autobiography of W. E. B. DuBois* (New York: International Publishers, 1968), 254. © International Publishers Co., Inc. Used with permission.

CHAPTER REVIEW

- Explain the formal definition of *adjective*.
- Write three sentences, each using an adjective in a different position.
- Write a sentence in which a noun functions adjectivally. How can you prove that the noun is not an adjective?
- Write a sentence containing a present participle used adjectivally.
- Write a sentence containing a past participle used adjectivally.
- Write a sentence containing an infinitive used adjectivally.
- Write a sentence containing a prepositional phrase used adjectivally.

12

Adjectivals: Clauses

CHAPTER PREVIEW

- Looking back, you remember that clauses can fill noun positions in sentences and that clauses, like sentences, have either TN or MOD. Thus, in

  Dick knew *that Jane had played hooky.*

  the clause *that Jane had played hooky* is the object of the verb *knew*.

- Clauses can also modify nominals—hence, adjective clauses.

  Naughty children must be punished.

  Children *who are naughty* must be punished.

- This chapter will explain adjective clauses and the word classes that relate these clauses to the nominals that they modify:

  Definite relative pronouns

  The dog *that howled all night* is Spot.

  Definite relative adjectives

  Jane met the neighbor *whose cat terrified Spot.*

  Definite relative adverbs

  Dick remembers the time *when Jane swallowed the goldfish.*

DEFINITE RELATIVE PRONOUNS, ADJECTIVES, AND ADVERBS

Definite Relative Pronouns

In noun clauses, the pronouns that link the clause to a nominal are indefinite relatives; they do not gain their meaning (their semantic content) from other words in the sentence.

In adjective clauses, the pronouns that link the clause to a nominal are definite relatives, gaining their semantic content from other words to which they relate. They have antecedents, in other words. In the noun clause *who ate the last M&M*, the relative pronoun *who* has no definite reference:

Father knew *who ate the last M&M.*

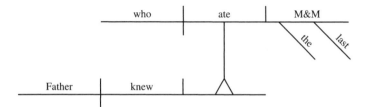

Figure 12.1   Reed-Kellogg diagram of *Father knew who ate the last M&M.*

But in the same clause used as an adjective, the relative pronoun *who* takes its meaning from its antecedent.

Father knew the child *who ate the last M&M.*

In this sentence, *who* and *the child* are semantic equivalents.

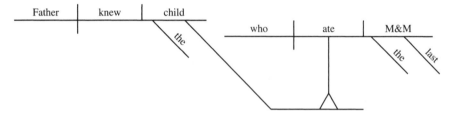

Figure 12.2   Reed-Kellogg diagram of *Father knew the child who ate the last M&M.*

The definite relative pronouns are:

We know *the woman who* obeyed the law now and then.

The driver whom the police arrested did not obey the law.

"I have not seen *a person who* loved virtue, or *one who* hated what was not virtuous. *He who* loved virtue would esteem nothing above it." (Confucius) [The antecedents are *a person, one,* and *he.*]

"In *men whom* men condemn as ill I find so much of goodness still, / In *men whom* men pronounce divine I find so much of sin and blot, / I do not dare to draw a line between the two, where God has not." (Joaquin Miller, 1841–1913) [The antecedents are *men* and *men.*]

The law, which keeps society safe, must be obeyed. [The antecedent is *law.*]

"*The business of eating, which* in common with a crisis or danger brings heterogeneous incompatibles comfortably together, was over and suddenly we were all now fallen apart." (Nadine Gordimer) [The antecedent is the nominal phrase *The business of eating.*]

"*Economies that* do not add new kinds of goods and services, but continue only to repeat old work, do not expand much nor do they, by definition, develop." (Jane Jacobs) [The antecedent is *economies.*]

THE DEFINITE RELATIVE PRONOUNS

who, whom, which, that

Sometimes *but* and *as* occur as definite relative pronouns:

The judge sentenced such felons <u>*as*</u> *appeared before him* to maximum sentences.

There was not a student <u>*but*</u> *hoped to graduate in June.*

These usages are rare. Do not confuse the coordinating conjunction *but* with *but* as relative pronoun, and distinguish *as* when it is a subordinating conjunction from *as* used as a relative pronoun:

As [subordinating conjunction] you slept, I did the dishes.

Functions of Definite Relative Pronouns

Within their own clauses, definite relative pronouns function just as do other nominals.

Subject

Dick is the lad <u>*who*</u> *sings in the choir.*

"Man is the only being <u>*who*</u> *feels himself to be alone* and the only one <u>*who*</u> *is searching for the Other.*" (Albert Camus) [<u>*who*</u> *feels himself to be alone* = <u>*being*</u> *feels himself to be alone;* <u>*who*</u> *is searching for the Other* = <u>*one*</u> *is searching for the Other*]

Direct Object

The choir sang the hymn <u>*that*</u> *Mother composed.* [<u>*that*</u> *Mother composed* = *Mother composed* <u>*the hymn*</u>]

"The last thing a woman will consent to discover in a man <u>*whom*</u> *she loves* or on whom she simply depends, is want of courage." (Joseph Conrad) [<u>*whom*</u> *she loves* = *she loves* <u>*a man.*</u> The *whom* in *on whom* she simply depends is, of course, object of a preposition. See below.]

Object of Preposition

Do you enjoy the food *of* <u>*which*</u> *you partake*? [*of* <u>*which*</u> *you partake* = *you partake of* <u>*the food*</u>]

"There is not a woman in the world *the possession of* <u>*whom*</u> *is as precious as that of the truths which she reveals to us by causing us to suffer.*" (Marcel Proust, 1871–1922) [*of* <u>*whom*</u> *is as precious.* . . . = *of* <u>*a woman*</u> *is as precious* . . . ; *which she reveals to us by causing us to suffer* is an adjective clause in which the relative *which* is the direct object]

Exercise 12.1

Find the definite relative pronouns in the following sentences.

1. Spot always guarded the bowl that contained his supper.
2. Jane gave the boy who lived next door his first kiss.
3. Dick bought the motorized scooter which he had saved for.
4. Father admired the woman whom the voters had elected.
5. "Strange new problems are being reported in the growing generations of children whose mothers were always there, driving them around, helping them with their homework—an inability to endure pain or discipline or pursue any self-sustained goal of any sort, a devastating boredom with life." (Betty Friedan)
6. "The yearning for an afterlife is the opposite of selfish: it is love and praise for the world that we are privileged, in this complex interval of light, to witness and experience." (John Updike)

Definite Relative Adjectives

The definite relative adjectives are *whose* and *which*.

In Chapter 10 we saw that indefinite relative adjectives can provide the syntactic connection between noun clauses and their frame clauses (page 146).

I know *whose* woods stand on the hill.

The noun clause *whose woods stand on the hill* is the object of the verb *know,* and, of course (to repeat a point), the indefinite relative adjective has no antecedent (i.e., no word or phrase from which it gains its meaning).

The definite relative adjective, on the other hand, has an antecedent, from which it gains its semantic value.

Mother is *the woman* <u>*whose*</u> *cakes are always burned.* [<u>*whose*</u> *cakes are always burned* = <u>*the woman's*</u> *cakes are always burned*]

"Here lies our sovereign lord the King, / _Whose promise_ none relies on; / He never said a foolish thing, / Nor ever did a wise one." (John Wilmot, Earl of Rochester, 1647–1680; written on the bedchamber door of Charles II) [_Whose promise none relies on_ = none relies on _the king's_ promise]

Exercise 12.2

Find the adjective clauses in the following sentences.

> **Examples**
>
> Shakespeare wrote plays that live through the ages.
>
> > _That live through the ages_ is an adjective clause modifying _plays. That_ is a definite relative pronoun.
>
> Joseph Conrad is a novelist whose works I enjoy.
>
> > The adjective clause _whose works I enjoy_ contains the definite relative adjective _whose._
>
> "It ain't those parts of the Bible that I can't understand that bother me, it's the parts that I do understand." (Mark Twain)
>
> > _that I can't understand_ modifies _parts of the Bible; that_ is a definite relative pronoun.
> >
> > _that bother me_ modifies _parts of the Bible that I can't understand; that_ is a definite relative pronoun.
> >
> > _that I do understand_ modifies _parts; that_ is a definite relative pronoun.

1. Everyone must find the vocation that is right for him or her.
2. Only the person whose life has helped others dies happy.
3. Is it failure of which you are afraid?
4. "A happy woman is one who has no cares at all; a cheerful woman is one who has cares but doesn't let them get her down." (Beverly Sills)
5. "Having a baby . . . brought home to me with real force the hopelessly unbalanced nature of a society which is organized solely for the needs of people without responsibility for children." (Angela Phillips, 1983)
6. "That man is little to be envied whose patriotism would not gain force upon the plain of Marathon, or whose piety would not grow warmer among the ruins of Iona." (Samuel Johnson)

7. "The age in which we live can only be characterized as one of barbarism." (Alva Myrdal)

8. "I am the kind of man who would never notice an oriole building a nest unless it came and built it in my hat in the hat room of the club." (Stephen Leacock)

9. "The classes that work least are those that wash most." (G. K. Chesterton)

10. "I don't care to belong to a club that accepts people like me as members." (Groucho Marx)

11. "He who has mastered any law in his private thoughts, is master to that extent of all men whose language he speaks." (Ralph Waldo Emerson)

12. "Conservative, *n*. A statesman who is enamored of existing evils, as distinguished from a liberal, who wishes to replace them with others." (Ambrose Bierce)

13. "Criticism is the art wherewith a critic tries to guess himself into a share of the artist's fame." (George Jean Nathan)

Definite Relative Adverbs

The definite relative adverbs are *where, when,* and *why.*

Pearl Harbor is *the place where World War II began.* [*where* relates to *the place*]

Christmas is *the time when everyone enjoys life.* [*when* relates to *the time*]

Dick and Jane make *the reason why children need discipline* obvious. [*why* relates to *the reason*]

These words are adverbs, they have antecedents, and they link dependent clauses to main clauses. Hence, they are definite relative adverbs.

DEFINITE RELATIVES

PRONOUNS
who, whom, which, that

ADJECTIVES
who, which

ADVERBS
where, when, why

FOR DISCUSSION: INFINITE SENTENCES

In Chapter 10, we saw that noun clause after noun clause can be added to a sentence, making it theoretically infinitely long. This is also the case with adjective clauses:

> This is the house *that Jack built.*
>
> This is the malt *that lay in the house* that Jack built.
>
> This is the rat *that ate the malt* that lay in the house that Jack built.
>
> This is the cat *that chased the rat* that ate the malt that lay in the house that Jack built.
>
> This is the dog *that worried the cat* that chased the rat that ate the malt that lay in the house that Jack built.

Make the following information into adjective clauses and add them, one after another, to the sentence above:

> A cow with a crumpled horn tosses the dog.
>
> A milkmaid all forlorn milks the cow with the crumpled horn.
>
> A man all tattered and torn woos the milkmaid all forlorn.
>
> A preacher all shaven and shorn marries the man all tattered and torn to the milkmaid all forlorn.

Exercise 12.3

Find the relative clauses in the following sentences and note the relative adverbs.

1. Greed is the reason why misers save their dough.
2. The day when Bill and Edna were married was cold and rainy.
3. Can you direct me to a place where I can find a good hamburger?
4. Explain the method how you did it? (Do you take this sentence to be grammatical? Explain.)
5. At the time when everyone was ready to go to the arena where the show was to be held, Reginald stated the argument why all should stay home.
6. "Know'st thou the land where the lemon trees bloom, / Where the gold orange glows in the deep thicket's gloom, / Where a wind ever soft from

the blue heaven blows, / And the groves are of laurel and myrtle and rose?" (Johann Wolfgang von Goethe)

7. "Oh, give me a home where the buffalo roam, / Where the deer and the antelope play, / Where seldom is heard a discouraging word / And the skies are not cloudy all day." (Anonymous)

8. "In order to progress, radio need only go backward, to the time when singing commercials were not allowed on news reports, when there was no middle commercial on a news report, when radio was rather proud, alert and fast." (Edward R. Murrow)

9. "If any man can show just cause, why they may not lawfully be joined together, let him now speak, or else hereafter forever hold his peace." (*The Book of Common Prayer,* 1928)

10. "There is a time of life somewhere between the sullen fugues of adolescence and the entrenchments of middle age when human nature becomes so absolutely absorbing one wants to be in the city constantly, even at the height of summer." (Edward Hoagland)

RESTRICTIVE AND NONRESTRICTIVE ADJECTIVE CLAUSES

Here is a sentence containing a restrictive adjective clause:

Students *who respect knowledge* do not cheat.

And here is a sentence containing a nonrestrictive adjective clause:

Students, *who do not cheat,* respect knowledge.

In paraphrase, the sentence containing the restrictive adjective clause means something like this:

Some students respect knowledge and some do not. The ones who respect knowledge don't cheat.

The clause restricts the group of students being referred to. On the other hand, the sentence containing the nonrestrictive relative clause means something like this:

All students respect knowledge, and no student cheats.

The great Mohandas K. Gandhi said,

Rights *that do not flow from duty well performed* are not worth having.

In other words, not all rights flow from duty well performed, and only those that do are worth having. That clause is restrictive.

In his biography of Samuel Johnson, James Boswell (1740–1795) wrote,

> I was before this time pretty well acquainted with Goldsmith, *who was one of the brightest ornaments of the Johnsonian circle.*

There was only one Oliver Goldsmith, and Boswell is giving information about him. If the adjective clause had been restrictive, the class "Goldsmith" would have included more than one person, and the clause would have singled out one of these:

> I was before this time pretty well acquainted with *the Goldsmith who was one of the brightest ornaments of the Johnsonian* circle (but I may or may not have known the other Goldsmiths).

In Chapter 8, we discussed close and loose apposition of nominals (pages 101–102), which are very similar to restrictive and nonrestrictive noun clauses:

Close Apposition of Nominal

> Tom *the manicurist* married Jane *the plumber.* [*The manicurist* renames *Tom,* and *the plumber* renames *Jane.*]

> "Our friend *the carpenter* spied us out: at least he was not my friend." (D. H. Lawrence) [*The carpenter* renames *our friend.*]

Restrictive Adjective Clauses

> The car *that I bought* was a lemon.

> "The world is made for people who aren't cursed with self-awareness." (Susan Sarandon) [Of all possible people, the restrictive adjective clause singles out only those *who aren't cursed with self-awareness.*]

Loose Apposition of Nominal

> Tom, *a manicurist by trade,* married Jane, *a plumber.* [The appositives do not merely rename, but give added information about.]

> "Thou art the Christ, *the Son of the living God.*" (Matthew 16:16) [*The Son of the living God* does not merely rename Christ, but gives added information about him.]

Nonrestrictive Adjective Clauses

> Tom's marriage, *which took place in Las Vegas,* was the greatest event of his life.

> "His [Herod's] son Antipater, d. 43 BC, was favored by Julius Caesar, *who made him* (c. 55 BC) *virtual ruler of all of Palestine.* The son of the second Antipater was Herod the Great, d. 4 BC, *who gave the family its name.*" (*The Concise Columbia Encyclopedia*) [*Who made him . . . virtual ruler of all Palestine* does not identify Caesar, but gives us information about him. The clause

who gave the family its name does not identify Herod, but provides information about him.]

Both close appositives and restrictive clauses imply that the item referred to is one of more than one; both loose appositives and nonrestrictive clauses imply that the item referred to is unique. Close appositives and restrictive clauses limit and identify; loose appositives and nonrestrictive clauses add information.

Exercise 12.4

Find the restrictive and nonrestrictive relative clauses in the following sentences and explain why these clauses are either restrictive or nonrestrictive. (Clauses other than adjective may be in the sentences.)

1. The class, which bored all of the students, was required for graduation.

2. The professor who taught the class was about to retire.

3. The dean said that the students, all of whom had cheated on the final, should be kicked out of the university.

4. Do you know the book that Alex checked out?

5. "Total loyalty is possible only when fidelity is emptied of all concrete content, from which changes of mind might naturally arise." (Hannah Arendt)

6. "Bore, *n.* A person who talks when you wish him to listen." (Ambrose Bierce)

7. "This has been due to cheap P. G. & E. power, which enables farmers to pump water from wells all over the valley." (*Time*)

8. "It's afterwards you realize that the feeling of happiness you had with a man didn't necessarily prove that you loved him." (Marguerite Duras)

9. "Love is an act of endless forgiveness, a tender look which becomes a habit." (Peter Ustinov)

CHALLENGER

Does the following sentence contain an adjective clause? If so, what is it? Where is the definite relative pronoun, adjective, or adverb?

The way students found the answers to the test is still a mystery.

USING GRAMMAR: RELATIVE CLAUSES

Relative clauses provide writers with useful stylistic options. For example, the following two sentences can be combined by inserting the second one into the first as a relative clause, with just a bit of rearranging of noun phrases:

Uncombined: Professor J. Melanogaster Druse was an expert on fruit flies. He had studied these insects for twenty-five years.

Combined: Professor J. Melanogaster Druse, who had studied fruit flies for twenty-five years, was an expert on these insects.

So which version is preferable? We could make such a judgment only if the sentences were in context and we had some idea of what the author wanted the passage to do. In the uncombined version, the information about the professor's expertise (he had studied fruit flies for twenty-five years), being isolated in its own sentence, is more emphatic than is the same information when it becomes part of the other sentence.

As a brief exercise in stylistics, rewrite the following examples. If the item contains two sentences, combine them, making one of them a relative clause. If the item consists of only one sentence, de-combine them, creating a two-sentence passage.

> **Examples**
> "Old age is an insult. It's like being smacked." (Lawrence Durrell)
>
> > Old age, which is like being smacked, is an insult.
>
> "We shape our buildings: thereafter they shape us." (Winston Churchill)
>
> > We shape our buildings, which thereafter shape us.
>
> "All God's children are not beautiful. Most of God's children are, in fact, barely presentable." (Fran Lebowitz)
>
> > All God's children, most of whom are, in fact, barely presentable, are not beautiful.

1. Dick sold his baseball cards to a dealer. The cards were valuable.

2. Jane, who seldom brushed her teeth, hated to visit the dentist.

3. Father wanted to restore his old Studebaker. He thought it might be worth a lot of money.

4. "A man's indebtedness . . . is not a virtue; his repayment is. Virtue begins when he dedicates himself actively to the job of gratitude." (Ruth Benedict)

5. "Obscenity is a moral concept in the verbal arsenal of the Establishment, which abuses the term by applying it, not to expressions of its own morality but to those of another." (Herbert Marcuse)

CLAUSES WITHIN CLAUSES

As we saw in Chapter 8 clauses can be embedded within clauses. For instance, here is a sentence in which an adjective clause is embedded within another adjective clause:

The lad *who wrote the poem that won the prize* said nothing.

The lad | who wrote the poem | that won the prize | said nothing

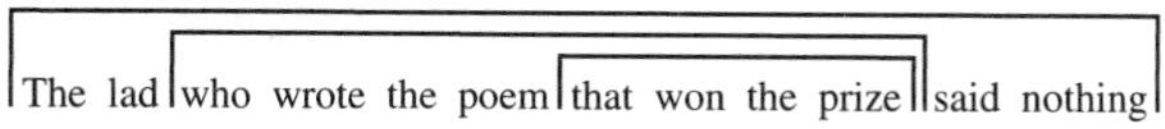

Figure 12.3 Constituent structure diagram of *The lad who wrote the poem that won the prize said nothing.*

Adjective clauses are frequently embedded in noun clauses, as in the following sentence:

The woman thought that *the man who dented her car was rude.*

The woman thought | that the man | who dented her car | was rude

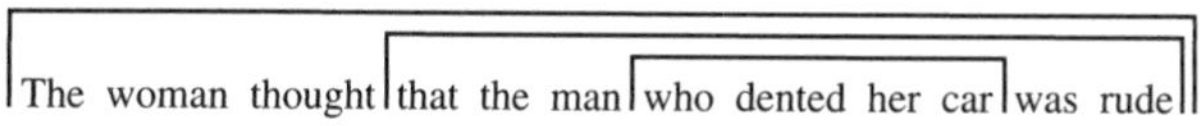

Figure 12.4 Constituent structure diagram of *The woman thought that the man who dented her car was rude.*

Deleting the Relative Pronoun

We will begin with an interesting but difficult exercise that will allow you to test your ability to analyze sentences and draw general conclusions about grammar from your analysis.

Exercise 12.5

The following sentence demonstrates that sometimes relative pronouns can be deleted without destroying grammaticality:

A girl whom we know won the tennis match.

A girl we know won the tennis match.

And the following sentence demonstrates that sometimes relative pronouns *cannot* be deleted without destroying grammaticality:

> The girl who won the tennis match sings in the choir.
>
> *The girl won the tennis match sings in the choir.

On the basis of the following examples, formulate the rule governing the deletion of definitive relative pronouns in sentences.

1. Bob knew who had borrowed the mower.

   *Bob knew had borrowed the mower.

2. Barbara resented the remark that Julie made.

   Barbara resented the remark Julie made.

3. Blatchford liked the man whom he gave one of his puppies.

   Blatchford liked the man he gave one of his puppies.

4. Billingsley admired the director from whom she had received a call.

   Billingsley admired the director she had received a call from.

5. Billy resented the name that the teacher had called him.

   Billy resented the name the teacher had called him.

6. Bultitude called the woman who was his accountant.

   *Bultitude called the woman was his accountant.

You guessed it! *If the definite relative pronoun is an object in its own clause, it can be deleted.* Now let's reexamine our six examples.

1. *Who* is the subject of the clause *who had borrowed the mower* and cannot be deleted.

2. *That* is the direct object of the verb *made* in *that Julie made* and thus can be deleted. [Julie made *that*.]

3. *Whom* is the indirect object in *whom he gave one of his puppies* and thus can be deleted. [He gave *whom* one of his puppies.]

4. *Whom* is the object of a preposition in *from whom she had received a call* and thus can be deleted. [She had received a call from *whom*.]

5. *Which* is the objective complement in *which the teacher had called him* and thus can be deleted. [The teacher called him *which*.]

6. *Who* is the subjective complement in *who was his accountant* and thus cannot be deleted. [His accountant was *who*.]

Reduced Clauses and Nonfinite Verbal Phrases

In many sentences, the adjective clause has been reduced or changed to leave a nonfinite verb or verbal phrase functioning adjectivally.

Present Participial Phrases

Let's work this through with an example sentence:

We saw a horse *running away with its rider.*

The phrase *running away with its rider* is made up of a nonfinite verb *running* and a prepositional phrase *with its rider.* The entire nonfinite verb phrase is functioning adjectivally; it is modifying the noun *horse.* We can think of a nonfinite verb phrase as originating in a clause with a finite verb:

We saw a horse *that was running away with its rider.*

By deleting the relative pronoun *that* and the auxiliary verb *was,* we end up with the nonfinite verb phrase.

We saw a horse ~~that was~~ running away with its rider.

U SING GRAMMAR: PRESENT PARTICIPIAL PHRASES

The following passage seems awkward and choppy:

"'I'd come back for just this dish,' said a friend. She was polishing off her *empanada de maduro* [a cheese-filled plantain turnover]. Another friend couldn't believe it cost only $1.75. She was running her finger through the last of the creamy sauce."

The actual passage, from a restaurant review in the *Los Angeles Times,* is much less awkward and choppy.

"'I'd come back for just this dish,' said a friend, polishing off her *empanada de maduro.* Another friend, running her finger through the last of the creamy sauce, couldn't believe it cost only $1.75."

The difference between the two versions is that the original uses present participial phrases to embed propositions within the sentences: *polishing off her empanada de maduro* and *running her finger through the last of the creamy sauce.*

Here are further examples of the usefulness of present participial constructions.

"Anyone _wishing_ to communicate with America should do so by e-mail, which has been specially invented for the purpose, _involving_ neither *physical proximity nor speech.*" (Auberon Waugh)

> "Knowledge is ancient error *reflecting on its youth*." (Francis Picabia)
>
> "The law is simply expediency *wearing a long white dress*." (Quentin Crisp)

As an exercise in style, combine the following pairs of sentences or coordinate clauses, transforming one of them into a present participial phrase.

1. The senator promised his constituents that he would vote to lower taxes. He was running for reelection.

2. Students spend many hours in the library. They are preparing to take the Graduate Record Examination.

3. The jet suddenly went into a dive. This terrified the passengers.

4. "In this unbelievable universe in which we live there are no absolutes. Even parallel lines, reaching into infinity, meet somewhere yonder." (Pearl S. Buck)

5. "A cruel story runs on wheels, and every hand oils the wheels as they run." (Ouida)

Past Participial Phrases

Past participial phrases can also function adjectivally.

Meat *left in the sun* will spoil.

The past participial phrase *left in the sun* is functioning adjectivally to modify the noun *meat*. We can think of this past participial phrase as having been derived from the adjective clause *that is left in the sun*. The words *that* and *is* have been deleted from the clause.

Meat ~~that is~~ left in the sun will spoil.

USING GRAMMAR: PAST PARTICIPIAL PHRASES

The following examples are, first, "decomposed" versions of the original sentences, followed by the originals with past participial phrases functioning adjectivally.

1a. A spirit of national masochism prevails. It is encouraged by an effete corps of impudent snobs who characterize themselves as intellectuals.

1b. "A spirit of national masochism prevails, *encouraged by an effete corps of impudent snobs who characterize themselves as intellectuals*." (Spiro T. Agnew)

> 2a. Undernourished intelligence becomes like the bloated belly of a starving child. It is swollen. It is filled with nothing the body can use.
>
> 2b. "Undernourished intelligence becomes like the bloated belly of a starving child: _swollen, filled_ with nothing the body can use." (Andrea Dworkin)
>
> 3a. Walpole was a minister. He was given by the King to the people. Pitt was a minister. He was given by the people to the King.
>
> 3b. "Walpole was a minister _given_ by the King to the people: Pitt was a minister _given_ by the people to the King." (Samuel Johnson)

Infinitive Phrases

Last, an infinitive (_to_ + verb) can function adjectivally. For example, in the sentence _She was baking a cake to take to the party,_ the infinitive phrase _to take to the party_ modifies the noun _the cake_ and is part of the noun phrase.

Here are more examples of infinitive phrases used adjectivally.

"The mind's passion is all for singling out. Obscurity has another tale _to tell._" (Adrienne Rich)

"An office party is not, as is sometimes supposed, the Managing Director's chance _to kiss the tea-girl._" (Katharine Whitehorn)

USING GRAMMAR: DANGLING PARTICIPLES

English teachers and editors often ask writers to revise sentences that contain dangling participles. For example:

Standing on one leg in the swamp, I saw the heron.

At first glance, the sentence creates a ridiculous picture: of someone standing on one leg in a swamp and watching a heron. Of course, our knowledge of the way the world works allows us to gain the meaning of the sentence: it's the heron that's standing on one leg, not the observer. The nonfinite participial (adjectival) phrase is an example of a dangling participle.

The problem is, of course, that the reader looks for the deleted subject of the verbal _standing_. The unexpressed question is "Who or what is standing on one leg in the swamp?" And the first nominal in the main clause usually supplies that information. Here are other examples of dangling participles:

Wanting to adopt a pet, the cat was chosen.

To become a chess master, the game must be an obsession with the player.

Administering vaccinations, Dick watched the nurse go from patient to patient.

PASSAGE FOR ANALYSIS

Find the adjective clauses in the following passage from *Taking the World in for Repairs* by Richard Selzer. What is the function of the definite relative pronouns, adjectives, or adverbs that link the relative clauses to the rest of the sentences?

It is May and, for whatever reason, I have been invited to serve on a jury that is to pass judgment on the final projects of a group of candidates for the degree of Master of Architecture at Yale University. But I am not an architect. I am a surgeon. Nor do I know the least thing about buildings, only that, like humans, they are testy, compliant, congenial, impertinent. That sort of thing. When I am faced with blueprints and drawings-to-scale, which are the lingua franca of architecture, something awful happens to the left half of my brain. It shrinks, or desiccates, collapses, and I fall into a state of torpor no less profound than that of the Andean hummingbird when it is confronted with mortal danger. Sadly, my acceptance of such an invitation by the Yale School of Architecture is just another example of the kind of imposturage of which otherwise honest men and women are capable.

The charge that has been given the students is to design and build an abattoir. It is understood that prior to this undertaking they have, as a class, made a field trip to a slaughterhouse in the New Haven area. For months afterwards they have been working toward this date. It is two days before we are all to meet for the examination in the seventh floor "pit" at the School of Architecture. But if I cannot know what they know of buildings, at least I can have seen what they have seen, so I telephone the owner of the slaughterhouse on the outskirts of New Haven, the one the students visited months before. "Yes," he says, "by all means." His voice is genial, welcoming.

It will be no great shock, I think. A surgeon has grown accustomed to primordial dramas, organic events involving flesh, blood, and violence. But before it is done this field trip to a slaughterhouse will have become for me a descent into Hades, a vision of life that perhaps it would have been better never to know.[1]

CHAPTER REVIEW

- Explain how a definite relative pronoun differs from an indefinite relative pronoun.

- Use each of the definite relative forms in a sentence.

- Definite relative pronouns function, within their own clauses, as either subject, direct object, object of preposition, or objective complement. Write four sentences, each of which contains a definite relative pronoun in one of the four functions.

- Write a sentence containing a definite relative adjective.

- Write a sentence containing a definite relative adverb.

---

[1] Richard Selzer, "How to Build a Slaughterhouse," in *Taking the World in for Repairs* (New York: Morrow, 1986), 115–116. Reprinted by permission of Georges Borchardt, Inc., for the author.

- In your own words, explain *restrictive* and *nonrestrictive* adjective clauses. Write two sentences, one containing a restrictive adjective clause and one containing a nonrestrictive adjective clause.

- Under what conditions can the relative pronoun be deleted? Write one sentence in which the relative can be deleted and one in which the relative cannot.

- What is meant by "reduced clauses and nonfinite participial phrases"? Write sentences to illustrate the principle.

Adverbials: Adverbs,
Prepositional Phrases, Nouns

CHAPTER PREVIEW

- Adverbials qualify verbs, nonfinite verbs, and adjectivals, answering questions about time, place, frequency, and manner:

  We played bridge *after supper./After supper,* we played bridge. [time]

  Father ate his supper *on the patio.* [place]

  Mother *often* cooks liver for supper./Mother cooks liver for supper *often.* [frequency]

  Jane ate the liver *reluctantly./Jane reluctantly* ate the liver. [manner]

  Adverbs are often movable within the sentence.

- In addition to adverbs, other forms that do not seem to have much in common function adverbially: Words such as *very* and *somewhat* are called *intensifiers* (or *qualifiers*) and are a subclass of adverbs.

  Spot was *very* stupid and was *somewhat* vicious.

  Intensifiers are not movable.

- Interrogative adverbs introduce questions: *When* did Jane last clean her room?

- Nouns and prepositional phrases can function adverbially.

DEFINITION OF ADVERBS

Notional Definition

As we have seen, the notional definition of verbs, nouns, and adjectives is not very helpful. However, the notional definition of adverbs is useful: "Adverbs relate to such meanings as time, place, manner, and degree."

  Time: Herbert will arrive *tomorrow.*

  Place: Hermione lives *there.*

Manner: Herkimer worked *diligently*.

Degree: Harold is *somewhat* fatigued.

Adverbs and adverbials also answer questions:

* Why?

  To find gold, thousands came to California in 1849. [The adverbial in this case is an infinitive phrase. See page 76.]

  Thousands came to California in 1849 *to find gold.*

* How often?

  Every Sunday Rev. Stackpoole conducts a service for the students. [The adverbial is a noun phrase. See page 94.]

  Rev. Stackpoole conducts a service for the students *every Sunday*.

* How much?

  They walked *for three miles*. [The adverbial is a prepositional phrase. See pages 213–214.]

  The fisherman came home *with five beautiful trout*.

Formal Definition

Because adverbs and adjectives have similar characteristics, the formal definition is minimally helpful. For example, the suffix *-ly* is typical of adverbs, but many adjectives also have that suffix.

Adverbs	Adjectives
walk *slowly*	*manly* action
talk *incomprehensibly*	*queenly* woman
unjustly accused	*portly* gentleman
win *easily*	*sickly* excuse

Both adverbs and adjectives can be compared: *slowly, more slowly, most slowly; manly, more manly, most manly*. However, *more manly* and *manlier* are equally acceptable forms whereas more *slowly* is preferable to *slowlier*.

The tortoise moved *more slowly* than the hare.

?The tortoise moved *slowlier* than the hare.

The snail moved *most slowly*.

?The snail moved *slowliest*.

Functional Definition

The common definition "Adverbs are words that modify verbs (think *quickly*) and adjectives (*devastatingly* beautiful), and other adverbs (*very* quickly)" is not awfully helpful. At least some adverbs are movable within their sentences:

>*Quickly* the thief pocketed the jewel and *madly* dashed from the house.

>The thief *quickly* pocketed the jewel and dashed *madly* from the house.

>The thief pocketed the jewel *quickly* and dashed from the house *madly*.

A frame sentence provides a useful test for adverbs but does not apply to adverbs (such as *very* or *awfully*) that modify other adverbs.

The NOUN	VERB	the NOUN _____.
The woman	drove	the car *expertly*.
The cat	ate	the food *greedily*.

Note that the adverb is not necessary for making a complete sentence.

>The woman drove the car.

>The cat ate the food.

TESTS FOR ADVERBIALS

MEANING

>Time: We leave *at eight.*

>Place: The family moved *to Utah.*

>Manner: The family moved *eagerly.*

>Degree: Marie is *pretty* sure she'll win the case.

>Why?: *To escape persecution,* the Christians hid in caves.

>How often?: *Every Monday* Norma washes the linen.

>How much?: They waited *for two hours.*

FORM

>*-ly* suffix: America will sure*ly* prevail.

>Comparison: quickly/more quickly/most quickly

SYNTAX

>Movability (for some): She ran *quickly* from the house./She ran from the house *quickly*.

TEST SENTENCE

>| The NOUN | VERB | the NOUN _____. |
>|----------|------|--------------------|
>| The girl | solved | the problem *easily*. |

Exercise 13.1

Find the adverbs in the following sentences and explain the tests that verify your choices.

Examples

People spend money freely.

Freely is an adverb. (1) It denotes manner. (2) It has the *-ly* suffix and can be compared (more freely, most freely). (3) It is movable (People *freely* spend money). (4) It fits the frame sentence.

"Today, age is needy and, as its powers decline, so does its income; but full-blooded youth has wealth as well as vigour." (Colin MacInness)

Today is an adverb. (1) It denotes time. (2) It is movable.

"What Romantic terminology called genius or talent or inspiration is nothing other than finding the right road empirically, following one's nose, taking short cuts." (Italo Calvino)

Empirically is an adverb. (1) It has the adverb suffix *-ly*. (2) It can be compared: more empirically, most empirically. (3) It is movable: finding the right road *empirically/empirically* finding the right road.

1. Marvin solved the puzzle cleverly.

2. We will go to Hollywood tomorrow.

3. Humorously the man in the ski mask told the bank teller to hand over the cash.

4. The train will pull out of the station soon.

5. "Colorless green ideas sleep furiously." (Noam Chomsky)

6. "Movements born in hatred very quickly take on the characteristics of the thing they oppose." (J. S. Habgood)

7. "Sharing food with another human being is an intimate act that should not be indulged in lightly." (M. F. K. Fisher)

8. "Across the narrow beach we flit, / One little sandpiper and I; / And fast I gather, bit by bit, / The scattered driftwood, bleached and dry." (Celia Thaxter, 1835–1894)

9. "In our world of big names, curiously, our true heroes tend to be anonymous." (Daniel Boorstin)

QUALIFIERS (INTENSIFIERS)

Qualifiers (sometimes called "intensifiers") are a subclass of adverbs or, depending on how one categorizes words in the language, a separate class altogether. However, since qualifiers typically show *degree,* we prefer to class them as adverbs.

The most common qualifier is *very.*

> I am *very* tired of your excuses.

> "The world breaks everyone and afterward many are strong at the broken places. But those that will not break it kills. It kills the *very* good and the *very* gentle and the *very* brave impartially. If you are none of these you can be sure that it will kill you too but there will be no special hurry." (Ernest Hemingway, *A Farewell to Arms*)

Other qualifiers are *somewhat, almost,* and *quite.*

Exercise 13.2

Find the qualifiers (intensifiers) in the following sentences.

1. The cat was very wild.

2. Even though the dog was vicious, it was extremely gentle with its owner.

3. When hiking on mountain trails, one must be somewhat careful.

4. The student's answer to the question almost completely overwhelmed the professor.

5. The trip to Madras totally wiped Hema out.

6. "The really great novel . . . tends to be the exact negative of its author's life." (André Maurois)

INTERROGATIVE ADVERBS

The interrogative adverbs are *where, when, how,* and *why.* (*Whence* and *whither* are now archaic and seldom used, but they do occur in writings dated earlier than about 1900.) Interrogative adverbs, of course, create interrogative sentences (also known as *wh-* questions), in which the subject and verb must be inverted.

> Declarative: Jane goes to school.

> Interrogative: Where does Jane go?

> "*Where* lies the land to which the ships would go?" (Arthur Hugh Clough, 1819–1861)

> *When* will the bull market end?

"How doth the little crocodile / Improve his shining tail, / And pour the waters of the Nile / On every golden scale!" (Lewis Carroll)

Why should we be in such desperate haste to succeed and in such desperate enterprises?" (Henry David Thoreau)

"Whence had they come, / The hand and lash that beat down frigid Rome?" (William Butler Yeats)

"Goosey goosey gander, / *Whither* shall I wander? / Upstairs and downstairs, / And in my lady's chamber; / There I met an old man who wouldn't say his prayers; / I took him by the left leg / And threw him down the stairs." (Anonymous nursery rhyme)

INTERROGATIVE ADVERBS

Where did you put the sugar bowl?

When does the semester end?

How did you prepare the salmon?

Why would anyone study for a final?

Whence came the law of supply and demand?

Whither goeth the sinner for eternity?

NOT

If we were to categorize all of the words in English strictly, one of the categories would contain a single item: the word *not*. We include *not* here because it is adverbial in its function; it qualifies the verb. As you know, it negates

- Sentences

  Dick could *not* find his shoes.

- Clauses

  Dick might attend a military academy, but Jane will *not* [attend a military academy].

- Phrases

  Dick likes to knit, *not* to crochet.

- Words

  Jane eats spinach, *not* cabbage.

When AUX in the sentence does not include MOD, *do* carries tense in negated sentences:

Mother disliked Spot. (AUX → PAST)

Mother *did not* dislike Spot. (PAST + *do* = *did*)

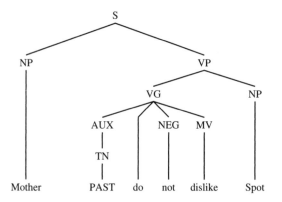

Figure 13.1   Branching tree diagram of *Mother did not dislike Spot.*

In Early Modern English, the verb could be negated directly, without the tense-carrying *do*:

They toil *not*, neither do they spin.

USING GRAMMAR: DOUBLE NEGATIVE

When two elements in a sentence are negated, the double negative results, and in English this is a nonstandard usage:

Informal: He doesn*'t* have *no* common sense.

Formal: He has *no* common sense./He hasn*'t* any common sense.

With some intensifiers such as *hardly*, negation creates a nonstandard usage:

Informal: William hasn*'t hardly* any money left.

Formal: William has hardly any money left.

ADVERBIALS

Nouns

Nouns often have an adverbial function. For example,

> When Jane saw the policeman, she went *quickly*.

> When Jane saw the policeman, she went *home*.

Out of context, the word *home* in the second sentence fills the criteria for nounhood: (1) it can be pluralized (home*s*); (2) it can take articles (*a* home, *the* home); (3) it can take the -'*s* possessive suffix (home'*s* owner). However, in *She went home,* the word *home* does not fill any of the nominal syntactic slots (subject, direct object, object of preposition, objective complement, subjective complement, appositive, vocative). Nor can *She went home* be made into a passive: **Home was gone by her.* In the sentence *She went home,* the word *home* fills an adverbial rather than a nominal slot. And it answers the adverbial question *where?*

Prepositional Phrases

As you have already surmised, prepositional phrases can and often do function adverbially.

- Time

  I like to drink tea *in the morning*.

  In the morning, I like to drink tea.

- Place

  You shop for bargains *at the swap meet*.

  At the swap meet, you shop for bargains.

- Manner

  He faces the future *with great joy*.

  With great joy, he faces the future.

Unlike the adverbial phrases in the sentences above, prepositional phrases that function adjectivally are not movable.

> The dean *of the college* is Dr. Cohen.

> **Of the college* the dean is Dr. Cohen.

> The teacher *with the most students* seems popular.

> **With the most students* the teacher seems popular.

> The student *from Poland* majored in physics.

> **From Poland* the student majored in physics.

Substituting a single-word adverb for the prepositional phrase is a handy, but not infallible, way to determine whether the phrase functions adverbially.

- Time

    I like to drink tea *in the morning.*

    I like to drink tea *early.*

- Place

    At the swap meet, you shop for bargains.

    There you shop for bargains

- Manner

    He faces the future *with great joy.*

    He faces the future *eagerly.*

Exercise 13.3

Find the adverbial prepositional phrases in the following sentences.

1. Marvin jogs in the morning.
2. After work, Marilyn works out at the gym.
3. The man from Georgia ate corn pone with great gusto.
4. From the evidence, we can draw the conclusion that Dillinger robbed the bank.
5. In several interesting cases the detective found that juvenile delinquents with long criminal records had swiped Twinkies from the market after school.
6. "God gives every bird his worm, but He does not throw it into the nest." (P. D. James)
7. "Always serve letters with a cup of tea and a footstool. Celebrate 'the reading' slowly. It is irreverent to read a letter fast." (Macrina Wiederkehr)
8. "The development of the national spirit in its present form leads into blind alleys." (Käthe Kollwitz)
9. "Media mystifications should not obfuscate a simple, perceivable fact: Black teenage girls do not create poverty by having babies. Quite the contrary, they have babies at such a young age precisely because they are poor—because they do not have the opportunity to acquire an education, because meaningful, well-paying jobs and creative forms of recreation are not accessible to them . . . because safe, effective means of contraception are not available to them." (Angela Davis)

PREPOSITIONS AND ADVERBS

Such words as *in, over,* and *up* can serve as either adverbs or prepositions. Prepositions (pages 213–215) link nouns and noun phrases to sentences and hence must be followed by nouns or noun phrases. Adverbs do not perform such a linking function and thus need not be followed by nouns or noun phrases.

Prepositions	Adverbs
The boy swam *in* the ocean.	The boy dived *in.*
The girl jumped *over* the fence.	The girl jumped *over.*
The man climbed *up* the ladder.	The man climbed *up.*

The words *in, over,* and *up* in these sentences do not fit the formal or syntactic definitions of adverbs, and many grammarians classify them as prepositions without objects.

CATEGORIES OF ADVERBS

SINGLE WORDS

Dick *cleverly* fooled Jane.

Dick fooled Jane *cleverly.*

Spot *quickly* wolfed down the steak.

QUALIFIERS (INTENSIFIERS)

Jane was *very* lucky.

Dick was *almost* ready.

INTERROGATIVES

Where did the day go?

When does the show start?

How can I make chocolate mousse?

Why does the beaver build a dam?

Whence came the Pilgrims?

Whither goest thou?

NOT

Father will *not* punish the children.

Mother did *not* cook supper.

NOUNS

Spot howled *day* and *night*.

PREPOSITIONAL PHRASES

At the game, we devour hotdogs.

We devour hotdogs *at the game*.

PREPOSITIONS AS ADVERBS

Dive right *in*.

Let Spot *out*.

Exercise 13.4

In the following sentences, find (a) the prepositions that can be used as adverbs and (b) the nouns that are used as adverbs.

1. Jane ran in, and Dick ran out.

2. After colliding with a bicycle, Spot crawled home.

3. "Go west, young man," said Horace Greeley.

4. The neighbors came over to share the seder.

5. My driver's license expires next year.

6. "You shoot me in a dream, you better wake up and apologize." (Harvey Keitel, as Mr. White in *Reservoir Dogs*)

7. "Drug misuse is not a disease, it is a decision, like the decision to step out in front of a moving car. You would call that not a disease but an error of judgment." (Philip K. Dick)

8. "It doesn't matter who you vote for, the government always gets in." (Graffito, London 1970)

9. "A foolish consistency is the hobgoblin of little minds, adored by little statesmen and philosophers and divines. With consistency a great soul has simply nothing to do. . . . Speak what you think today in hard words and tomorrow speak what tomorrow thinks in hard words again, though it contradict everything you said today." (Ralph Waldo Emerson)

10. "The contents of [Sitting Bull's] pockets were often emptied into the hands of small, ragged little boys, nor could he understand how so much wealth should go brushing by, unmindful of the poor." (Annie Oakley)

CHALLENGER

To each of the following sentences, add an adverbial prepositional phrase of the kind indicated in parentheses. Into how many sentence positions can you move each phrase without creating ambiguity or nonsense and without making the sentence so awkward as to be grammatically dubious?

Example

"You can tell a lot about a fellow's character by his way of eating jelly beans." (Ronald Reagan)

Through intelligent analysis, you can tell a lot about a fellow's character by his way of eating jelly beans.

You can, *through intelligent analysis,* tell a lot about a fellow's character by his way of eating jelly beans.

You can tell, *through intelligent analysis,* a lot about a fellow's character by his way of eating jelly beans.

You can tell a lot, *through intelligent analysis,* about a fellow's character by his way of eating jelly beans.

?You can tell a lot about a fellow's character by his way of eating jelly beans *through intelligent analysis.*

1. "Children's liberation is the next item on our civil rights shopping list." (Letty Cottin Pogrebin) [time]

2. "After all, crime is only a lefthanded form of human endeavor." (John Huston) [place]

3. "An alcoholic has been lightly defined as a man who drinks more than his own doctor." (Alvan L. Barach) [manner]

4. "Children's talent to endure stems from their ignorance of alternatives." (Maya Angelou) [frequency]

5. "I became a feminist as an alternative to becoming a masochist." (Sally Kempton) [time, place]

PASSAGE FOR ANALYSIS

In the following passage from *Table of Contents* by John McPhee, find the adverbials. Notice the variety and their positions in the sentences. Move them around and see how the passage changes.

Sue Cochran entered Radcliffe College in 1969, and after two years felt a need to go away and develop a sense of purpose. She went to work for a rural doctor. Her brother, her brother's wife, her sister, and her sister's husband were all on their way to becoming specialists in internal medicine. Her father, a teacher at Harvard Medical School, was a neonatologist—in her words, "a high-tech physician." The rural doctor was her great-aunt, who was scornful of specialists of every kind. For decades, the aunt had looked after a large part of the population around two mountain towns, and she passed along to her grandniece not only a sense of what Sue Cochran calls "the psychosocial input into physical illness" but also a desire to practice medicine in a rural area and to concentrate on prevention at least as much as cure. Of her medical siblings and siblings-in-law, she says now, "They think I'm flaky." She goes on to say, "The one who's the most supportive is my father, and even he thinks I'm pretty crazy."[1]

CHAPTER REVIEW

- Explain the notional definition of adverbs.
- Explain the formal definition of adverbs.
- Explain the functional definition of adverbs.
- What is an intensifier (qualifier)? Write a sentence containing one.
- Write three sentences, each containing a different interrogative adverb.
- Write a transitive sentence with a modal in AUX; then negate the sentence.
- Write a sentence in which AUX = PAST (without any other elements). Negate that sentence. What carries tense in the negative sentence?
- Write a sentence in which a noun functions adverbially.
- Write a sentence in which a prepositional phrase functions adverbially.
- Write a sentence in which a word that can function as a preposition is used adverbially.

---

[1] John McPhee, "Heirs of General Practice," in *Table of Contents* (New York: Farrar, Straus and Giroux, 1985), 76. Copyright © 1985 by John McPhee. Reprinted by permission of the publisher.

Adverbials: Clauses and Adverbial Conjunctions

CHAPTER PREVIEW

- Clauses can function as adverbials. In the following sentence, *yesterday* is an adverb of time:

  Yesterday Spot bit the letter carrier.

  And in the following sentence, the clause is an adverbial of time:

  When the mail came, Spot bit the letter carrier.

  Spot bit the letter carrier *when the mail came.*

- Adverbial clauses express ideas of time, cause and effect, and contrast and condition.

  After the family ate supper, they all chewed antacid tablets. [time]

  Since no one claimed the puppy, the children took it home as a companion for Spot. [cause and effect]

  Although the sky was cloudy, a warm breeze blew from the ocean. [contrast and condition]

- Adverbial clauses are movable. They can occur before or after the independent clause.

  After the ceremony ended, the bride and groom left for Niagara Falls.

  The bride and groom left for Niagara Falls *after the ceremony ended.*

- Conjunctive adverbs such as *however* or *moreover* are used in independent clauses and can be moved within the clause. A semicolon must be used when two independent clauses are joined with a conjunctive adverb.

  The stew was inedible; *however,* the pie was delicious.

  The stew was inedible; the pie, *however,* was delicious.

  The stew was inedible; the pie was delicious, *however.*

ADVERB CLAUSES

If you examine and think about the dependent clauses in the following sentences, you will discover an important principle about adverb clauses.

> *That rabbits multiply so fast* worries some people.
>
> *Worries some people *that rabbits multiply so fast.*
>
> *Worries *that rabbits multiply so fast* some people.
>
> People *who steal rabbits* don't care about the pets' owners.
>
> **Who steal rabbits* people don't care about the pets' owners.
>
> *People don't care about the pets' owners *who steal rabbits.*
>
> *If they know about crime,* detectives will catch the rabbit thief.
>
> Detectives, *if they know about crime,* will catch the rabbit thief.
>
> Detectives will, *if they know about crime,* catch the rabbit thief.
>
> Detectives will catch the rabbit thief *if they know about crime.*

As you undoubtedly know, *that rabbits multiply so fast* is a noun clause, and *who steal rabbits* is an adjective clause. *If they know about crime* is an adverb clause; unlike noun and adjective clauses, adverb clauses are usually movable.

Exercise 14.1

In the following passages, which clauses are adverbials? How do you know?

1. If wishes were fishes, we'd all have a fry.
2. The students gorged themselves on pizza after they had finished the test.
3. I relax, when I have spare moment, with a good book.
4. "Confront a man in his office with a nuclear alarm, and you have a documentary. If the news reaches him in his living room, you have a drama. If it catches him in the lavatory, the result is comedy." (Stanley Kubrick)

SUBORDINATING CONJUNCTIONS

Adverb clauses are introduced by subordinating conjunctions: *as, after, although, as if, as though, because, before, even though, except that, if, in order that, provided that, since, so that, that, till, unless, until, when, wherever, where, whereas, while.*

> *After the winter snow had melted,* George raked up the soggy leaves on his front lawn.
>
> *Although some did not believe Murgatroyd,* I had complete faith in his excuse.
>
> The fog begins to roll in *as night grows colder.*

The clerk ignored Milicent *as if she didn't exist.*

As though he had a billion dollars, Wallace traveled in the greatest luxury.

Everyone should have an ample supply of water on hand *because the inevitable earthquake will destroy the city's infrastructure.*

It is unwise to cross highways *before the walk signal appears.*

The future looks good *except that I lost all my money in Las Vegas.*

If winter comes, can spring be far behind?

In order that we can get reservations for the show, we'll stand in line all night.

I'll bring the sandwiches *provided you'll supply the drinks.*

Provided that Marsha brings the dessert, the picnic will be a success.

Why don't you buy some eggs *since you're going to the store anyway?*

So that everyone could hear, the speaker shouted loudly.

That sinners might be reformed, the preacher told of the horrors of hell.

I will persist in my belief *till hell freezes over.*

The business will grow *unless management commits serious errors.*

Until all citizens achieve equal rights, the nation is not a true democracy.

When the bell rings, the boxing match begins.

Marvin eats a Cadbury chocolate bar *whenever he feels downcast.*

Where there are no winners, there are also no losers.

Several folks bought the new gadget, *whereas no one knew how to use it.*

In Nevada, *wherever you look* you find beauty.

While everyone likes jazz, few really enjoy oboe solos.

Three tests will help you identify adverb clauses:

1. Like noun and adjective clauses, adverb clauses have either TN or MOD.

   In order that we can get reservations: AUX → MOD; *whereas* no one knew how to use it: AUX → PAST.

2. Unlike noun and adjective clauses, adverb clauses are usually movable:

   When the bell rings, the boxing match begins./The boxing match begins *when the bell rings.*

3. Single-word adverbs can be substituted for the clauses:

   I will persist in my belief *till hell freezes over.*/I will persist in my beliefs *forever.*

   The business will grow *unless management commits serious errors.*/The business will grow *steadily.*

   Until all citizens achieve equal rights, the nation is not a true democracy./ *Actually* the nation is not a true democracy.

Reed-Kellogg diagrams can help one visualize the syntax of adverb clauses, as in Figure 14.1, in which the clause is placed under the verb, showing the modification.

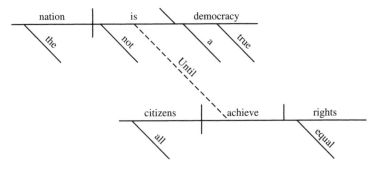

Figure 14.1   Reed-Kellogg diagram of *Until all citizens achieve equal rights, the nation is not a true democracy*. The broken line in the diagram, connecting the adverb clause with the verb, indicates the subordinating conjunction and explicitly shows the modification.

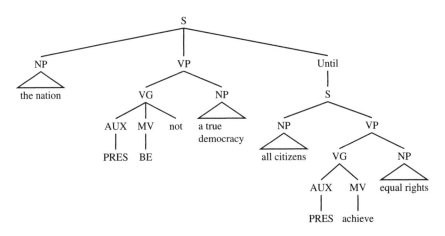

Figure 14.2   Branching tree diagram of *Until all citizens achieve equal rights, the nation is not a true democracy*. Note that the subordinating conjunction *until* is at the topmost node of the tree analyzing the adverb clause. This notation indicates that the sentence in question is subordinate.

Tests for Adverb Clauses

- Like other clauses, adverb clauses have either TN or MOD.
- Adverb clauses are usually movable.
- Single-word adverbs can be substituted for an adverb clause.

Exercise 14.2

Find the adverb clauses in the following sentences. (These sentences also contain noun and adjective clauses.)

1. Although the city council voted to rezone the neighborhood, no businesses seemed willing to move into the area.

2. Because the weather is so uncertain, I wonder if the game will be postponed.

3. The man who had asked whether the computer was fixed grew angry when the repairman said the job would take another week.

4. The territory looked barren, as though it had been swept by a giant bulldozer.

5. "When I'm good I'm very good, but when I'm bad I'm better." (Mae West)

6. "Life is something to do when you can't get to sleep." (Fran Lebowitz)

7. "City people try to buy time as a rule, when they can, whereas country people are prepared to kill time, although both try to cherish in their mind's eye the notion of a better life ahead." (Edward Hoagland)

REDUCED CLAUSES AND NONFINITE VERBS

A nonfinite phrase "reduced" from adverbial clauses consists of a subordinator and a nonfinite verb form (and its objects or modifiers):

While reading the newspaper, Peter was thinking about his work for the day.

We can think of this adverbial phrase as reduced from *while he was reading the newspaper.* In the adverbial phrase, the subject (*he*) and the auxiliary verb (*was*) have been deleted because they are identical to the subject and auxiliary in the main clause (sometimes called the frame sentence). More examples illustrate how this reduction can work with past participles as well:

When we were awakened by the wind, we ran to the window.

When awakened by the wind, we ran to the window.

Sometimes the adverbial subordinator is also deleted and the adverbial relationship has to be inferred:

Because I had a horrible headache, I went to the pharmacy.

Having a horrible headache, I went to the pharmacy.

Infinitives also form nonfinite adverbial modifiers:

You must study hard *to pass this course.*

To build this house, I will need to hire a fine carpenter.

Exercise 14.3

Find the nonfinite adverbial clauses and the finite adverbial clauses in the following sentences. Find and identify other clauses, too, for review.

1. Singing the song of the wind, we were on our way to the moon.

2. The Bach that she played at the concert is beautiful whether performed on harpsichord or piano.

3. Not having been aware of the power shortage, Milly installed thousands of Christmas lights.

4. Millard knew that he was doomed whether judged guilty or innocent.

5. When arriving late, audience members are asked to wait in the lobby until the end of the first act.

CHALLENGER

The following sentence contains a clause that can be interpreted in two ways. Explain.

No one can be sure of the future when world conditions are so unsettled.

CONJUNCTIVE ADVERBS

The forms most frequently used as conjunctive adverbs are

- Accordingly

    The recipe called for a liberal amount of garlic; *accordingly*, I chopped twelve buttons.

    "In the prologue (1–2) [to the book of Job], Satan obtains God's permission to test the 'upright man' Job; *accordingly*, all Job has is destroyed, and he is physically afflicted." (*The Concise Columbia Encyclopedia*)

- Besides

    Garlic helps control blood pressure; *besides,* it's delicious.

    "Executions, far from being useful examples to the survivors, have, I am persuaded, a quite contrary effect, by hardening the heart they ought to terrify. *Besides,* the fear of an ignominious death, I believe, never deterred anyone from the commission of a crime, because in committing it the mind is roused to activity about present circumstances." (Mary Wollstonecraft Godwin)

- Consequently

    The flight was canceled; *consequently,* I took a bus to Reno.

    "Man is an animal with primary instincts of survival. *Consequently,* his ingenuity has developed first and his soul afterwards. Thus the progress of science is far ahead of man's ethical behavior." (Charlie Chaplin)

- Hence

    The electricity was off; *hence,* the house was dark.

    "Two members of the Order should be sent together among the infidels to treat about the ransom of Christian slaves, and they are *hence* called Ransomers." (Alban Butler, 1710–1773)

- However

    It is too late for lunch; *however,* it is too early for supper.

    "I, too, dislike it. / Reading it, *however,* with a perfect contempt / for it, one discovers in / it, after all, a place for the genuine." (Marianne Moore, *Poetry*)

- Indeed

    Students don't resent homework; *indeed,* they enjoy it.

    "Art, it seems to me, should simplify. That, *indeed,* is very nearly the whole of the higher artistic process; finding what conventions of form and what detail one can do without and yet preserve the spirit of the whole—so that all that one has suppressed and cut away is there to the reader's consciousness as much as if it were in type on the page." (Willa Cather)

- Likewise

    Grandma was convicted of embezzlement; *likewise,* Grandpa swindled the power company.

    "The heaping together of paintings by Old Masters in museums is a catastrophe; *likewise,* a collection of a hundred Great Brains makes one big fathead." (Carl Jung, on committees)

- Moreover

    Rolls Royces are expensive; *moreover,* they're ugly.

    "The first law for the historian is that he shall never dare utter an untruth. The second is that he shall suppress nothing that is true. *Moreover,* there shall be no suspicion of partiality in his writing, or of malice." (Marcus Tullius Cicero)

- Nevertheless

    Roy hated horses; *nevertheless,* he played polo.

"For God created man to be immortal, and made him to be an image of his own eternity. *Nevertheless* through envy of the devil came death into the world." (Wisdom 2:23–24)

* Nonetheless

    Lobster was expensive; *nonetheless,* Betty ordered it.

    "What is called a high standard of living consists in considerable measure in arrangements for avoiding muscular energy, increasing sensual pleasure, and enhancing caloric intake beyond any conceivable nutritional requirement. *Nonetheless,* the belief that increased production is a worthy social goal is very nearly absolute." (John Kenneth Galbraith)

* Then

    Cholesterol clogs the arteries; I must, *then,* avoid cheese and butter.

    "Oh, that it were my chief delight / To do the things I ought! / *Then* let me try with all my might / To mind what I am taught." (Ann Taylor and Jane Taylor)

* Therefore

    Some television programs are worth watching; *therefore,* I sit in front of the set all evening, waiting for something worthwhile.

    "Nobody can deny but religion is a comfort to the distressed, a cordial to the sick, and sometimes a restraint on the wicked; *therefore,* whoever would laugh or argue it out of the world, without giving some equivalent for it, ought to be treated as a common enemy." (Lady Mary Wortley Montagu)

Conjunctive adverbs are often confused with subordinating conjunctions that begin adverbial clauses. These adverbial subordinators are not movable within their own clauses, but the clauses are movable:

Aerobic exercise is good *because* it strengthens the heart.

Because it strengthens the heart, aerobic exercise is good.

*It *because* strengthens the heart, aerobic exercise is good.

Conjunctive adverbs are movable within their clauses:

Aerobic exercise strengthens the heart; *therefore* Alvin lifts his hand to his mouth 100 times a day.

Aerobic exercise strengthens the heart; Alvin, *therefore,* lifts his hand to his mouth 100 times a day.

Aerobic exercise strengthens the heart; Alvin lifts his hand, *therefore,* to his mouth 100 times a day.

Aerobic exercise strengthens the heart; Alvin lifts his hand to his mouth 100 times a day *therefore.*

Be sure to differentiate the conjunctive adverb *however* from the intensifier *however*. For example, here is a sentence in which *however* is used a conjunctive adverb:

"The cross of the Legion of Honour has been conferred on me. *However,* few escape that distinction." (Mark Twain)

Notice that *however* is movable:

Few, *however,* escape that distinction

Few escape that distinction, *however.*

However, in the next sentence, *however,* is an intensifier. (In the next sentence, however, *however* is an intensifier.) It is not movable.

"Faithfulness to the truth of history involves far more than a research, *however* patient and scrupulous, into special facts." (Francis Parkman)

*Faithfulness to the truth of history involves far more than a research, patient *however* and scrupulous, into special facts.

Some adverbs that modify sentences (i.e., sentential adverbs) are similar to conjunctive adverbs:

Adverb	Conjunctive Adverb
Myrtle liked candy; *unfortunately,* she was diabetic.	Myrtle liked candy; *however,* she was diabetic.
She controlled her craving; *obviously,* she had an iron will.	She controlled her craving; *indeed,* she had an iron will.

Notice that the adverbs that modify whole sentences are derived from adjectives: unfortunate/unfortunate*ly*; obvious/obvious*ly*; sure/sure*ly*. Conjunctive adverbs are connectives, linking clauses. Sentential adverbs modify the clauses with which they occur. Compare the following two sentences:

Dick doesn't like cauliflower; *furthermore,* he detests broccoli.

Jane enjoys caviar; *regrettably,* her parents can't afford this treat.

The word *furthermore* in the first sentence allows readers to understand how the two clauses relate to one another. In the second sentence, the word *regrettably* adds meaning to the whole clause (in paraphrase, *It's too bad that her parents can't afford this treat*).

A word about punctuation with conjunctive adverbs. Usually, a semicolon separates clauses when the second one is introduced by a conjunctive adverb:

Marla loved root vegetables; *thus,* she often prepared rutabagas.

When the conjunctive adverb is not at the beginning of the clause, it is set off by comma.

Marla loved root vegetables; she, *thus,* often prepared rutabagas.

A period may be used to separate the clauses:

Parsnips are nutritious. *Nonetheless,* they are not popular.

Parsnips are nutritious. They, *nonetheless,* are not popular.

Parsnips are nutritious. They are not popular, *nonetheless.*

Conjunctive Adverbs

accordingly, besides, consequently, hence, however, indeed, likewise, moreover, nevertheless, nonetheless, then, therefore

- They are movable within their own clauses.
- They should not be confused with subordinating conjunctions.
- When conjunctive adverbs are used in independent clauses, the clause is set off with a semicolon:

  The student was late; however, the class had not started.

Using Grammar

Your knowledge of grammar will enable you to develop an explanation for the following sentence, in which the conjunctive adverb *hence* introduces a noun phrase, *the constant popularity of dogs,* not a clause (since the phrase has neither TN nor MOD).

"To his dog, every man is Napoleon; *hence* the constant popularity of dogs." (Aldous Huxley)

If we write a clause that means roughly the same as the noun phrase, we get *dogs are constantly popular.* To explain how the noun phrase relates to the equivalent clause, answer the following questions:

1. What was deleted from the clause?
2. What word was changed from an adjective to a noun?
3. What word was changed from an adverb to an adjective?
4. What word became the object of a preposition?

Exercise 14.4

Find the conjunctive adverbs in the following sentences.

1. The used auto was a real creampuff; however, it was too expensive.
2. The TV was broken; the children, nevertheless, sat staring at the blank screen.
3. Sloth is a cardinal sin. Moreover, slothful people do not get ahead in life.
4. Rain ruined the rhubarb. Farmer Graham, hence, had no rhubarb pie that spring.
5. Carrots improve the eyesight; besides, they taste good.
6. "I had thought on starting this composition, that I should define what humor means to me. However, every time I tried to, I had to go and lie down with a cold wet cloth on my head." (Dorothy Parker)
7. "The insight that peace is the end of war, and that therefore a war is preparation for peace, is at least as old as Aristotle, and the pretence [*sic*] that the aim of an armament race is to guard the peace is even older, namely as old as the discovery of propaganda lies." (Hannah Arendt)
8. "We are well advised to keep on nodding terms with the people we used to be, whether we find them attractive company or not. Otherwise they turn up unannounced and surprise us. . . ." (Joan Didion)
9. "What you have to do is enter the fiction of America, enter America as fiction. It is, indeed, on this fictive basis that it dominates the world." (Jean Baudrillard)
10. "The Church welcomes technological progress and receives it with love, for it is an indubitable fact that technological progress comes from God, and, therefore, can and must lead to Him." (Pope Pius XII)

PASSAGE FOR ANALYSIS

Find the adverbials in the following passage from *Moses* by Jonathan Kirsch. Remember that adverb clauses are often movable, and by the process of elimination you can determine that if a clause is not a nominal or an adjectival, it must be adverbial.

[T]he Bible does not always depict Moses as a well-behaved monotheist who toted the Ten Commandments wherever he went. Sometimes he shows up in the guise of a sorcerer with as many tricks up his sleeve as a lounge-act magician in Las Vegas. Armed with the so-called rod of God—a shepherd's wooden staff, but we might as well call it a magic wand—Moses worked all kinds of sideshow legerdemain to impress both Pharaoh and the ever dubious Israelites. First he announced the divine commandment against making graven images, then he fashioned a bronze snake that he used to cure snakebite. And he was equipped with the mysterious Urim and Thummim, a tool of divination that may have consisted of a pair of inscribed gemstones used to consult God for answers to yes-or-no questions, not unlike a Magic 8 Ball at a children's birthday party.

Some of his tricks, of course, are famous. Moses engaged in a contest of dueling magicians in the court of Pharaoh by casting his staff to the ground and turning it into a snake. The Bible, which sometimes allows us to glimpse a livelier sense of humor than do the sermonizers who came later, renders the encounter as a kind of burlesque: when Pharaoh's magicians matched Moses by turning *their* staffs into snakes, too, Moses' snake promptly devoured the other snakes as if to make the point that all magicians may be created equal, but some are more equal than others.

Other works of magic were not so playful. Moses used the rod of God to call down upon Egypt the Ten Plagues—boils, vermin, plague, pestilence, and so on. The sufferings of the Egyptians built to a bloodthirsty crescendo when God himself struck down the firstborn children of Egypt, rich and poor, guilty and innocent. And the Bible describes a magic-soaked ritual that Moses used to protect the Israelites when God ranged across Egypt in search of the firstborn—the blood of slaughtered lambs was smeared above the doorways of the slave dwellings to catch the attention of a deity who was so intent on killing that he might not have noticed if he had alighted on one of his Chosen People. Compared to the pristine and even prissy preachments of the Ten Commandments, the blood ritual strikes us as raw and primitive.[1]

CHAPTER REVIEW

- How can you differentiate adverb clauses from noun and adjective clauses?
- Write three sentences, each containing a different subordinating conjunction.
- Explain the term *reduced clause*.
- Write two sentences, each with a different reduced adverb clause.
- What are the characteristics of conjunctive adverbs? How do they differ from subordinating conjunctions?

---

[1] Jonathan Kirsch, *Moses: A life* (New York: Ballantine, 1998), 7–8. Copyright © 1998 by Jonathan Kirsch. Used by permission of the publisher, a division of Random House, Inc.

Prepositions and Particles: Review of Prepositional Phrases as Nominals, Adjectivals, and Adverbials

CHAPTER PREVIEW

- Prepositions are connectives. In

    Dick threw Jane *into* the pool.

    the preposition *into* connects the noun phrase *the pool* with the verb *threw*. As you already know, *into the pool* is an adverbial modifying the verb. Prepositional phrases can also function as nominals, adjectivals, and complements.

- Words we recognize as prepositions can also be analyzed as particles, adverbs, and adjectives when they are not followed by a noun phrase.

THE FUNCTIONS OF PREPOSITIONAL PHRASES: REVIEW

AS ADVERBIALS
As adverbials, prepositional phrases modify

- Verbs

    Lionel worked *until midnight.* [adverb of time]

    Leona lived *near the hospital.* [adverb of place]

    Lolita seduced Humbert *with her charms.* [adverb of manner]

- Adjectives

  Dale is free *with his money.* [*free* is the adjective being modified]

  Donna looks haggard *with cares.* [*haggard* is the adjective]

- Adverbs

  Luckily *for Leon,* the patrolman didn't give him a citation. [*luckily* is the adverb]

  It was done well *in part.* [*well* is the adverb]

  In part it was done well.

AS NOMINALS

Strangely enough, in a few usages, prepositional phrases can function as nominals.

  Over the fence is out. [subject of sentence]

  A tiger came out from *behind the bush.* [object of the preposition *from*]

AS ADJECTIVALS

Typically, prepositional phrases that are adjectival follow the nominals they modify:

  A good education is *money in the bank.* [*Money* is the nominal; *in the bank* is the prepositional phrase.]

  Friends of the Earth worry about global warming. [*Friends* is the nominal; *of the Earth* is the prepositional phrase.]

  Have you read *the letter from Arlen?* [*The letter* is the nominal; *from Arlen* is the prepositional phrase.]

PREPOSITIONAL PHRASES AS COMPLEMENTS

Subjective Complements

From our work with basic sentence types, you may recall that *be* verbs (*am, was, are, were, is, was, has been, have been*) and *linking* verbs, such as *seem* and *become,* are followed by structures called complements.

- Sentences with adjectives as subjective complements:

  The scene was *beautiful.*

  The answer seems *doubtful.*

- Sentences with prepositional phrases as subjective complements:

  The meal was *out of this world.*

  The price seems *in the ballpark.*

Objective Complements

And prepositional phrases can also be objective complements.

* Sentences with adjectives as objective complements:

    The neighbors found Spot *vicious.*

    Dick called Spot *gentle.*

* Sentences with prepositional phrases as objective complements:

    The neighbors found Spot *beyond endurance.*

    Dick thought Spot *out of sorts.*

Compare *The neighbors found Spot beyond endurance* with *The neighbors found Spot in the garage.* Why would we say that *beyond endurance* is adjectival while *in the garage* is not adjectival? A single-word adjective substitutes nicely for *beyond endurance:* The neighbors found Spot *intolerable.* However, the phrase *in the garage* answers the adverbial question regarding location: *where?* Thus, an adverb substitutes for *in the garage*: the neighbors found Spot *there.*

Exercise 15.1

Some of the following sentences contain prepositional phrases as complements, both subjective and objective. Identify these.

1. Your excuse is beyond belief.
2. Everyone considered the movie in bad taste.
3. Since the stock market is volatile, investors seem on edge.
4. The ride of Paul Revere has become a legend in America.
5. The necessity for caution grows with each passing day.
6. The proposal is under consideration.
7. My attorney deemed the settlement within reason.

PREPOSITIONS AND PARTICLES

Working inductively, see if you can articulate the rules that make the first three sentences in each group grammatical while the fourth sentence is not grammatical. Sentences 4, 8, and 12, that is, do not seem to be English sentences. Use the sentences below to help you figure out the rules.

1. The curator hung *up* the newly acquired Rembrandt.
2. The curator hung the newly acquired Rembrandt *up.*

3. The hiker climbed *up* the mountain.

4. *The hiker climbed the mountain *up*.

5. The tourist choked *down* the fried grasshoppers.

6. The tourist choked the fried grasshoppers *down*.

7. The inn was a good way *down* the road.

8. *The inn was a good way the road *down*.

9. The miser hated to pay *out* his money.

10. The miser hated to pay his money *out*.

11. The land is mountainous *out* West.

12. *The land is mountainous West *out*.

Some grammarians would argue that when words like *up, down,* and *out* are movable, they are not prepositions at all because prepositions are always heads of phrases. Other grammarians, wanting to make the descriptive rules more elegant and simple, would argue that they are prepositions and that prepositions are not always followed by noun phrases. In this book, we are going to make a distinction between prepositions and particles.

Just close your eyes and think *of* England. [*England* is a proper noun.]

The same *to* you, pal. [*You* is a personal pronoun.]

Thank you *for* helping me. [*Helping me* is a verbal phrase.]

Margot made do *with* what she earned. [*What she earned* is a noun clause.]

That's the plan *of* which I was thinking. [This sentence can be transformed thus: *That's the plan I was thinking of.* Even though the nominal *which* is deleted in the "surface" structure of the sentence, it is there in the meaning.]

When the prepositions are moved so that they follow the nominals, the sentences become ungrammatical.

*Just close your eyes and think England *of*.

*The same you *to,* pal.

*Thank you helping me *for*.

*Margot made do what she earned *with*.

When they are movable, words such as *up, down,* and *out* are particles, not prepositions. But there is one catch. (Isn't there always at least one catch?) If the verb to which the particle relates is intransitive (i.e., not followed by a nominal), the particle obviously cannot be moved.

The player gave *up* after the first game.

*The player gave after the first game *up*.

However, if you insert a nominal, making the sentence transitive, then the particle becomes movable.

The player gave *up* the challenge after the first game.

The player gave the challenge *up* after the first game.

(Once again, manipulating language—moving elements around, making substitutions, asking questions, and deducing patterns—is the best way to understand grammar.)

U SING GRAMMAR: PARTICLES

Uses of particles differ according to dialect. One example is a husband and wife, both of whom speak a dialect of might be called "broadcast standard," the dialect of Dan Rather and Peter Jennings.

The couple have been happily married for more than fifty years and have never solved this problem: Should one put things *away* or *up*?

Husband: Please put the dishes *away*.

Wife: Please put the dishes *up*.

Making the situation more difficult, the husband's beloved uncle always used *by*:

Put the dishes *by*.

In your own native "dialect," do you put things *away, up,* or *by*? Is the usage question really worth considering?

The good news is this. The husband and wife make this usage matter an ongoing subject of affectionate banter.

Wife: Dear, please put these pans *up*.

Husband: I can't put the pans *up*. The cupboard is *down*.

F OR DISCUSSION: PARTICLES

Both the following sentences are perfectly grammatical, but one is clearly preferable.

The baby threw up the mush his mother had forced down.

The baby threw the mush his mother had forced down up.

Explain why the first sentence is preferable to the second.

Exercise 15.2

Find the particles in the following sentences.

1. Spot threw up his dinner.

2. The knight threw down the gauntlet.

3. Get out the door before the smell knocks you out, but don't let the secret out.

4. "There is but one way left to save a classic: to give up revering him and use him for your own salvation." (José Ortega y Gasset)

5. "My love for you is mixed throughout my body . . . / So hurry to see your lady, / like a stallion on the track, / or like a falcon swooping down to its papyrus marsh. / Heaven sends down the love of her / as a flame falls in the hay." (*Love Songs of the New Kingdom,* c. 1550–1080 BCE)

6. "Polly, put the kettle on, / We'll all have tea." (Anonymous nursery rhyme)

7. "It takes far less courage to kill yourself than it takes to make yourself wake up one more time." (Judith Rossner)

8. "Most men who run down women are only running down a certain woman." (Rémy de Gourmont, 1858–1915)

9. "A passage is not plain English—still less is it good English—if we are obliged to read it twice to find out what it means." (Dorothy L. Sayers)

10. "If you get hung up on everybody else's hang-ups, then the whole world's going to be nothing more than one huge gallows." (Richard Brautigan)

11. "We test and then they test and we have to test again. And you build up until somebody uses them." (John F. Kennedy).

CHALLENGERS

Find the particles in the following sentences.

1. "I will not blot out his name out of the book of life." (Revelation 3:5)

2. "1992 is not a year I shall look back on with undiluted pleasure." (Elizabeth II)

CONGLOMERATE PREPOSITIONS

Phrases such as *in front of, alongside of, together with, in regard to,* and *out of* are often considered to be simple prepositions:

The mailbox stood *before* the house./The mailbox stood *in front of* the house.

The garage was *beside* the house./The garage was *alongside of* the house.

The meal consisted of liver and onions *with* bacon./The meal consisted of liver and onions *together with* bacon.

The auditor questioned me *about* my deductions./The auditor questioned me *in regard to* my deductions.

The children ran *from* the rain to the shelter of the porch./The children ran *out of* the rain to the shelter of the porch.

PREPOSITIONS AND OTHER FORMS AND FUNCTIONS

Adverbs

Many words such as *on, off, about,* and *around* function both as prepositions and as adverbs.

Not stopping for a breath, the senator spoke *on* and *on.* [adverb]

Not stopping for a breath, the senator spoke *on* the national budget. [preposition]

The little girl ran *off.* [adverb]

The little girl ran *off* the playground. [preposition]

Maurice looked *about.* [adverb]

Maurice looked *about* the room. [preposition]

Don't just hang *around.* [adverb]

Don't just hang *around* the video games. [preposition]

Many grammarians would not classify *on* in *The senator spoke on and on* or *off* in *The little girl ran off* and other such uses as adverbs, but would categorize them as prepositions without objects.

Adjectives

Some forms that usually function as prepositions can also function adjectivally. Here are some examples of prepositional forms that function adjectivally:

The sentences *above* provide perfect examples. [adjective]

The boxes *above* the door are heavy. [preposition]

The theater was *inside* the mall. [preposition]

The robbery was an *inside* job. [adjective]

The temperature was *below* normal. [preposition]

For an answer, look at the chart *below*. [adjective]

In these sentences, we see that *above, inside,* and *below* are functioning adjectivally because they are movable

The sentences *above*

The *above* sentences

and because they stand between nouns and determiners.

1. The mountain towered *above* the town.
2. *The mountain towered the town *above*.
3. *The mountain towered the *above* town.
4. The speaker points to a photo of a mountain in a travel book and says, "On our trip to Nevada, we saw the mountain *above*."
5. In a photo we saw the *above* mountain.
6. In a photo we saw *above* the mountain.

In a photo we saw above the mountain is perfectly grammatical, but it has a different meaning from *In a photo we saw the mountain above* or *In a photo we saw the above mountain*. Sentences 4 and 5 are synonymous; sentence 6 has a different meaning.

SAME WORD, DUAL FUNCTIONS

PARTICLE

Preposition: Get *off* the field.

Particle: When you leave, turn *off* the lights./When you leave, turn the lights *off*.

ADVERB

Preposition: The parade went *up* the street.

Adverb: The price of gasoline went *up*.

ADJECTIVE

Preposition: The cat crouched *in* the corner.

Adjective: We don't belong to the *in* crowd.

As

The word *as* is particularly troublesome. Sometimes it appears to be a preposition:

We prefer our salad *as* dessert.

We prefer our salad *with* mayonnaise.

However, prepositions always have nominals as objects:

Many go *on* cruises *to* Alaska *in* the summer.

Unlike prepositions, *as* can be followed by adjectivals.

The children thought of Kolya's act *as* very heroic.

Heroic is clearly an adjective: it has the suffix *-ic*; it can be compared

more heroic

most heroic

it is modified by the intensifier *very;* and it fits the adjectival sentence pattern

The heroic act was very heroic.

Often *as* appears as a word introducing the objective complement:

The committee named Melanie *as* chairperson.

In this case, the *as* can be deleted:

The committee named Melanie chairperson.

But in some sentences when *as* stands before the objective complement, it cannot be deleted:

Marvin knew Natasha *as* a friend.

*Marvin knew Natasha a friend.

And, of course, there is the common structure *as* + ADJECTIVE + *as* + NOUN:

The check was *as* good *as* gold.

My mood is *as* black *as* night.

The thunder was *as* loud *as* a cannon.

It seems to us that the best solution to the problem of *as* is to treat it as unique in the language and call it an *operator.*

Exercise 15.3

Find the prepositional phrases in the following sentences. Indicate whether they are adverbial or adjectival.

1. Mother went to the store every day.
2. Father enjoyed his wedge of pie.

3. Dick served time in reform school.

4. Jane enjoyed her weeks of freedom from Dick's teasing.

5. "There are only three things that can kill a farmer: lightning, rolling over in a tractor, and old age." (Bill Bryson)

6. "It has to be acknowledged that in capitalist society, with its herds of hippies, originality has become a sort of fringe benefit, a *mere* convention, accepted obsolescence, the Beatnik model being turned in for the Hippie model, as though strangely obedient to capitalist laws of marketing." (Mary McCarthy)

7. "All things truly wicked start from an innocence." (Ernest Hemingway)

8. "If men as individuals surrender to the call of their elementary instincts, avoiding pain and seeking satisfaction only for their own selves, the result for them all taken together must be a state of insecurity, of fear, and of promiscuous misery." (Albert Einstein)

9. "I'm not gonna change the way I look or the way I feel to conform to anything. I've always been a freak. So I've been a freak all my life and I have to live with that, you know. I'm one of those people." (John Lennon)

10. "Ultraliberalism today translates into whimpering isolationism in foreign policy, a mulish obstructionism in domestic policy, and pusillanimous pussyfooting on the critical issue of law and order." (Spiro T. Agnew)

11. "Loneliness is never more cruel than when it is felt in close propinquity with someone who has ceased to communicate." (Germaine Greer)

12. "The real trouble with the doctor image in America is that it has been grayed by the image of the doctor-as-businessman, the doctor-as-bureaucrat, the doctor as medical-robot, and the doctor as terrified-victim-of-malpractice-suits." (Shana Alexander)

13. "Hollywood is a place where people from Iowa mistake each other for stars." (Fred Allen)

PASSAGE FOR ANALYSIS

In the following passage from *Among the Lowest of the Dead* by David von Drehle, find the particles and the prepositional phrases. Identify the prepositional phrases as nominals, adjectivals, or adverbials. Note patterns in usage of prepositional phrases and think about the stylistic effects of this usage.

On Florida's death row, in the bloom time of spring, grimy windows beyond the cell bars glow with the beauty *of* freedom, and reminders of the living world stream through in a ceaseless taunt. Sunshine teases but doesn't touch the men *of* death row.

You can tell just by looking at them, especially the white guys, whose skin, after a couple of years, goes as pale and doughy as a lump *of* mozzarella. Blue skies and sunshine beyond the prison's windows set a caged man to thinking, and the inhabitants of the row live lives that don't bear much thinking about. There's the ugly past that got them to that place, the miserable present, and the future they don't want to come.

May 18, 1979, was a glorious spring morning, the sun warm in a Wedgwood sky: heaven to the tourists on their beach towels, paradise to the retirees along their neat green fairways. A postcard Florida day. Perhaps John Spenkelink reflected that morning on the fact that he would be inching up on parole—if only he had been smart enough to cop a plea. Some six years earlier, John Spenkelink had killed a man in a Tallahassee motel room. Spenkelink was a bad young man, but the victim was at least as bad, and arguably worse. The prosecutor and the *defense* attorney danced around the matter of a plea bargain to second-degree murder, and it seemed like a good solution to most everyone involved—except Spenkelink. He thought he could get on the witness stand, explain why he did it, and talk his way out of the whole lurid matter. As with most men on death row, thinking was not Spenkelink's strong suit.

What ultimately happened was that the prosecutor filed first-degree murder charges, and the jury convicted. The jurors thought so little of Spenkelink's testimony that they recommended the death penalty, and the judge took their advice. So there he sat on that fine May morning, taunted by the view, in a cell the size of a bathroom on Florida State Prison's R-wing, home to 134 condemned men, the largest death row population in America at the time. And there, at about 9 A.M., a guard arrived, handcuffed Spenkelink, and walked him to a nearby office to meet with the warden.

"I have something to read to you, John," said the warden, David Brierton. But the piece of paper on the warden's desk spoke for itself. It was bordered with a quarter inch of black. A death warrant is a curiously bloodless government document, one dry "whereas" after another, culminating in a businesslike "therefore." A busy governor signs thousands of papers much like it every year, so the black border was added to avoid confusion.[1]

CHAPTER REVIEW

- As adverbials, prepositional phrases modify verbs, adjectives, and adverbs. Write three sentences illustrating these functions of prepositional phrases.

- Write a sentence in which a prepositional phrase (as adjectival) modifies a noun phrase.

- Write a sentence in which a prepositional phrase is a subjective complement.

- Write a sentence in which a prepositional phrase is an objective complement.

- What test can you apply to determine whether a word such as *up*, *down*, or *over* is functioning as a preposition or as a particle?

---

[1] David von Drehle, *Among the Lowest of the Dead* (New York: Times Books/Random House, 1996), 3–5. Reprinted with permission by the author.

- Write a sentence in which *down* functions as a preposition.
- Write a sentence in which *up* functions as a particle.
- Write a sentence in which *up* functions as an adverb.
- Write a sentence in which *up* functions as a preposition.
- Write a sentence in which *after* functions as a preposition.
- Write a sentence in which *after* functions as an adjective.

16

Sentence Types, Clauses, Conjunctions

CHAPTER PREVIEW

- A sentence will consist of at least one independent clause.

  Kenneth writes essays.

- In addition to an independent clause, a sentence may have one or more dependent clauses that could not function as sentences by themselves.

DEPENDENT CLAUSE	INDEPENDENT CLAUSE	DEPENDENT CLAUSE
Because he is wise,	Kenneth writes essays	when he has time.

  *Because he is wise.

  *When he has time.

- Sentences can be described as

  Simple (one clause)

  Dogs chase cats.

  Compound (multiple independent clauses joined by coordinating conjunctions)

  Dogs chase cats, *and* cats chase mice.

  Complex (one independent and any number of dependent clauses joined by subordinating conjunction(s))

INDEPENDENT CLAUSE	DEPENDENT (ADVERBIAL) CLAUSE
Dogs chase cats	because canines hate felines.

  Compound-complex (at least two independent clauses and at least one dependent clause)

  Because canines hate felines, dogs chase cats, *and* cats avoid dogs.

- Conjunctions come in three forms:

  Subordinating conjunctions join dependent (or subordinate) clauses to main clauses.

Coordinating conjunctions join independent clauses or phrases.

Correlative conjunctions are pairs of words (e.g., *both . . . and*) that join phrases.

Sentences

A sentence may consist of any number of clauses, from 1 to infinity. When a sentence has more than one clause, the sentence can be described by the relationship of the clauses to each other.

SENTENCE TYPES ACCORDING TO CLAUSE STRUCTURE

Clauses that can stand alone are called *independent.* An independent clause may, of course, have a dependent clause as subject

> *That the weather turned cold in August* amazed the forecasters.

direct object

> The meteorologist knew *that August would be a cold month.*

object of preposition

> The forecaster was wrong about *what the weather would be.*

and so on. These embedded clauses are simply nominals and can be replaced by nouns or noun clusters

> *The weather* amazed the forecaster.

> The meteorologist knew *the climate.*

> The forecaster was wrong about *his prediction.*

An independent clause may also have compound verbs:

> The children *moaned and groaned;* Father *snored* all night and *kept* Mother awake.

Simple Sentences

Sentences consisting of one independent clause are called *simple,* a misleading term since a "simple" sentence can be hundreds of words long and contain any number of verbals (infinitives and present and past participles).

> Dick *flunked* his geography test. [The verb *flunked* is in past tense.]

> Jane *may* need braces. [The modal *may* anchors this sentence.]

"I never *hated* a man enough *to give* him his diamonds back." (Zsa Zsa Gabor) [The verb *hated* is in past tense; *to give* is a verbal.]

"The fame of heroes *owes* little to the extent of their conquests and all to the success of the tributes *paid* to them." (Jean Genet) [The verb *owes* is in present tense; *paid* is a past participle modifying the noun *tributes*.]

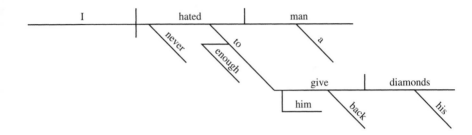

Figure 16.1   Reed-Kellogg diagram of *I never hated a man enough to give him his diamonds back*.

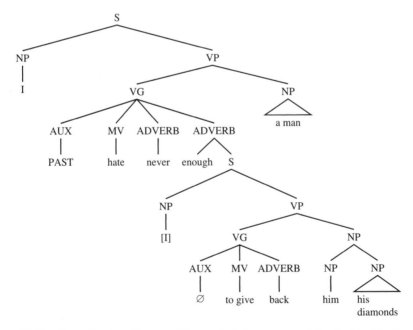

Figure 16.2   Branching tree diagram of *I never hated a man enough to give him his diamonds back*. In this sentence, *enough* is an adverb of degree modifying *hated,* and the infinite phrase *to give him his back diamonds* is an adverbial of degree modifying *enough*. The subject of the infinitive, the personal pronoun *I*, does not appear in the surface structure of the sentence. To indicate that the pronoun is present in meaning but not in the "surface" of the sentence, we have put the pronoun in brackets. Also, the null sign [∅] indicates that the phrase has no AUX.

Compound Sentences

Sentences that consist of two or more independent clauses are compound. Independent clauses are joined by coordinating conjunctions.

Coordinating Conjunctions

The coordinating conjunctions below are used in compound sentences.

Spot whined pitifully, *and* Father plugged his ears.

Jane swiped a buck from Mother's purse, *but* Dick ratted on her.

Mother will prepare dinner, *or* Father will starve.

Father did not tell Jane to mow the lawn, *nor* did he ask Dick to help.

Jane sulked and pouted, *for* she believed Father was unfair.

Father had ordered Jane to mow the lawn, *yet* he did not make her carry out the order.

Father had fallen asleep on the couch, *so* Jane went to the video arcade.

Coordinating Conjunctions

and, but, or, nor, for, yet, so

More examples:

"A right is not what someone gives you; it's what no one can take from you." (Ramsey Clark) [A semicolon joins the clauses, replacing a coordinating conjunction.]

"My imagination makes me human and makes me a fool; it gives me all the world and exiles me from it."[1] (Ursula K. Le Guin)

It goes without saying that each clause in a compound sentence can stand alone. Thus, the compound sentence *Mother coughs, Father sneezes, Dick whines, and Jane cries* could be written as *Mother coughs. Father sneezes. Dick whines. Jane cries.*

Unsurprisingly, there are a few tricky aspects in the use of coordinating conjunctions. For instance, compare the following two sentences:

The chairperson rapped his gavel, *but* the delegates would not settle down.

No one *but* Murgatroyd could operate the chain saw.

---

[1] In this compound sentence, *makes me a fool* is not a clause because the subject of the verb is *imagination; makes me human and makes me a fool* is a clause that contains coordinate verbs.

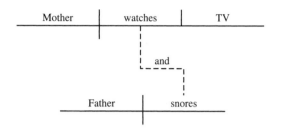

Figure 16.3   Reed-Kellogg diagram of *Mother watches TV, and Father snores*.

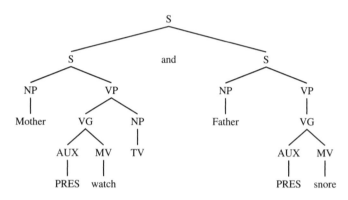

Figure 16.4   Branching tree diagram of *Mother watches TV, and Father snores*.

In the first sentence, the *but* is clearly a coordinating conjunction. Others can be substituted for but:

> The chairperson rapped his gavel, *for* the delegates would not settle down.

> The chairperson rapped his gavel, *yet* the delegates would not settle down.

On the other hand, in the second sentence we can substitute prepositions for *but*:

> No one *except* Murgatroyd could operate the chain saw.

> No one *besides* Murgatroyd could operate the chain saw.

In other words, *but* can be used as either a coordinating conjunction or as a preposition. The word *so* also has two functions. Compare the following two sentences:

> Wilbur couldn't solve the problem, *so* he just gave up.

> Wilbur had never been *so* angry.

In the first sentence, *so* is a coordinating conjunction, for which at least one other coordinating conjunction can be substituted:

> Wilbur couldn't solve the problem, *and* he just gave up.

In the second sentence, *so* is an intensifier.

>Wilbur had never been *very* angry.

>Wilbur had never been *pretty* angry.

U SING GRAMMAR: COMMA SPLICE (COMMA FAULT)

Grammar books often state the "rule" that either coordinating conjunctions or semicolons link independent clauses:

>Father knitted sweaters, *and* Mother did ceramics.

>Father knitted sweaters; Mother did ceramics.

However, writers often use commas to link independent clauses:

>"I don't believe in evil, I believe only in horror." (Isak Dinesen)

Many editors and grammarians consider this use of commas to be an error.

Clauses linked by commas are sometimes called *contact clauses;* the writer feels that the ideas expressed are so closely related that a semicolon or a conjunction would simply disrupt the semantic linkage.

However, when the clauses joined are fairly long or complicated, the so-called comma splice merely results in confusion for the reader.

>Confusing: Andrew Carnegie viewed himself as an intellectual, getting to know cultural lions such as Matthew Arnold, the great American industrialist also endowed libraries throughout the United States.

>Rewritten: Andrew Carnegies viewed himself as an intellectual, getting to know cultural lions such as Matthew Arnold. The great American industrialist also endowed libraries throughout the United States.

Complex Sentences

Sentences that consist of one independent clause and one dependent clause (noun, adjective, adverb) or more than one dependent clause are *complex.*

Dependent Clauses Once More

Let's review the types of dependent clause. The dependent clauses—noun, adjective, and adverb—are by definition parts of other clauses and conventionally do not stand alone.

Noun Clauses

In Chapter 10 you studied noun clauses.

- Sentence with noun clause as subject:

    What Dick told Jane revolted her.

- Sentence with noun clause as direct object:

    Dick knew *that Jane had skipped her piano lesson.*

- Sentence with noun clause as indirect object:

    Mother gave *whoever passed her on the street* the evil eye.

- Sentence with noun clause as object of preposition:

    Mother was afraid of *what she would find under Jane's bed.*

- Sentence with noun clause as subjective complement:

    Father's hobby was *whatever took no skill or exertion.*

- Sentence with noun clause as objective complement:

    Jane called Dick *what I can't repeat.*

Adjective Clauses

In Chapter 12 you studied adjective clauses.

- Adjective clause modifying a noun:

    The boy *who set the fire in the wastebasket* was (you guessed it!) Dick.

- Adjective clause modifying a pronoun:

    He *who hesitates* is lost.

Adverb Clauses

And in Chapter 13 you studied adverb clauses.

  When the time comes, everyone will be ready.

  Everyone will be ready *when the time comes.*

  "Why should I study arithmetic, *since I have a pocket calculator?*" asked Dick.

  "*Since I have a pocket calculator,* why should I study arithmetic?" asked Dick.

Noun, adjective, and adverb clauses are dependent; that is, they normally do not stand alone but are parts of a sentence. Adverbial clauses are introduced by subordinating conjunctions. Subordinating conjunctions are not movable within their own clauses, but the clauses are movable:

  Aerobic exercise is good *because* it strengthens the heart.

Because it strengthens the heart, aerobic exercise is good.

*It *because* strengthens the heart, aerobic exercise is good.

Examples of Complex Sentences

Dick thinks *that Jane believes all of his stories.* [noun clause]

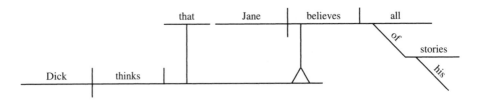

Figure 16.5   Reed-Kellogg diagram of *Dick thinks that Jane believes all of his stories.*

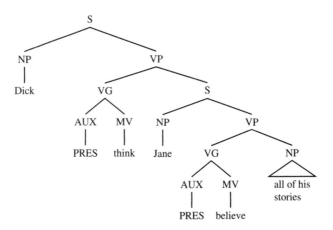

Figure 16.6   Branching tree diagram of *Dick thinks that Jane believes all of his stories.*

Father was the man *who terrified the neighborhood.* [adjective clause]

If Mother doesn't watch carefully, Spot will snatch food from the coffee table. [adverb clause]

"I have always believed that opera is a planet where the muses work together, join hands and celebrate all the arts." (Franco Zefferelli) [*That opera is a planet where the muses work together, join hands and celebrate all the arts* is a noun clause, the object of *believed; where the muses work together . . .* is an adjective clause modifying *planet.*]

I have always believed | that opera is a planet | where all the muses work together, join hands and celebrate all the arts

Figure 16.7   Constituent structure diagram of *I have always believed that opera is a planet where the muses work together, join hands and celebrate all the arts.*

Compound-Complex Sentences

Sentences that contain two or more independent clauses and one or more dependent clauses are compound-complex.

> Dick swiped some apples, and Jane ate the ones that he didn't want. [*Dick swiped some apples* and *Jane ate the ones* are independent clauses. *That he didn't want* is an adjective clause modifying *ones.*]

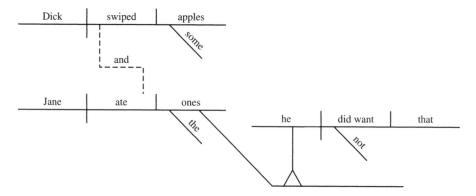

Figure 16.8   Reed-Kellogg diagram of *Dick swiped some apples, and Jane ate the ones that he didn't want.*

> "Those who talk about individuality the most are the ones who most object to deviation, and in a few years it may be the other way around." (Andy Warhol) [*Those . . . are the ones . . .* and *in a few years it may be the other way around* are independent clauses. *Who talk about individuality the most* is an adjective clause modifying *those. Who most object to deviation* is an adjective clause modifying *ones.*]

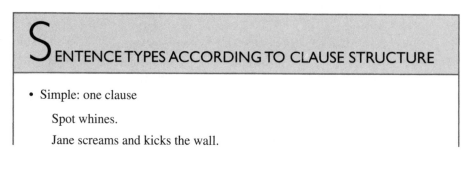

S ENTENCE TYPES ACCORDING TO CLAUSE STRUCTURE

• Simple: one clause

Spot whines.

Jane screams and kicks the wall.

- Complex: one independent clause (italicized) and one dependent clause (underlined), or more than one dependent clause

  Dick threw his oatmeal on the floor <u>because he was angry at Mother.</u>

  Children <u>who misbehave</u> *need discipline* <u>if they are to become decent adults.</u>

- Compound: two or more than two independent clauses

  Jane detests Dick, and *he hates her.*

  Mother tolerates Father, Spot ignores everyone, and *the children are simply oblivious.*

- Compound-complex: two or more independent clauses (italicized) and at least one dependent clause (underlined)

  Dick plucks the guitar, and *Jane tootles the flute* <u>while the neighbors plug their ears.</u>

  Dick turns up the volume on the TV <u>because the noise bothers the family;</u> *Jane,* <u>who has a headache,</u> *screams at Dick;* and *Father leaves the house* <u>when he can stand no more.</u>

Exercise 16.1

Classify the following sentences according to their clause structure as simple, compound, complex, or compound-complex.

1. The children stood quietly in line.
2. The band played, and the children sang.
3. When the concert was over, Dick and Jane were happy.
4. Jane knew that Dick hated music, for he had destroyed the Beatles albums that she had collected.
5. "I hate the word housewife; I don't like the word home-maker either. I want to be called—domestic goddess." (Roseanne Barr)
6. "Cleaning your house while your kids are still growing is like shoveling the walk before it stops snowing." (Phyllis Diller)
7. "I used to think that everything was just being funny but now I don't know. I mean, how can you tell?" (Andy Warhol)
8. "When your dreams tire, they go underground and out of kindness that's where they stay." (Libby Houston)

9. "We have so many people who can't see a fat man standing beside a thin one without coming to the conclusion that the fat man got that way by taking advantage of the thin one!" (Ronald Reagan)

10. "I was brought up to believe that the only thing worth doing was to add to the sum of accurate information in the world." (Margaret Mead)

USING GRAMMAR: SENTENCE VARIETY

Writers are often advised to vary their sentence structure, but this variation goes beyond the three basic sentence types—and, in fact, involves much of what you have learned from *The Uses of Grammar*. The following items demonstrate how structures that you have learned about can be used to create lucid, graceful sentences.

1. Norma tried to control her moral outrage. She blushed as she listened to a passage from Ray's latest tale.

   Trying to control her moral outrage, Norma blushed as she listened to a passage from Ray's latest tale.

2. Mary's romantic idyll had lifted Wesley's spirits. He poured himself a glass of wine.

   Mary's romantic idyll having lifted Wesley's spirits, he poured himself a glass of wine.

3. Mary writes poetry. She seeks inspiration among the flowers in her garden.

   To write poetry, Mary seeks inspiration among the flowers in her garden.

4. Beverly shows great promise as a writer. Her work doesn't offend Norma.

   Beverly, *whose work doesn't offend Norma,* shows great promise as a writer.

5. Jean took the leader to task. She is an astute woman.

   Jean, *an astute woman,* took the leader to task.

6. The group waited. They were expectant and nervous.

   The group, *expectant and nervous,* waited.

7. *In even the most respectable journals,* the stories about Harding were shocking.

The stories about Harding *in even the most respectable journals* were shocking.

The stories about Harding were shocking, *in even the most respectable journals.*

To demonstrate to yourself that you are a versatile prose stylist, try the following:

A. Write a sentence using a structure like that in item 1 above. (Example: *The puppy, <u>shivering in the cold</u>, whined and awaked the boy*).

B. Write a sentence using a structure like that in item 2 above.

C. Write a sentence using a structure like that in item 3 above.

D. Write a sentence using a structure like that in item 4 above.

E. Write a sentence using a structure like that in item 5 above.

F. Write a sentence using a structure like that in item 6 above.

G. Write a sentence using a structure like that in item 7 above.

And now for an even more vivid demonstration of your versatility:

1. Write a sentence using a 1 and a 2 from the numbered items above. (Example: *<u>Gasping for breath</u>, the hiker staggered toward the summit, <u>the cold having lowered the air pressure</u>.*)

2. Write a sentence using a 4 and a 6.

3. Write a sentence using a 3 and a 5.

4. Write a sentence using a 2 and a 7.

5. Write a sentence using a 1, a 3, and a 5.

USING GRAMMAR: BLOATED SENTENCES

We begin with a simple sentence, adding bloat seven times, for illustrative purposes.

- The glutton ate the pie.
- *Slobbering with greed,* the glutton ate the pie.

- Slobbering with greed, the glutton ate the pie, *whipped cream and spittle dribbling down his ample belly.*

- Slobbering with greed, the glutton, *to prove his prowess as a trencherman,* ate the pie, whipped cream and spittle dribbling down his ample belly.

- Slobbering with greed, the glutton, *whose bestial moans and belches offended all,* to prove his prowess as a trencherman, ate the pie, whipped cream and spittle dribbling down his ample belly.

- Slobbering with greed, *one of the cardinal sins,* the glutton, whose bestial moans and belches offended all, to prove his prowess as a trencherman, ate the pie, whipped cream and spittle dribbling down his ample belly.

- Slobbering with greed, one of the cardinal sins, the glutton, whose bestial moans and belches offended all, to prove his prowess as a trencherman, ate the pie, *sweet and gelatinous,* whipped cream and spittle dribbling down his ample belly.

- *In an absolutely disgusting display,* slobbering with greed, one of the cardinal sins, the glutton, whose bestial moans and belches offended all, to prove his prowess as a trencherman, ate the pie, sweet and gelatinous, whipped cream and spittle dribbling down his ample belly.

The sentences toward the end of the series become unwieldy and certainly wouldn't be composed by any competent writer (except, perhaps, as a joke). Find the subject and the verb in each case. Can you identify the other units in the sentence? Can you find another example sentence that is also unwieldy?

CONJUNCTIONS

Coordinating Conjunctions and Phrases

As we have seen beginning with the discussion of *and* in Chapter 2, the coordinating conjunctions connect phrases as well as independent clauses.

Spot and Father whined pitifully all night long. [connected noun phrases functioning as the subject]

Father will cook *dinner and breakfast* all week long. [connected noun phrases functioning as the object]

Jane turned over the job *to Father and Dick.* [connected objects of the preposition *to*]

Dick *moaned and complained* long into the night. [verbs connected with *and*]

Exercise 16.2

Find the coordinating conjunctions in the following sentences, and identify the units being coordinated.

1. Taking vitamins and minerals can improve your health.

2. Literacy consists of both reading and writing.

3. Eat, drink, and be merry, for tomorrow you die.

4. "Talk to me about the truth of religion and I'll listen gladly. Talk to me about the duty of religion and I'll listen submissively. But don't come talking to me about the consolations of religion or I shall suspect that you don't understand." (C. S. Lewis)

5. "The choice is whether you start sober and end drunk, or start drunk and end sober. The former is much better, both for the health of the speaker and for the effect on the audience." (Oswald Mosley)

6. "I reckon—when I count at all— / First—Poets—Then the Sun— / Then Summer—Then the Heaven of God— / And then—the List is done— / But, looking back—the First so seems / To Comprehend the Whole— / The Others look a needless Show— / So I write—Poets— All—" (Emily Dickinson)

7. "The Moving Finger writes; and, having writ, / Moves on: nor all your Piety nor Wit / Shall lure it back to cancel half a Line, / Nor all your Tears wash out a Word of it." (Edward FitzGerald, *The Rubáiyát of Omar Khayyám*)

8. "Call no man foe, but never love a stranger." (Stella Benson)

9. "We knew that winter had arrived, for our neighbors took in their patio umbrella." (Student)

10. "Talent is a misfortune, for on the one hand it entitles a person to neither merit nor respect, and on the other it lays on him tremendous responsibilities; he is like the honest steward who has to protect the treasure entrusted to his keeping without ever making use of it." (Andrey Tarkovsky)

11. "The trouble with tea is that originally it was quite a good drink. So a group of the most eminent British scientists put their heads together, and made complicated biological experiments to find a way of spoiling it." (George Mikes)

12. "My imagination longs to dash ahead and plan developments; but I have noticed that when things happen in one's imaginings, they never happen in one's life, so I am curbing myself." (Dodie Smith)

CHALLENGER

Find the coordinating conjunctions in the following poem and identify the units being coordinated. Explain why some words in the passage that are normally used as coordinating conjunctions are not so used in this passage, and identify how they are being used.

> *The night has a thousand eyes,*
> *And the day but one;*
> *Yet the light of the bright world dies*
> *With the dying sun.*
> *The mind has a thousand eyes,*
> *And the heart but one;*
> *Yet the light of a whole life dies*
> *When love is done.*
> *—Francis William Bourdillon*

U SING GRAMMAR: PARALLELISM AND COORDINATING CONJUNCTIONS

When coordinated elements in a sentence are not the same grammatically, the sentence is not parallel.

Not parallel: Dick likes to watch *Romper Room* on TV and eating caramel popcorn.

Parallel: Dick likes to watch *Romper Room* on TV and to eat caramel popcorn./Dick likes to watch *Romper Room* on TV and eat caramel popcorn.

In the unparallel sentence, an infinitive phrase (*to watch* Romper Room *on TV*) is coordinated with a participial phrase (*eating caramel popcorn*), destroying balance in the sentence.

Unparallel: Americans, who are passionate about football and with their devotion to baseball, spend a good part of each week viewing spots on TV.

Parallel: Americans, who are passionate about football and who are devoted to baseball, spend a good part of each week viewing sports on TV./ Americans, with their passion for football and their devotion to baseball, spend a good part of each week viewing sports on TV.

In the unparallel sentence, a clause (*who are passionate about football*) is coordinated with a prepositional phrase (*with their devotion to baseball*). In the first revision, clauses are coordinated (*who are passionate about football* and *who are devoted to baseball*); in the second revision, noun phrases as objects of the preposition *with* are coordinated (*their passion for football* and *their devotion to baseball*).

Correlative Conjunctions

Some conjunctions come in pairs:

> *Both* Dick *and* Jane watched TV all day Saturday.

> The programs were *not* educational *but* trashy.

> They were *either* violent *or* pornographic.

> They were *neither* intelligent *nor* amusing.

Correlative conjunctions can join any sentence elements. For example:

- Nouns

  > Both *the teachers* and *the counselors* thought Dick and Jane would come to no good.

- Adjectives

  > The children were neither *courteous* nor *obedient.*

- Adverbs

  > The children planned their capers both *diabolically* and *cleverly.*

- Prepositional phrases

  > They plotted not only *with great care* but also *in detail.*

- Clauses

  > They suspected either *that Mother was secretly watching them* or *that Father would discover the bomb in the shed.*

U SING GRAMMAR: CORRELATIVE CONJUNCTIONS

In formal English, the words, phrases, or clauses following correlative conjunctions must be of the same grammatical form. For example, if a nominal follows *either,* a nominal must also follow *or.*

> Informal: *Either* the dog [noun] has run away *or* is hiding [verb group] in the garage.

Formal: The dog *either* <u>has run away</u> [verb group] *or* <u>is hiding</u> [verb group] in the garage.

Informal: The classroom was *both* <u>stuffy</u> [adjective] *and* <u>it was smelly</u> [clause].

Formal: The classroom was *both* <u>stuffy</u> [adjective] *and* <u>smelly</u> [adjective].

CONJUNCTIONS

SUBORDINATING
as, after, although, as, as if, as though, because, before, even though, except that, if, in order that, provided that, since, so that, that, till, unless, until, when, whenever, where, whereas, wherever, while

CONJUNCTIVE ADVERBS
accordingly, besides, consequently, hence, however, indeed, likewise, moreover, nevertheless, nonetheless, otherwise, then, therefore

COORDINATING
and, but, or, nor, for, yet, so

CORRELATIVE
both . . . and, not . . . but, either . . . or, neither . . . nor

USING GRAMMAR: RUN-ON SENTENCES

The term *run-on sentence* describes problems of several types: often it is synonymous with comma splice; at other times it refers to a sentence that runs on and on, the elements pasted together with coordinators or subordinators. The third type of run-on is not a grammar error, per se. The sentence may be awkward or difficult to read, but nothing is technically wrong with the punctuation. (The bloated sentence on pages 236–237 is an example.) Finally, the term *run-on* can mean "fused sentence," an error in which two or more independent clauses are not separated by a comma, period, or semicolon.

Fused sentence: The noise of helicopters and planes flying sightseers over the Grand Canyon has become a serious problem the National Park Service has tried to restrict such flights.

> Corrected: The noise of helicopters and planes flying sightseers over the Grand Canyon has become a serious problem. The National Park Service has tried to restrict such flights.
>
> Whereas writers often use comma splices for stylistic effects, fused sentences have no stylistic value and simply confuse and frustrate readers.

Exercise 16.3

Find the prepositions, particles, adverbial prepositional phrases, adjectival prepositional phrases, conglomerate prepositions, subordinating conjunctions, coordinating conjunctions, conjunctive adverbs, and correlative conjunctions in the following sentences.

1. In May, Norma Nell has much to say.
2. Norman vowed never to give up the struggle.
3. The fun of the game is playing, not winning.
4. The old car stood in front of the house for months.
5. Because gasoline is so expensive, the family canceled their plans.
6. Everyone was disappointed, but such is life.
7. No one volunteered to clean up the mess, yet the smell was horrific.
8. The hero chose a haircut, for a duel might be dangerous.
9. The day was cloudy and cold; however, the tourists enjoyed the sights in Rome.
10. They neither complained about the weather nor growled about the high prices.
11. "The difference between our decadence and the Russians' is that while theirs is brutal, ours is apathetic." (James Thurber)
12. "Deconstruction . . . insists not that truth is illusory but that it is institutional." (Terry Eagleton)
13. "If the federal government had been around when the Creator was putting His hand to this state, Indiana wouldn't be here. It'd still be waiting for an environmental impact statement." (Ronald Reagan)
14. "If you have formed the habit of checking on every new diet that comes along, you will find that, mercifully, they all blur together, leaving you with only one definite piece of information: french-fried potatoes are out." (Jean Kerr)
15. "When my mother had to get dinner for eight she'd just make enough for sixteen and only serve half." (Gracie Allen)

16. "People like watching people who make mistakes, but they prefer watching a man who survives his mistakes. . . . The so-called rebel figures are not popular because they're rebels, but because they've made mistakes and got over them." (David Bowie)

17. "Both men and woman are fallible. The difference is, women know it." (Eleanor Bron)

18. "Virtue is simply happiness, and happiness is a by-product of function. You are happy when you are functioning." (William Burroughs)

19. "I find it interesting that the meanest life, the poorest existence, is attributed to God's will, but as human beings become more affluent, as their living standard and style begin to ascend the material scale, God descends the scale of responsibility at a commensurate speed." (Maya Angelou)

EXPLETIVE *IT* AND *THERE*

It

Now a penultimate concern about sentences. To understand syntax, one must differentiate *it, it, it,* and *it,* for even though they are identical in form, they serve quite different functions. One function is nominal, as pronoun.

The children bought a kitten. *It* was skinny, flea-bitten, and vicious.

In this example, *it* is coreferential with *kitten* (means the same as "kitten"). But what about the next three uses of *it*?

It is raining.

It is Mother.

It is difficult to understand Father.

Impersonal *It*

The *It* in *It is raining* has no reference, simply filling the "subject slot" in the sentence. We would not say, for instance, **The sky is raining* or **The clouds are raining,* and we also would not say **is raining* or **rains.* Impersonal *it* satisfies the grammatical need, in English, for a subject.

Situation *It*

The *It* in *It is Mother* does "point to" a referent, *Mother.* But note the strangeness of the following:

Who belched just now?   *She was Mother.

What caused the turmoil?   *He was Dick.

When the grammatical context does not provide information necessary to determine gender or number of the referent, situation *it* supplies the bridge to the referent. Here are further examples:

> *It* was Dick who made the fudge.
>
> *It's* Uncle George and Aunt Mary.
>
> Was *it* Spot?

Expletive *It*

The sentence *It is difficult to understand Father* can be transformed into *To understand Father is difficult*. Like the impersonal *it* and situation *it*, expletive *it* fills the subject slot in the sentence and often makes sentences easier for readers to process. For example, think about the following:

> That Mother thinks that Father believes that Jane is horrid is odd.
>
> It is odd that Mother thinks that Father believes that Jane is horrid.

In a way, *odd* is the most important word in each sentence, the nucleus around which the other sentence elements are organized. Until readers have the organizational pivot, they cannot make sense of the propositions (the embedded clauses). In the first sentence, the pivotal *odd* is the last word; in the second sentence, with expletive *it*, the pivotal *odd* is up front, enabling the reader to organize the propositions in the sentence.

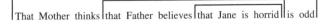

Figure 16.9   Constituent structure diagram of *That Mother thinks that Father believes that Jane is horrid is odd.*

Figure 16.10   Constituent structure diagram of *It is odd that Mother thinks that Father believes that Jane is horrid.*

Exercise 16.4

In the following sentences, identify each *it* as a personal pronoun or as impersonal, situation, or expletive.

1. It was Dick who dropped the vase on the floor.

2. It is very cold outside today.

3. It is hard to save money.

4. It had seemed strange for Jane to believe it was too hot to roller skate.

5. When it is raining, it is difficult to mow the grass.

6. "The worst thing about movies is, no matter how far you can go, when it comes to violence you are wearing a pair of handcuffs that novelists don't wear." (Quentin Tarantino)

7. "I misremember who first was cruel enough to nurture the cocktail party into life. But perhaps it would be not too much to say, in fact it would be not enough to say, that it was not worth the trouble." (Dorothy Parker)

8. "A State in the grip of neo-colonialism is not master of its own destiny. It is this factor which makes neo-colonialism such a serious threat to world peace." (Kwame Nkrumah)

9. "It made me gladsome to be getting some education, it being like a big window opening." (Mary Webb)

10. "It is the function of a liberal university not to give right answers, but to ask right questions." (Cynthia Ozick)

Expletive *There*

And now the last point about sentences, the use of *there* as a "slot filler," the so-called expletive *there*. In a sentence such as *There are many reasons for hope,* expletive *there,* like expletive *it,* fills the subject slot. Whereas sentences with expletive *it* can easily be transformed (It is amazing that Dick passed his algebra class./That Dick passed his algebra class is amazing.), sentences with expletive *there* cannot be thus transformed:

There are good reasons for exercising./*Good reasons for exercising are there.

The expletive and adverbial forms of *there* are easy to differentiate. Expletive *there* is always in the subject position of its clause; adverbial *there* is never in the subject position.

- Expletive *there*

   There seem to be many problems in life.

   Many people think *there* are good reasons for saving money.

   There are many people who think *there* are good reasons for saving money.

- Adverbial *there*

   The new dishes are *there*.

   Where are the old shoes? *There* they are. [The subject of the sentence is not *there,* but *they*.]

Exercise 16.5

Identify expletive *there* in the following sentences.

1. "There is the guilt all soldiers feel for having broken the taboo against killing, a guilt as old as war itself." (Philip Caputo)

2. "Would you go out there and win one for the Gipper?" (Ronald Reagan)

3. "There often seems to be a playfulness to wise people, as if either their equanimity has its source in this playfulness or the playfulness flows from the equanimity. . . ." (Edward Hoagland)

4. "We are volcanoes. When we women offer our experience as our truth, as human truth, all the maps change. There are new mountains." (Ursula K. Le Guin)

5. "There is no female Mozart because there is no female Jack the Ripper." (Camille Paglia)

6. "Where the whole man is involved there is no work. Work begins with the division of labor." (Marshall McLuhan)

7. "Washington is a very easy city for you to forget where you came from and why you got there in the first place." (Harry S. Truman)

8. "So much of our lives is given over to the consideration of our imperfections that there is no time to improve our imaginary virtues." (Edward Dahlberg)

9. "There must be a reason why some people can afford to live well. They must have worked for it. I only feel angry when I see waste. When I see people throwing away things that we could use." (Mother Teresa)

U SING GRAMMAR: PERIODIC AND LOOSE CONSTRUCTIONS

A periodic construction is one in which modifiers are placed toward the front of the clause or sentence:

> *Before going to bed,* many people have a glass of warm milk.

> *Because warm milk soothes the nerves,* many people drink it at bedtime.

> *Wanting to enjoy a good night's sleep,* Albert drank a glass of warm milk.

A loose construction is one in which modifiers are placed at the end of the clause or sentence.

> Many people have a glass of warm milk *before going to bed.*

Many people drink warm milk at bedtime *because it soothes the nerves.*

Albert drank a glass of warm milk, *wanting to enjoy a good night's sleep.*

As we have seen, adverb clauses are often movable within sentences:

> "*If you watch a game,* it's fun. *If you play it,* it's recreation. *If you work at it,* it's golf." (Bob Hope)

> It's fun *if you watch a game.* It's recreation *if you play it.* It's golf *if you work at it.*

From this example, we can see that placement of the adverb clauses determines emphasis in the sentences. The last position in a sentence generally gains more emphasis and is more important than other positions. Thus, in the original version by Bob Hope, the nominals *fun, recreation,* and *golf* receive the emphasis; in the rewrite, that emphasis has shifted to the adverbial clauses, which qualify the predications in the main clauses.

Which version is better? That, of course, is a nonsense question, for the answer depends on the effect that the writer (or speaker) was trying to achieve.

Move the modifiers in the following sentences and discuss how emphasis is affected by the move. Note also the instances in which moving the modifier creates awkwardness.

1. "At 50, everyone has the face he deserves." (George Orwell)

2. "If you join government, calmly make your contribution and move on." (Peggy Noonan)

3. "Women have face lifts in a society in which women without them appear to vanish from sight." (Naomi Wolf)

4. "The ones we choose to love become our anchor when the hawser of the blood tie [is] hacked, or frays." (Tony Harrison)

5. "Repudiating the virtues of your world, criminals hopelessly agree to organize a forbidden universe." (Jean Genet)

6. "No one can terrorize a whole nation, unless we are all accomplices." (Edward R. Murrow)

7. "When two people marry they become in the eyes of the law one person, and that one person is the husband!" (Shana Alexander)

8. "One becomes aware in France, after having lived in America, that sex pervades the air." (Henry Miller)

9. "Every time a woman makes herself laugh at her husband's often-told jokes she betrays him." (Germaine Greer) [Hint: *every time = when*]

PASSAGE FOR ANALYSIS

1. Can you explain the structure of the second sentence in Shelley's "Ozymandias"? Why have we included "My name is Ozymandias, king of kings: Look on my works, ye Mighty, and despair!" as components of the second sentence rather than setting them apart as simple sentences?

2. Do you find any verbal modifiers (present or past participles or infinitives) in the sentences? Where?

3. Explain why you think that some stylistic features of the poem are effective or ineffective (variation in sentence structure and length, word choice, figures of speech such as metaphor and simile).

Ozymandias

(1) I met a traveller from an antique land
Who said: Two vast and trunkless legs of stone
Stand in the desert . . . (2) Near them, on the sand,
Half sunk, a shattered visage lies, whose frown,
And wrinkled lip, and sneer of cold command,
Tell that its sculptor well those passions read
Which yet survive, stamped on these lifeless things,
The hand that mocked them, and the heart that fed:
And on the pedestal these words appear:
"My name is Ozymandias, king of kings:
Look on my works, ye Mighty, and despair!"
(3) Nothing beside remains. (4) Round the decay
Of that Colossal wreck, boundless and bare
The lone and level sands stretch far away.

CHALLENGER

Take a piece of your own writing (anything—a letter, a term paper, a poem, an essay, etc.) and analyze its style. What could you say about the style of this piece of your writing? Do you think your style is consistent in this genre?

CHAPTER REVIEW

- Define *simple sentence*. Write a simple sentence.
- Define *compound sentence*. Write a compound sentence.

- Define *complex sentence.* Write a complex sentence.
- Define *compound-complex sentence.* Write a compound-complex sentence.
- What are the functions of coordinating conjunctions?
- What are *correlative conjunctions*? Write a sentence containing correlative conjunctions.

17

Using Grammar

In writing this book, we have discovered that nearly everything associated with the word *grammar* provokes anxiety. Some people worry about their own grammar (and the possibility for error). Others self-righteously judge everyone else's grammar. Some express concern that immigrants are learning standard English grammar slowly or poorly and that they are contributing to social problems: in the opinion of the American Immigration Control Foundation, nonnative speakers "create countries within our own . . . take jobs and social services from our poorest citizens. . . . Expand our welfare rolls."[1] In addition, many social and educational ills are blamed on the fact that in the United States grammar study has been virtually absent from the public school curriculum for the last twenty years.

In this vein, many students who dislike studying grammar actually come to the conclusion that if they had nevertheless studied it earlier in their lives, they would now be more successful at school, at work, or even in social relationships. This is magical thinking. Unfortunately, all too often students who have been taught prescriptive grammar have not gained an understanding of grammar as usage. Those who know (or think they know) the rules of traditional prescriptive grammar frequently become martinets, giving friends advice about their language and correcting errors that do not even really exist.

F OR DISCUSSION

Return to the "For Discussion" box in Chapter 1, page 2, about using grammar as part of the writing process. Now that you have had time to reflect on your use of grammar, how has your opinion changed? (Or has there been no change?) Do you use grammatical knowledge? If your answer is yes, how do you use it? If no, why?

In finishing this book, we will want to examine what grammar study can and cannot do. Knowledge of grammar must be contextualized and must be examined. Only when members of the multilingual society that is America understand the contradictions in

---

[1] Bruce Horner and John Trimbur, "English Only and U.S. Composition," *College Composition and Communication* 53, no. 4 (2002): 609.

what people believe and do with grammar will conflicts over language be defused and productive uses of grammar begin.

SO, WHAT ABOUT ERROR?

We will begin with questions about error, knowing that our later topics such as diversity and dialect are interconnected with our anxieties about error. In the preceding chapters, we discussed prescriptive grammar rules and what violations of these rules may entail. If, for example, you make many mistakes with capital letters, you may be judged uneducated or just generally incompetent. Such errors are easily fixed, particularly because they often show up only in printed text and can be corrected through the process of learning to edit one's prose. We call these errors "point-at-ables" because the places in which they occur can be pointed at. Such errors are then picked out of sentences, fixed, and inserted back into sentences, usually without rearranging other words or phrases. Point-at-ables generally do not require a complete revision of the sentence. To edit for these problems, a lot of grammar terminology or complex analysis is unnecessary.

P OINT-AT-ABLES

Apostrophes

Capital letters

Commas

Pronoun forms

Reference/agreement with pronouns

Sentence boundaries and punctuation accompanying them: periods, semicolons

Subject-verb agreement

The rules for these forms may vary, depending on the dialect of English being considered. For example, in Standard Edited Academic English (SEAE) this sentence would be grammatical: *He goes to the store.* However, in African American Vernacular English (AAVE), the correct verb form would be *go: He go to the store.*

What Are Other Types of Error? What Are Their Sources?

Error generally does not result from laziness or stubbornness—that is, a refusal to learn. In many ways, errors are inevitable. When language learners stop making errors, they stop learning. As learners of both first and second languages, adults and children alike share learning processes that create error: learners may omit an element that is mandatory because they are trying to simplify a rule. They may overgeneralize by applying a rule in a context where it does not belong. (By "rule," we mean the concept that a learner has, not "rule" in the sense of a statement found in a grammar book.) The learner might, for example, overgeneralize and develop a rule that says "Put -ed on the end of the verb for the past tense." This rule, of course, does not take irregular verbs into account, and would produce forms such as *comed* and *goed,* which are obviously in error. In addition, second-language learners may transfer rules (or the absence of rules) from their first language. For example, the lack of determiners preceding nouns in Japanese may lead Japanese speakers learning English to omit determiners.

Native speaker of Japanese learning English: Mary enjoyed cake I baked.

Native speaker of English: Mary enjoyed *the* cake I baked.

The term *interlanguage* was coined to refer to the system of rules that learners develop while they are learning a language. This system of rules, however, is faulty; it contains erroneous as well as correct forms. Interlanguage rule systems are very unstable. That is their nature. Sometimes a learner appears to be making steady progress, learning for example, the word *went* as the past tense of *go.* Later, the learner may appear to regress by producing the form *goed* instead of *went.* In actuality, the learner may have used *went* as an isolated bit of knowledge, without having learned the rule for past tense regular verbs. Then, when the learner has incorporated the past tense regular rule, she may overgeneralize for a time (applying -ed everywhere) until she learns that irregular verbs exist and that *go* is one of them. Of course, we do not mean to suggest that the rules are spelled out quite like this in the learner's head.

Important Concepts

Interlanguage

Omission

Overgeneralization

Simplification

Transfer [applicable particularly to second-language acquisition]

For Discussion

Parents of a young child are extremely distressed because the boy has begun to produce the form *amn't:*

I *amn't* hungry.

> I *amn't* going to bed.
>
> They think the boy has lost the ability to learn correct English. They are partic-
> ularly worried because their son used to say "I am not hungry," which they view
> as even more correct than "I'm not hungry," with the contraction. What could
> you say to these parents to allay their fears and clear up their confusion about
> language acquisition?

How *are* the rules spelled out in learners' heads? Are they formulated much like
the rules of a grammar book? Do learners have a conscious rule for inserting *do* to
make questions or negatives? We don't know exactly how rules are represented in our
brains, especially the more or less tacit ones of which we are unaware. Linguist Noam
Chomsky has argued that we are all born with a set of general guidelines for language.
These guidelines he calls "principles." Because the brains of all human beings are
equipped for language, we do not have to be explicitly taught everything about the lan-
guage(s) we speak. But this ability to acquire language appears to decline with age.
(The debate about the differences in child and adult language acquisition is summa-
rized at the companion website.) However, because some language learning processes
are universal, language learners go through similar sequences of development, whether
they are children or adults learning first or second languages. For example, negation
(see Chapter 7) is acquired in a series of stages that begins with inaccurate placement
of the negative *no* (*No touch that*) and ends with the correct insertion of an auxiliary to
support the negative *not* (*Don't touch that*).

What Can Be Done to Help Learners with Language Acquisition and Error?

Is the language acquisition process completely "natural"? Does correction help? Do
grammar lessons help? What is necessary? What is useful?

Error Correction

Children learning their first language appear to go through necessary stages in acquiring the grammar and sound systems of their respective native languages. Correcting
their errors does not help, nor do explicit lessons in the language. Obviously, children
need to have input in their language to learn it. But all children leading "normal" lives
receive this input; parents and other adults do not need to do anything special for children to learn language. Error will mostly (if not entirely) disappear as children acquire
their first language.

Adults lose some and retain much of their inborn language-learning capabilities.
They are generally worse than children at acquiring nativelike pronunciation in a second language, but clearly they have some advantages in language learning. They are
more mature cognitively and emotionally and have more world knowledge, which
helps them to learn languages. Understanding and using grammar terms and analysis
can also be of help to adults.

The results on error correction are very mixed, even for adults. Research has shown that much error correction is inconsistent and even wrong. For error correction to help the learner, the correction must be clear and consistent and perfectly adjusted to fit with the learner's stage of language acquisition. (More easily said than done!) For example, if the learner is not using any determiners at all, error correction will be useless if it meticulously differentiates between *the* used for a definite noun (the tiger = one specific tiger) and *the* used for a generic category (the tiger = the species as a whole). The learner would not be at a stage to use this very particular rule. Another problem with error correction arises when some adults try to simplify what they say. To avoid making mistakes, they avoid complex constructions. They may not be making any errors because they do not want to be corrected. However, they must make errors and use new language forms if they are ever to acquire these forms.

For DISCUSSION

Do you ever avoid language forms as a means of avoiding the possibility of error? What are the forms you avoid? Try to figure out what you avoid, and then learn the correct forms through discussion with your class and use of this book.

Form-Focused Instruction

While elaborate analysis of grammatical terminology and sentence parsing may not speed up second-language learning or enable first-language writers to produce graceful, error-free prose, some instruction can make correct forms salient for learners. In what has been called "form-focused instruction," rather than necessarily using grammar terminology or explicating grammar rules, the teacher may instead simply point out errors and model new and correct language forms for the learner.[2]

CHALLENGER

If you were to try form-focused instruction with a group of students, what could you do? How could you draw learners' attention to correct or incorrect forms in their own speech and in the language they hear or read without embarrassing them or discouraging them from trying to use this grammar? Think of a specific group of students you might be working with and imagine some teaching strategies.

---

[2] M. Pienemann, "Is Language Teachable?" *Applied Linguistics* 10, no. 1 (1989): 52–79.

Errors, Acquisition, Motivation, and Identity

We began by asserting that learners do not speak and write incorrectly because they are lazy or stubborn. But we need to complicate the picture slightly. Learners are motivated to change their language for many reasons: extrinsic rewards such as a job or a grade in a class or intrinsic ones such as identifying with the people who use the language forms they are trying to learn.

Often we are *not* motivated to change our language by ourselves. Friends, family, teachers, and employers motivate us and provide resources for language change. For example, it would be very difficult (and even pointless) to learn to write academic research papers without being part of an academic community in which students are taught to write these papers and are given credit for having done so. Or because they do not know anyone who speaks a particular language, students may have a really hard time learning and speaking a new language.

On the other hand, a high school student we know is an excellent speaker of Spanish but will not speak it around the native speakers of Spanish at his school. He says that some of these students would not appreciate his speaking Spanish and would see it as an incursion on their "territory." The point here is that grammar use is tied up with issues of identity, both individual and group. Often we need to identify with or have some affiliation with a group to (want to) use their language/grammar. Group affiliation and identity change, however, so it is possible to use a language/grammar easily in one situation and then be unable to use grammar/language at all in another.

FOR DISCUSSION

Think about something that was hard for you to do. What motivated you? Did your motivation stay the same, or was it variable? Did it feel as though it came from within you or from a variety or sources—outside and inside of you? What would motivate you to use more formal grammar structures such as *whom* or *whomever?* Or, what would motivate you to use the slang of a social group with whom you are not usually affiliated?

FOR DISCUSSION

We have a friend who says "She give me the flowers," leaving off the third person singular *-s* ending on the verb. She says she wants to speak perfect English, but she still produces a lot of errors that to a fluent adult appear simple to correct. Her errors occur on structures (like the *-s*) that she has studied repeatedly and hears correctly many times a day.

What might be the reasons for the seeming contradiction between our friend's stated desires to speak perfect English and her actual use of grammar? Do you know of similar examples you can share with the class?

A Last Word on Error

It is very important to remember that errors (and correct forms) come and go. In many ways we are always learning to use our language; when we are in a new context, whether intellectual or physical, we are more likely to produce utterances that are incorrect or difficult to understand. Native speakers of a language trying to articulate new or difficult ideas will produce errors in grammar in speech and writing (as they will when nervous). Teachers or tutors who clearly and elaborately explain and correct an error for a student writer may believe that the student is now producing the correct form consistently, only to have the error occur again because the student's situation of language use has changed. This problem is fairly easy to deal with in writing because student writers can be taught to revise and edit their texts.

For DISCUSSION

Students often have a repertoire of incorrect but rigid ideas about what is and isn't an error. None of the rules below are actually "correct":

> All short sentences are wrong.
>
> Long sentences are incorrect.
>
> Do not begin a sentence with *because*.
>
> Do not use *I*.

Can you add to this list of incorrect rules? Can you speculate about how these "rules" came to be?

DIALECT AND DIVERSITY

So far we have been considering the language use and development of individuals. Now we are going to shift perspective from individual language use to the use of dialects, in effect focusing on the grammar and language use of groups. This move throws us into the maelstrom of anxiety about language divergence, diversity, and difference.

The United States has long been a multilingual country with an uneasiness about its linguistic diversity. Although English does not have the status of an "official" language, for all practical purposes, English is considered to be *the* language of the United States. English and English only is "our" language, the tongue of "we the people." In other words, often using a language other than English marks one as an alien, an "other." There is nothing inevitable about this attitude toward linguistic difference. Many other countries in the world are multilingual without official or popular distress over their linguistic diversity.

FOR DISCUSSION

Many residents of East Los Angeles speak little English, their main language being Spanish. In Little Saigon in Orange County, California, Vietnamese is the primary language. Throughout the United States are many language "enclaves" like these. What are the implications of this fact? Why should people (e.g., Vietnamese immigrants in Orange County) attempt to become fluent in English when they live in a thriving community of folks who speak their language? Do you know of other "islands" of folks whose primary language is one other than English? Describe these societies within the larger society of the nation, and discuss the economic and political implications of such groups.

Many dialects of English are spoken in the United States. In truth everyone speaks a dialect, which can be defined as a variety of a language that is shared by a group of speakers. Dialects differ from one another in vocabulary, grammatical structure, and pronunciation. No one dialect is intrinsically better than another, but some dialects have more prestige than others.

African American Vernacular English (introduced in Chapter 5) is a dialect of English, but not a prestige dialect, and its use in the public sphere often provokes intense emotional responses. This dialect is maligned and misunderstood as a collection of errors, or sloppy attempts at Standard Edited Academic English (SEAE). In fact, AAVE has a system of rules that diverge and differ from the rules of SEAE. But the response to AAVE has little to do with language per se; rather it is a product of racism and fear of the "other." One example from the verb structure of AAVE will illustrate grammar that deviates from SEAE, and thus may be erroneously judged by some to be attempts to speak "properly." These examples, however, follow the rules of the AAVE dialect:

- In Standard English the word *been,* the past participle of be, is used in the present or past perfect active *He has/had been sick* and the present or past perfect passive: *The cake has/had been eaten.* (See Chapter 6 for review of the present and past perfect.) In AAVE, one can say *He been sick.* Without stress on the word *been,* this form is similar to the present perfect in SEAE. This form, for example, can co-occur with adverbials such as "since last week." Furthermore, in AAVE, one can put stress on the past participle as in the sentences *He been married.* or *He been ate it.* This stressed form of *been* means that the action happened a long time ago.

- AAVE differs from SEAE in use as well as the structure (and pronunciation). Because slaves were deprived of literacy instruction and materials (books, paper, writing implements, etc.), a highly developed oral culture grew on the basis of African traditions such as storytelling and praise songs. This oral culture can be seen today in the verbal expertise of rappers and other forms of oral poetry performance (slam poetry, etc.).

CHALLENGER

If you are interested in rap and the verbal politics of hip-hop culture, read the book *Spectacular Vernaculars* (Russell Potter, Albany: State University of New York Press, 1995). Report to your class on what you learned about the uses of grammar in hip-hop culture.

BILINGUAL GRAMMARS

People who speak more than one language have, of necessity, more than one grammar. Thus bilinguals may also alternate between two languages (or codeswitch) in the same conversation. Bilinguals codeswitch because of the social situations they are in or the topics they are talking about. By codeswitching, bilinguals can create, maintain, and change social relationships. For example, Susan, who speaks only English, had made friends with Va, a Hmong-English bilingual in her math class. While the two young women were waiting for the bus together, a group of Hmong students arrived at the bus stop, speaking to Va in Hmong. Va switched to Hmong but peppered the sentences with English so that Susan would not be completely excluded by the conversation. Va used her codeswitching to maintain affiliations and relationships with both Susan and her Hmong friends throughout this conversation.

FOR DISCUSSION

Have you ever been the situation of having someone switch into a language you couldn't speak or understand. How did you feel? What was the effect of this use of language on your relationship with the bilingual person?

By switching between the two languages, bilinguals can make the best use of their linguistic resources. Grammatically, the switches tend to occur between phrases or clauses and not in the middle of them.

Codeswitching does not occur by mistake. Bilinguals codeswitch because their expertise in two languages helps them to communicate. Even though codeswitching may not always be a conscious act, it is deliberate, and it is the norm in some communities such as among the Puerto Ricans in Spanish Harlem section of New York City.[3] Misunderstandings about bilingualism have resulted in the idea that some bilinguals don't really speak any language at all. The derogatory term *Spanglish,* for example, connotes a random mishmash of Spanish and English that is supposedly spoken by Spanish-English bilinguals in the United States.

IMPORTANT TERMS

African American Vernacular English (AAVE)

Codeswitching

Dialect

Standard Edited Academic English (SEAE)

CHALLENGER

Hunger of Memory by Richard Rodriguez and *Growing Up Bilingual* by Ana Maria Zentilla are books about bilingualism. They are very different not only in style but also in the meaning they attribute to Spanish-English bilingualism in the United States. Read one or both and report to the class on what either author thinks about bilingualism.

FOR DISCUSSION

Do you codeswitch in the use of vocabulary? Pronunciation? Grammar? What provokes the switches? What do you use the switches for? What do they accomplish?

---

[3] Shana Poplack, "Sometimes I'll start a sentence in Spanish yiemino en español: Toward a typology of code switching," *Linguistics* 18 (1980): 581–616.

WHAT ABOUT EDUCATION AND SCHOOLING?

Perhaps the place to end this discussion is with the topic of schooling and education. What should educators do about both our uses of grammar and our *ideas* about uses of grammar? Clearly students need to know about language and diversity in other countries so that they can see that fear of linguistic diversity is part of a belief system; it is not natural or unavoidable. By the same token, students can be made aware that language change is inevitable, in both individuals and groups. Prescriptive rules and attitudes themselves change over time. Students can choose when, where, and how they will adhere to which prescriptive rules.

CHALLENGER

The work of Joshua Fishman provides social and historical context for issues of language diversity and grammar in the United States. We find this article particularly useful: "The Displaced Anxieties of Anglo-Americans," *International Journal of the Sociology of Language* 74 (1988): 125–140. Read this article and report on it to your class.

Students can use descriptive grammar to analyze their own language for its grammatical and stylistic features. As students become interested in experimenting with language and style, they can analyze the grammatical structures of prose or oral language that they admire. In an effort to ascertain how language achieves its varied effects, students can imitate a variety of styles.

Finally, knowledge about language acquisition, both first and second, by adults and by children, will help us to know what and when language anxiety is appropriate and when it is foolish or, at the very least, a waste of energy.

It turns out, then, that understanding grammar and its uses may help us achieve peace and understanding among people of varying language backgrounds—among the citizens of a multicultural nation such as the United States—and that, after all, is a purpose worth pursuing in the grammar class, through a grammar book, and in our day-to-day relationships with that strange breed of creatures who talk and write, that is, with our fellow humans.

Glossary

Acronym   Word formed with the first letter of each important word in a phrase (e.g., National Council of Teachers of English = NCTE).

Adjectival   Structures that function to modify nouns: adjectives, nouns, prepositional phrases, nonfinite verbs, adjective clauses, and reduced clauses (nonfinite verb phrases).

Adjective   A category of words that modify nouns and fit in these blanks: *The* _____ *dog was very* _____. Adjectives cannot be made plural; they can be compared. They precede nouns in the attributive position; they follow nouns in the appositive position.

Adjective clause   Sometimes called relative clauses for the definite relative pronouns, adjectives, and adverbs that begin these clauses. They follow nouns and modify nouns. [*The table that was covered in paper was being used by the students.*]

Adverb   A member of the category of words that modify verbs and tell about place, time, manner, or degree. Adverbs include intensifiers (*so, very*), qualifiers (*somewhat*), interrogative adverbs that form questions (*when?*), the word *not,* and the more commonly thought of *-ly* adverbs (e.g., *quickly*).

Adverbial clause   Dependent clause that functions adverbially; can precede, follow, or occasionally interrupt, the independent clause. [*When I began school, the weather was hot.*] Adverbial clauses begin with a subordinating conjunction: *as, after, although, as if, as though, because, before, even though, except that, if, in order that, provided that, since, so that, that, till, unless, until, when, wherever, where, whereas, while.*

African American Vernacular English   AAVE is a dialect of English spoken by many people in the United States, it is but one of the dialects of English used by some who speak it. AAVE is completely grammatical; that is, AAVE has constitutive rules that its speakers follow, but these rules differ from the rules of other dialects of English. For example, AAVE speakers might describe a woman who is usually happy by saying *She be happy.* That is, happiness is a characteristic of her personality.

Agreement   Subject-verb agreement. In formal usage, singular verbs must have singular subjects: *The bird sings* [*-s* on the verb does not make it plural; it makes it third person singular]. In formal usage, plural subjects must have plural verbs: *The birds sing.*

Antecedent   A word or phrase that a pronoun refers to and draws both its form and its meaning from. *The boy is a great dancer. He* [referring to the antecedent, *the boy*] *wants a career on the stage.*

Appositive   A noun phrase that follows another noun phrase and renames the first noun. *My student the genius will do great things with her life.* (See Chapter 8 for comma rules with appositives.)

Aspect   This term refers to the nature of the action of the perfect and progressive forms of a verb: whether it is or is not continuing, whether it has or does not have an effect in the present, whether it occurs in contrast to another action in the past, and so on.

Auxiliary verbs   A verb group (i.e., a verb consisting of more than one word) has a main verb and an auxiliary verb, sometimes called a "helping" verb. Auxiliary verbs carry the tense for the verb group. The verbs *be, do,* and *have* all function as auxiliary verbs (as well as being main verbs themselves). *I am running that race.*

Back-formation   A word formed by removing parts of another word; the act of producing such a word.

Blend   A word formed by fusing parts of words together (*sm*oke + f*og* = *smog*).

Clause   A subject and verb unit. A clause is either independent, in which case it could be a sentence on its own, or dependent, in which case it has a function with respect to another clause. For example, a clause can function adverbially, adjectivally, or nominally with respect to another clause. *Braydon, who is a senior in high school, is very talented with technology.* The underlined clause is functioning adjectivally, modifying *Braydon.*

Codeswitching   The act of a speaker (or writer) who moves between two or more dialects or languages in a single conversation or piece of writing. Codeswitching is a deliberate action that builds social bonds and adds meaning to a conversation or text. Codeswitching is done between phrases and clauses, usually not in the middle of them.

Comma splice   Two independent clauses spliced together with a comma (i.e., without any conjunction to join the clauses). Generally considered an error. *Houa works very hard in my class, his grades are excellent.*

Complement   A noun, adjective, or prepositional phrase will function as a complement when it follows a linking verb (*be, become, appear, feel,* etc.). *The sun is hot.*

Complex sentence   A sentence with at least one dependent clause (adverbial, adjectival, or nominal). *When we read that poem, we wanted to cry.*

Compound-complex sentence   A sentence with at least two coordinate clauses and one dependent clause (adverbial, adjectival, or noun). *I went to the beach, and I learned to surf because it was a wonderful challenge.*

Compound personal pronouns   *myself, yourself, himself, herself, itself, ourselves, yourselves, themselves.* These pronouns are used for emphasis as intensifiers. *I myself wrote that poem.* These pronouns are also used reflexively. *I washed myself.*

Compounds   Two words joined to form a new word (cup + cake = cupcake).

Compound sentence   A sentence with two or more independent clauses joined by the appropriate number of coordinating conjunctions. *I went to the beach, and I learned to surf.* A compound sentence has coordinate clauses.

Conglomerate prepositions   Phrases such as *together with* are considered to be a single (but conglomerate) preposition.

Conjunctive adverbs   *however, furthermore, therefore, thus, then,* etc. These adverbs join ideas between two clauses. *I like summer; however, it is very hot in my town.* Conjunctive adverbs are often mistaken for subordinating conjunctions and used to join two independent clauses. Note the semicolon in the example sentence above. The semicolon allows for the joining of the two clauses and not the conjunctive adverb which links ideas and not structures.

Constitutive rule Statements or rules that describe the structures that constitute a language. For example, "A sentence consists of a noun phrase and a verb phrase" is a constitutive or descriptive rule. See also *Descriptive grammar.*

Coordinating conjunctions *and, but, so, for, yet, or, nor.* Conjunctions that coordinate (join) independent clauses.

Correlative conjunctions These conjunctions come in pairs: *not only . . . but also; both . . . and; either . . . or; neither . . . nor.* It is important that the structures following each conjunction have the same grammatical form. That is, these structures should be grammatically parallel. *We went to the museum with both his family and our friends.*

Definite relative adjectives These words begin relative clauses and work similarly to adjectives in that they precede a noun. *The boy whose book was lost was upset.*

Definite relative adverbs These words begin adjective clauses and relate to time, place, manner, or degree. *At noon when the clock strikes, I will leave the office.*

Definite relative pronouns *who, whom, that, which.* These pronouns (unlike indefinite relative pronouns) have an antecedent and begin adjective clauses.

Demonstrative pronouns *this, that, these, those.* See also *Pronouns.*

Dependent clause A clause that is not a sentence on its own; it depends on another clause to form a sentence. Clauses that function nominally, adverbially, and adjectivally are dependent clauses.

Descriptive grammar Statements or rules that describe a language. Descriptive grammar is based on constitutive rules.

Determiners Function words that qualify nouns: *the, a* (articles); *this, these* (demonstratives); *his/her* (possessives); *one/first* (numbers); *several/few* (indefinites), and so on. A noun phrase consists of optional determiners, optional adjectives and a noun.

Dialect A variety of a language that is spoken by a group of people defined either geographically or socially. For example, Southern dialects of American English differ in some of their verb forms and their lexicon or vocabulary from many Northern dialects. Everyone speaks a dialect of a language. An idiolect, the variety of a language that one person speaks, is an individual version of a dialect.

Error Deviation by a speaker or writer from either constitutive or regulative rules of the language. Error occurs more often when a speaker or writer is trying to learn or to say something new. Errors occur in patterns and are not random or due to laziness.

Expletive *that* See *Strategic that.*

Finite verb forms The set comprising a main verb accompanied by an auxiliary that has either tense or a modal, with the verb as the head of the predicate.

Form Forms are associated with parts of speech terminology (e.g., noun, verb, adverb, adjective, preposition, conjunction) that refer to categories of words or language forms.

Function This term refers to the grammatical roles such as subjects, objects, and complements— the work that words, phrases, and clauses perform in sentences (e.g., the *forms* noun and clause can both *function* as subject, object, or complement).

Fused sentence A sentence in which two independent clauses one placed back to back without any punctuation or conjunctions to join them. *They worked all summer in the restaurant the work was extremely tiring.* This type of sentence is considered an error.

Gerund   A present participle functioning nominally. *Eating is fun. I like eating.*

Grammaticality   A sentence (or any part of a sentence) is grammatical if it would be spoken or written by a native speaker of the language. A native speaker would not generate an ungrammatical sentence, except inadvertently or perhaps to create humor. Native speakers use their language grammatically.

Imperative   Forms of sentences that are sometimes referred to as commands or requests. *Put the book down. Turn in your homework.*

Indefinite relative pronouns, adjectives, and adverbs   Words that establish the link between a noun clause and the sentences of which they are a part. They are indefinite because they do not have an antecedent. Pronouns: *which, who, whom, whomever, whose, whosoever, whichever, what, whatever, whatsoever.* Adjectives: *whose, which, whichever, what, whatever.* Adverbs: *when, why, how, where.*

Independent clause   An independent clause has a subject and a verb phrase and can stand alone, meaning that it is not an adverbial, adjectival, or nominal clause itself; of course, it may have a noun clause as its subject, which complicates the idea that it can "stand alone." *What I like is coffee ice cream.*

Intensifier   A type of adverb that modifies another adverb or adjective (e.g., *so, very, quite*): *He is very studious.*

Interlanguage   An unstable grammar or set of constitutive rules that is developed by a second-language learner. Some of the rules in an interlanguage are not accurate; they are not the rules that native speakers of that language possess. These rules will change as the learner progresses in acquiring the second language.

Interrogative   Refers to questions, both yes/no (*Is the baby asleep?*) and wh- (*What are you doing?*).

Interrogative adverbs   Adverbs referring to place, time, manner, degree, and reason. These adverbs are used to form questions: *Where are you going?*

Intransitive   A verb that does not take an object is intransitive. The verb does not transfer action to a noun. *The man sleeps like a baby.*

Lexicon   A dictionary; a person's vocabulary; the words in a language.

Linking verb   A verb that takes complements (*be, appear, seem, feel, become, taste, smell,* etc.).

Modal auxiliaries   The most common modals are *can, could, might, may, shall, should, will, would.* See *Auxiliary verb.*

Morpheme   Parts of words that change meanings (happy/*un*happy), make one part of speech into another (beauty/beauti*ful*), or show grammatical functions such as tense or plurality (walk/walk*ed;* cat/cat*s*). Morphemes are sometimes called the smallest unit of meaning. Some morphemes are free (e.g., life*like*); they are words themselves. Other morphemes are bound; they are connected to words (*dis*honor).

Negative   The word *not* is used with an auxiliary (unless the main verb is *be*) to make a statement negative.

Nominal(s)   The name of a group of functions in the sentence: subject, object, complement, vocative, and appositive. Nouns, noun clauses, and nonfinite verbs function nominally.

Noncount nouns   Nouns that in most cases do not have plural forms (e.g., *milk, oxygen, rice*).

Nonfinite verb forms   When present or past participles are used without auxiliaries, they are called nonfinite verbs. Infinitives are also nonfinite verbs. They are not the head of the verb phrase or predicate. They may function nominally or adjectivally; they may be the head of a nonfinite verb phrase.

Noun Generally thought of as a category of words denoting a person, place, thing, or idea. It can be preceded by a determiner in a noun phrase. A noun functions nominally, adjectivally, and adverbially. Common nouns (e.g., city) are not capitalized and proper nouns (the names of specific persons or places, e.g., Miami) are capitalized.

Noun clauses These are clauses (subject and verb units) that function nominally with respect to another clausal unit. They can function as subjects, objects, complements, vocatives or appositives (e.g., _What I want is a vacation_). The underlined clause is functioning as the subject of the verb _is_. See _Clauses_.

Noun phrase Could be a single noun or could be a group of words consisting of optional determiners, optional adjectives, and a noun. The group functions as a unit with a noun as the head word.

Object Direct objects receive the action of the verb: _I ate the apple._ A verb may entail a direct and an indirect object: _I gave my friend flowers._ The noun phrase _my friend_ is the indirect object (in some senses, the receiver of the direct object) and the noun phrase _flowers_ is the direct object. A preposition (_in, on, above, during, at,_ etc.) is generally followed by a noun phrase functioning as its object.

Objective complement An adjective or a noun phrase following an object is referred to as an objective complement. These structures occur with a limited number of verbs (_call, elect, christen, name,_ etc.). _I called that man a fool._

Operator This is the term we are using for _as_ when it is used in the one-of-a-kind structure: _as black as night._

Parallelism When units of a sentence are coordinated, they need to be grammatically similar. This is called parallelism. The sentence _I like to swim and run_ shows parallel construction. The ungrammatical sentence _I like to swim and running six miles every weekend_ does not show parallel construction.

Particle Words that could be classified as prepositions but are not functioning as the head of a prepositional phrase. These words are associated with verbs, and if the verb is transitive, they can be moved around in the sentence (prepositions cannot be moved). _I gave up the puppy. I gave the puppy up._

Passive voice If the receiver of the action, rather than the doer of the action, is the grammatical subject of a sentence, the text is in the passive voice. In passive voice the verb group is formed with _be_ as the auxiliary and the past participle of the main or lexical verb.

Past participle A form of the verb that is made with the base form V and the _-ed_ morpheme in some verbs (walk_ed_), or with the _-en_ morpheme in others (eat_en_). Many verbs have irregular past participle forms (_thrown_). The past participle is used in forming the perfect aspect of a verb.

Perfect aspect When a verb group is formed with _have_ as the auxiliary and the main verb is in the past participle form (HAVE + V + EN). The auxiliary _have_ will carry tense. _The man has eaten twenty cookies._ [present perfect] _The war had ended tragically._ [past perfect]

Periphrastic modals Modals made of more than one word; they can be marked for tense (unlike other modals). _I have to go. I had to go._ See also _Modals_.

Phrase A word or a group of words that functions as a unit in the sentence. A phrase has a head word that determines how the whole phrase will function in the sentence. For example, a noun phrase (NP) always consists of a noun but may also have an optional determiner followed by an optional adjective. In a sentence, a noun phrase can function as a subject, object, complement, appositive, or vocative (just as an individual noun can).

Plurals Most nouns can be made plural by adding *-s* to the end. Some irregular or mutation plurals (e.g., *children*) are formed in a variety of ways other than adding *-s*. (See Chapter 8 for discussion of irregular plural rules and foreign language influence on English.)

Predicate Another term for *verb phrase,* which includes a verb and all of the structures that form a unit with the verb—objects and modifiers.

Preposition Prepositions (e.g., *in, on, from, at, during*) are connectives that often have to do with space and time (but not always). Prepositions are followed by noun phrases, which function as their objects. Prepositional phrases function adjectivally, adverbially, and as complements; occasionally they may function nominally. Words that are classified as prepositions can also be analyzed as particles, adverbs, and adjectives when they are not followed by a noun phrase. (See Chapter 15.)

Prescriptive grammar and rules Statements or rules about what makes language use proper or correct. Prescriptive grammar is made of regulative rules. See also *Regulative rules.*

Present participle A form of the verb: base form V + ING. The present participle (e.g., *jumping, running, singing, eating, sleeping*) is used in forming the progressive aspect. *The queen is <u>retiring</u> to her chambers.*

Progressive aspect When a verb group is formed with *be* as the auxiliary and the main verb is in the present participle form (BE + V + ING), the auxiliary *be* will carry the tense. *He is <u>studying</u> now.* [present progressive]
I <u>was calculating</u> the answer to the problem. [past progressive]

Pronouns A category of words that function nominally and most often derive their meaning through reference to noun antecedents. *Liz had a beautiful dress for the dance. She had hired a friend to make it. She* is a personal pronoun referring to *Liz,* and *it* is also a personal pronoun referring to *dress.* In other words, *Liz* and *dress* are the antecedents for *she* and *it.*

Qualifier A type of adverb that modifies another adverb or adjective (e.g., *somewhat*): I was *somewhat* hungry.

Reduced clauses Adverbial clauses can be reduced to a subordinator and a nonfinite verb by deleting the subject and the auxiliary. These structures (e.g., *While reading the book, I fell asleep.*) are sometimes called nonfinite clauses or adverbial phrases. Adjectival clauses can also be reduced by eliminating the relative pronoun and the auxiliary. *I saw that heron fishing for koi in my pond.*

Regulative rule Rules that describe proper or "correct" language; regulative rules tend to have a "hard and fast" quality and are not sensitive to the situations in which language is used. An example of a regulative or prescriptive rule is "Do not end a sentence with a preposition."

Restrictive and nonrestrictive adjective clauses Restrictive adjective clauses limit and identify the nouns they modify and are not separated by commas. Nonrestrictive or loose clauses give additional but not defining information about the noun they are modifying. They are separated by commas.

Run-on sentence A sentence in which clauses and phrases are strung together, often with *and . . . and . . . and.* The run-on sentence may involve a comma splice (linking two independent clauses with only a comma). While a comma splice counts as a grammatical error, run-on sentences are not grammatical errors, but are violations of the norms of usage.

Sentence A basic unit of language in English that consists of a subject and a predicate or verb phrase (which together constitute an independent clause). In writing, sentences begin with capital letters and end with periods, exclamation points, or question marks.

Sentential adverbs Derived from adjectives (such as *unfortunate*), in some sense these adverbs modify an entire clause: *Unfortunately, my friend cannot run in the race.*

Simple sentence A sentence with a single, independent clause.

Strategic (expletive) *that* When the word *that* begins a noun clause, it is not a pronoun. It can often be deleted (see Chapter 10). It begins the noun clause and links it to the other clause of which the noun clause is a part.

Subject Except for imperatives (*Get the ball*), sentences consist of a subject and a predicate. Many forms may function as subjects: nouns, nonfinite verbs, noun clauses, pronouns. The subject could be thought of as the topic of the sentence.

Tense Tells the form of a verb. English has two tenses, past (formed with -*ed* suffix in regular verbs) and present (formed with -*s* suffix with he/she/it and other third person singular subjects). Tense does not necessarily correspond to ideas of time. Present tense verbs refer to habitual actions and not actions in the present. *He eats yogurt for breakfast.*

Transitive Verbs that can take objects are called transitive. The verb, in some sense, transfers the action to a noun phrase functioning as an object. *We ate the couscous.* Some verbs can take a direct and an indirect object and they may be called ditransitive. *I gave the patient some flowers.*

Verb The head of the verb phrase or predicate, an essential part of all sentences. A verb has five principal parts: infinitive or base form (*to walk*); present tense (*walk/walks*); past (*walked*); present participle (*walking*); past participle (*walked*).

Verb group The verb (as head of the predicate) may consist of more than one word; it may have one or more auxiliaries and a main or lexical verb.

Verb phrase A group of words functioning as a unit with a verb as its head, sometimes called a predicate.

Vocative One function of nominals, to call a name(s). *Students, sit down.*

Index